The

PICKUP
ARTIST

ALSO BY MYSTERY

The Mystery Method

The
PICKUP
ARTIST

THE NEW AND IMPROVED
ART OF SEDUCTION

Mystery

WITH CHRIS ODOM

VILLARD

NEW YORK

Published in the United States by Villard Books, an imprint of The Random House
Publishing Group, a division of Random House, Inc., New York.

VILLARD and "V" CIRCLED Design are registered trademarks of Random House, Inc.

Library of Congress Cataloging-in-Publication Data

Mystery
The pickup artist : the new and improved art of seduction / Mystery, with
Chris Odom.
p. cm.
ISBN 978-0-345-51819-4
eBook ISBN 978-0-345-51821-7
1. Dating (Social customs) 2. Mate selection. 3. Single women—Psychology.
4. Single men—Psychology. I. Odom, Chris. II. Title.
HQ801.M973 2010
306.730973—dc22   2009045133

Printed in the United States of America on acid-free paper

www.villard.com

2   4   6   8   9   7   5   3   1

First Edition

Book design by Christopher M. Zucker

THIS BOOK IS DEDICATED
TO ALL THE LONELY HEARTS.

MAY YOU FIND LOVE.

Contents

Pssst

NEIL STRAUSS

Hey, you.

Yeah, I'm talking to you. With the eyes. Staring right at me.

Come a little closer.

That's better.

Listen, I need to tell you something. But this is just between us, okay? Don't tell the authors of this book I've been talking to you. If they knew, they'd be really pissed.

You promise?

Okay, good. Here's the deal: You don't really need this book.

I know. I know. Shh. It's just us here. It's okay.

Look at you. You are a perfect specimen of manliness.

Rip off your shirt. Do it. No one will mind. You're a Greek god. All any other guy can do is compare himself to you, and weep at his own inadequacies.

Yeah, strut your stuff. Strut it down the self-help aisle. Strut it through the cookbooks section. Show them a body for life.

Now leap up on a table. Pull your pants off. That's right. Yank 'em clean off and swing them over your head like a Chippendale. Let go. See what lucky lady they land on.

What's that? This isn't working for you?

No, you don't say. That can't be true.

Okay, so maybe you don't have the perfect body. No big deal. Not everyone can be a Greek god. That's not all it's about. You've got something more important: experience. Plenty of it. You've got natural charm, charisma, and confidence. Something these seduction gurus and method meisters know nothing about. They order people to recite scripted lines, rehearse artificial gestures, and follow all sorts of crazy pie charts and bar graphs. They make this whole boy-meets-girl thing overly complex, like some sort of nerdy scientific formula. But you and I know the truth: Some guys were born with it and some guys weren't. It's as simple as that. And you, my friend, were clearly born with it.

All you have to do is just walk up to a woman and talk to her. You don't need a script. All you need is you. So show them how it's done.

Okay, just wait for it. The first attractive woman you see. Ready? Go!

There she is. Just receding out of sight. That's the one. With that silken hair, that perfect body, that enticing swing of the hips. Hurry. You're going to miss her. Run!

She's turning around, looking back at you. Now. Make that eye contact you do so well.

She saw you. She's running now too. That's good. She's mirroring you. You've got her right where you want her. Keep running. Show all those wanna-bes staring at you in admiration how to approach.

She's run right into a corner. This is great for you. It's what they call an indicator of interest. Now's your chance. Lock her in.

Her eyes are widening. Yes, that's fear, but you know that with your natural charm, you can turn that fear into lust. After all, it's just another emotion that's four letters long.

Now say something. Anything. The first thing that comes into your head, because you don't need scripted lines and artificial routines. Go. Now.

"Bladouwahhh"? That was the first thing that came to your head? Maybe you should —

No, wait. She's opening her mouth to speak. Maybe she's going to tell you she wants you or loves you or needs you. Hold on. Let's see. Your natural-born confidence and charisma just may have worked.

Okay, maybe not. She's screaming for help. She's yelling "police!" now.

Okay, quick, follow me. I know where we can go. There's a book. It's called *The Pickup Artist*. It will help. It's safe. I've read it already. It has words. Words that have been proven to work much better than "bladouwahhh." Trust me on this.

Oh, wait? That's the book you were reading when we started talking? And I interrupted you and said you didn't need it?

Well, you didn't need it then. But now maybe you do. Times change, people change. You've been through some hard times recently; some pretty embarrassing things have happened in the last five minutes. It couldn't hurt to spend a couple of hours reading. Just in case there's something useful to be gleaned from all this nonsense.

After all, it is confusing out there these days. If what you do naturally isn't working well enough, then several hundred men have appeared in the last few years willing to charge several thousand dollars to teach you the right way. And all several hundred of those right ways are mutually exclusive. You can't do indirect game if you want to do direct game. And you can't do direct game if you want to do natural game. And you can't do natural game if you want to do alpha game.

So where do you start when every time you want to try something new, a friend or expert tells you it's wrong or stupid? A good place to begin is by considering what all the competing theories and schools and methods have in common. For starters, almost all of them are not methods but marketing tactics, designed to differentiate themselves through criticizing the competition. In addition, they all contain one common denominator, the word *game*. And finally, the teacher behind almost every single one began as a student of Mystery's.

So why not simplify things and start at the source? The marketers may not want you to be aware of this, but in reality, all you need to know are two forms of game: game that works for you and game that doesn't. So try a few of the suggestions here— particularly the ones that seem the most unnatural to you, because you've been doing what seems natural your whole life—and see which ones yield results. Then start your own school of seduction. And while you're at it, go ahead and move in with Mystery. He seems to love having business competitors as roommates. It keeps life exciting.

We are all stuck. We're stuck in our own small reality, trapped in a miasma of petty little problems, anxieties, insecurities, resistance to change, and worries about being judged that won't matter one bit when we're dead, because all they'll add up to is regret. Fortunately, there's an escape from this trap. It's called approaching. After all, the best way to expand our small reality is to invite someone else into it. It keeps life exciting.

What's the worst that can happen? They can say no. And then do you know what you can do? You can beat them with your belt. That will teach them for not letting you expand your reality.

Or you can read this book. It has ideas. And a good idea is more powerful than any belt. After all, belts hold up pants. Ideas lower them.

A Message from Mystery

I've found that the pickup community can attract all sorts of interesting characters, and in order to cover my ass from hangers-on, copycat competitors, and jealous ex-girlfriends, I've changed a few names, altered some identifying characteristics, formed a few composite characters, and fudged the timeline a bit to make your reading experience all the more enjoyable. If in doing so I've created similarities to you, or your father, or anyone else living or dead, it was entirely coincidental.

The women, however, are another matter.

Introduction

I AM A PICKUP ARTIST.

I'm not a player, but I have devoted a large portion of my time to the art of seduction. I have read many books, dress cool, have many girlfriends, and believe I am rather charming at times. I once felt very much alone in this art. My friends did not enjoy the "chase" at all. I attempted to advise them on the reasoning behind the techniques, but they would just freeze up. I had a tough time coming to grips with the fact that I am what I just said I am. Why?

Truth is, though, I have had sex with hundreds of girls so far, and many have been beautiful. I mean 10s. I am very good at what I do. At the risk of sounding arrogant, I am the best pickup artist I've ever met. It *is* an art. I worked very hard to get good. There are many rules I may give you. Please take them only as considerations. They are *my rules*, and they have helped me greatly.

I honestly feel like I am a master at this. Not because I can get any woman—that, of course, is impossible—but because my pick-ups are so controlled and smooth; not sleazy, but rather natural.

I love women. I especially love the adventure and the companionship. I love being in a strange girl's apartment. She takes care of me and I feel like a king. And when I leave, I go to another girl's place and get the same great treatment all over again. I love back scratchings and baths. They're so clean and the girls smell so good.

You might feel lonely and decide to go out, and within two hours your life changes. You meet a girl and she is attracted to you. And she's hot. And you are at her house listening to new music and eating new foods and exploring a new life. They have issues you can listen to and learn from. It's a great big soap opera and you are the star.

I love it when my ideas actually help people. That's what I live for. All the pain I endured to finally learn these techniques has paid off. I bled for you. I will impart some minor pearls of wisdom to you. I myself have been greatly enriched by conversing with other pickup artists who truly enjoy the game, so I hope to do the same for you.

It is a very simple system, really.

1. Find
2. Meet
3. Attract
4. Close

Say it with me: Find, meet, attract, close. Find, meet, attract, close. The details and subtleties, however, are the heart of the system.

The

PICKUP
ARTIST

Chapter One

WELCOME TO MIAMI

"I AM INDULGING IN MY HUMANITY," I said.

I took a long drag from my spliff and then passed it matter-of-factly to the blonde seated next to me (without looking at her). She took it as I continued, "And I can say to all of you now, beyond a shadow of a doubt, that I"—pause—"have *earned* it. Eh, brother?" I smiled at Lovedrop, my trusty wingman.

"Mystery, you're damn right," said Lovedrop, "and this is going to be a great year." He raised a glass of chocolate protein shake and took a swig.

"I'm just living in the Now," I said, making a grand, sweeping gesture with my hands. "The Universe presents itself. I mean, look at all the math. It's absolutely brilliant." My straight, dark hair was pulled back into a ponytail, an expression of fascination fixed on my angular face.

The blonde next to me wore my trademark fuzzy black hat. I had used it earlier in the night as a lock-in prop. It was too big on her, and she looked very cute with it on. She had almond-shaped doe eyes and wide, Slavic features—my favorite type. She smiled at me. It was on. I'd been working on this one for a few hours; I was just comfort building now.

"This couch looks like something out of *The Jetsons!*" said the other girl, a brunette with long, straight hair. She wore a green cocktail dress and dark eye makeup. "I love this rug, though. It must cost you a fortune to have it cleaned."

The four of us—Lovedrop, the two women, and I—relaxed on a white shag rug. Lining the wall around us was a futuristic, white leather couch. Everything was white. The fourteen-thousand-dollar custom curtains were white. The giant avant-garde, plastic light fixtures around the house were white. Even the dog was white.

Seated in a nook nearby at a glass table was our acquaintance, the Rat. He was using his debit card to crush a few small blue pills on the surface of the table. The Rat flashed a sagging, loose smile from wet lips.

"Hey LD," he said, a slight whine to his voice, slurring, "you want one of these Roxies?"

Lovedrop smirked. "Haven't you had enough already? You look like you're about to drool all over that table."

The girls giggled.

"Is that a no?" The Rat kept smiling greasily as if to say, *You know you want some.*

A projector played music videos on the far wall of the room, and a bouncy hip-hop song came on. Lovedrop got up and started to dance to the music, bathed in the changing light of the projector. "I love this song," he said, and he was only half lying. It wasn't what he would actually sit around listening to through a pair of headphones, but it was perfect for dancing with girls.

The brunette stood up and started to dance with him. "Do you guys own this house?" she asked, the shag rug feeling oh-so-soft under her bare feet. All the pieces came together as a vibe: the beat of the music, the light from the projector, the dancing, the laughter, the smoke in the air. He put one hand on her hip and circled the other in the air like swinging a lasso.

"Hey Mystery," said Lovedrop, "remember the Matthew McConaughey chicken dance? In Vegas." He started flapping his arms like a chicken.

"I don't know about Matthew McConaughey, but you're in Miami now," said the Rat. "Hey LD, you look like the Backstreet Boys with that dance you're doing." He snickered under his breath and licked his lips.

"I guess I was lucky all I got was their dance moves," said Lovedrop. "And meanwhile you got stuck with their goatee, smack-dab in the middle of your face."

"Ouch," said the brunette. She smiled at Lovedrop and tucked her hair behind one ear.

The Rat scooted back in his futuristic chair and placed his hand on his chest indignantly. "LD, I'm hurt," he said in his whiny voice. "I'm hurt that you would say that. After everything that I would do for you." He actually sounded sad; it was good.

The Rat paused and then pushed it a little further. "LD, you know I love you like a brother, don't you? You guys, you're like brothers to me. I love you guys."

The brunette joked, "The girl is supposed to say 'I love you' first." She tossed her hair back and forth with the music, little green earrings swinging.

"Do you really know Matthew McConaughey?" the blonde asked me as she handed me the spliff. She touched her cheek and then ran her fingers back through her hair.

"No, no," I said, holding the spliff daintily. My nails were freshly painted black, matching my toes. I paused to take a drag. "I met him once in Vegas. In a small club. Not Tangerine, but near there. I saw him do his chicken dance."

The girls both said, "What's the chicken dance?" and then they looked at each other and giggled.

Lovedrop explained: "It's how McConaughey was picking up women. It's his game."

The blonde shook her head. "Matthew McConaughey doesn't need game to pick up women. He's *hot*."

"I deduced his game plan," I continued, "at least for that night. But I presumed he must have used this particular tactic before." I took a final drag from the spliff and then extinguished it directly onto the glass coffee table, then continued: "I was at this club in Vegas and there he was, doing this weird chicken dance, and of course it gets a reaction. McConaughey's flapping his arms around and walking low, and bobbing his head up and down. Just drunk as a skunk—"

"It provokes people!" said Lovedrop.

My voice took on a conspiratorial tone as I continued: "They make comments to each other about how funny he looks, and they start to ask each other, 'Who is that guy?' And then finally someone says, 'Wait, that's Matthew McConaughey!' and it starts to get around."

I spoke with a certain rhythm, and a fascinated glint in my eye. "Soon, McConaughey's got everyone whispering, 'He's that movie star' and 'Wasn't he dating so-and-so?' His value demonstrations got uploaded into everyone's head. People are looking at him, talking about him; the whole room is warmed up for him."

I paused, opened both of my hands, and continued: "And it worked. He started chicken dancing with this girl. And he was crossing some barriers, he was socially violating a little bit, but knowingly. I'm more than certain he knew what he was doing."

I suddenly produced a plastic eyeball and held it up for everyone to see. Then I tossed it into the air and it vanished, eliciting a gasp. I grinned and said, "McConaughey made his own chicken splash, all over the room."

Everyone laughed. "Did you talk to him?" asked the blonde.

"Well, I talked to him for a few minutes," I said. "He and I had dated the same girl, Jackie, and we talked about our dogs . . ."[1]

The blonde squeezed my skinny arm and said, "Do you guys know what Mystery said to me tonight, when I walked by? He

---

1. By mentioning the girl Jackie, I activate an attraction switch in the blonde's mind: that I am preselected by other women.

looked over at me like he's curious about something and then he says, 'You ever dump in a gold toilet?'"

The brunette's jaw dropped open. "Are you serious?" she said.

The blonde giggled. She started to apply some lip gloss and said, "I couldn't believe it at first: That was his opener! And then he says it again: 'I said, you ever dump in a gold toilet? It's *divine!*'"

Both of the girls burst out laughing, and the brunette looked at me and said, "Oh my God! I never would have talked to you if you had said that to me!"

The blonde continued, " . . . I mean who talks like that?"

No one talks like that, my dear, I thought; *not when they're trying to impress you. That's the point.* I'm a firm believer in disqualifying myself as a potential suitor early on; the pickup just seems to go easier that way.

The blonde started toying with the strap on her purse, and then she said, "We *were* curious about you guys, though. We thought you were in a band or something. *Are* you in a band?"

The brunette said, "Yeah really, what do you guys do? Were you serious about that pickup artist stuff?"

You couldn't blame them for being curious. Our house, Project Miami, was a fifty-four-hundred-square-foot mansion in Coconut Grove. It looked like a work of modern art, white, angular, and rising above the surrounding lush vegetation. Our driveway was like a luxury auto dealership, filled with different models of Mercedes, a white Bentley, and the Rat's black Lexus with cheesy custom rims. With the exception of the Lexus, not a single car was worth less than a hundred thousand dollars. Not that we had paid for any of them with pickup artist money—we were onto a new caper in Miami.

"It's true, in a way," Lovedrop admitted. "We teach seminars on how to be social and meet people. We call it the Venusian Arts. And we help guys learn how to talk to girls." He paused and then said, "We just want everyone to have as much fun as we do, because so many guys in the bar don't know what they are doing."

The blonde nodded in agreement. "That's for sure. Most of the guys in the club are such douchebags! Seriously, you guys were the most fun of any guys that we talked to all night." *She's pretty*, I thought as I looked at her. *She reminds me of my ex-girlfriend.*

"For sure," echoed the brunette. "You guys were definitely the most fun."

"Yeah," said Lovedrop, strutting with faux arrogance. "All the other girls were jealous of you guys because you got to hang out with us."

The brunette laughed. "Oh my God, you are so full of yourselves." She shook her head.

"Oh, hey guys," I said suddenly, "do you want to see the piece I did for Current TV?" I pulled out my iPhone, started a video, and handed it to the blonde. There I was on TV before her eyes, being interviewed like a big shot. The whole night I had been uploading my own value demonstrations into her head. It was like I was going down a checklist:

Fame? Current TV clip. Check.

Center of attention? Matthew McConaughey Story, everyone listens eagerly. Check.

Preselection? I dated this beautiful girl. Check.

Leader of men? "Are you ready for this? I am the tribal leader." Check.

Strong identity? Grounding routine. Check. Avatar. Check.

Social alignments? "I want you to meet my cool friends." Intro Lovedrop. Check.

Presently, the blonde said, "'World's Greatest Pickup Artist,' that's what it says on this video." She looked up at me.

I said, "Yeah, are you ready for this?" My pale skin gave me a vampiric charm in the glow of the projector, a reminder of my nocturnal lifestyle. "Turns out, some people think I'm the world's greatest pickup artist! Isn't that crazy?" I said it as if I found it strangely surprising.

The blonde snorted derisively. "Yeah right. *I'm* the one who picked *you* up tonight. And you were easy."

"*Easy* is just a word that people use when they're feeling over-confident," I replied. "But beauty is common. There are models all over South Beach. Personally, I prefer a woman with more flaws, more character. That's what I like about you. There is beauty in imperfection." I nodded at her seriously and continued: "You're one of us! I can tell. All that boy/girl stuff aside. You're in your humanity like the rest of us."

The Rat rolled up a one-dollar bill and made it into a straw, and then he leaned forward and snorted a fat line of blue powder from the glass table in front of him. His spiky black hair glistened from too much hair gel. "Hey LD," he said, "you should check out my modeling portfolio. I was a professional model, you know. I used to be in really good shape. I was even skinnier and more ripped than you."

"And you can be again," said Lovedrop. He took another swig from his protein shake and said, "I was overweight when I moved here a few months ago."

"Really?" asked the brunette, squeezing his bicep. "You look good now."

"Do you really mean that?" he flexed proudly.

"Of course." She giggled. "You're buff."

"Now I feel validated," Lovedrop said, beaming like a little boy. Then, as if with resignation, he said, "Oh, all right, you can have a hug . . ." and he rolled his eyes and looked away, opened his arms to her, and gave her a big hug. Squeezing her close, he paused momentarily. He was about to say, *You smell good,* but then he felt her stiffen just a little, and so to err on the side of caution, he said, "All right, that's all you get, now get off of me," then he pushed her away and rolled off.

Lovedrop thought to himself, *I'll just keep plowing her comfort levels and see how far I can get tonight. No big deal. I'll just go back and escalate again in a minute . . .*

Just then, we all heard a sharp muffled crack, followed by a distant sound like a woman's moan.

Everyone stopped.

"What was that?" asked the brunette.

"What was what?" said Lovedrop.

Then we heard it again, a distinct slapping sound followed by a woman's moan, and then again. It sounded like she was being spanked.

"That's Johnny," said the Rat. "He's down in his room with that flight attendant girl."

The brunette raised an eyebrow.

"Who all lives here?" asked the blonde.

Too many questions, I thought.

"Johnny just rents a room here," said Lovedrop. "He has his own place across town. He's a good guy. And he's also into bondage." Then he joked, "You should see the dungeon at his other house!"

"Wait a sec," said the brunette reservedly. "Are you saying there is a dungeon down there, with whips and chains and stuff?"

"No, no," I said, "he just has a bedroom here. She visits sometimes; they're into spanking." I sounded certain, sincere, no big deal.

I better make this quick, I thought. *Next thing you know Matador will come walking out here with his shirt off.* "Oh!" I said suddenly, "that reminds me. Have you guys ever seen Google Earth?" I thought, *bullshit baffles brains.*

"Oh yeah," said the blonde, "you were talking about that at the bar, right?"

"Oh my *God,* you *have* to see it." I was enthusiastic. "It's the most amazing thing. I have already flown all around Miami in Google Earth. Come on, I'll show you on my projector." I stood up, tall and skinny, and grabbed her by the hand. I looked like Tommy Lee; my avatar was an image I had created through years of experimentation. She looked at the brunette, and the two locked eyes.

Lovedrop turned to the brunette. "I'll show you around the house," he offered.

"Actually," she said, "I'm going to stay with my friend. No offense." She picked up her high heels and started slipping them back on.

Damn it, thought Lovedrop.

Another spank rang out from below, followed by another moan.

I led the blonde by the hand, and both girls followed me across the fluffy white rug, up the white marble steps, past the stainless-steel kitchen, around the pool table, into my bedroom, and up onto my white custom California king-size bed.

Lovedrop remained for a moment while the Rat snorted another blue line off the table. *Now I can't invite myself along without coming off like a try-hard,* he thought. *I have to wait it out. Hopefully she'll get bored. Maybe I should have just thrown her over my shoulder.* The gray of morning was starting to show through the windows.

"By the way," said the Rat, "you've got a conference call with the lawyers tomorrow. I forgot to tell you, your phone was off today and they called the office line. You guys are all being sued."

Another spank rang out, followed by another moan.

"Sure you don't want any of this?" the Rat slurred, and grinned as he held up the rolled dollar bill. His eyes defocused slightly and some drool began to leak from the corner of his mouth and into his Backstreet Boy goatee. He kept grinning and stared off into the distance somewhere.

Lovedrop snatched the dollar from him. "Give me that thing," he said.

MYSTERY'S TOP 10 TIPS

1) Get into the habit of starting conversations just for the practice. Release your outcome and be relaxed in the process.

2) Between approaches, always remember to smile while mingling.

3) Lean back and relax when you initiate conversations. Don't lean in. Speak slowly and expressively. This alone will improve your game by 300 percent.

4) Be chatty—really—and convey a strong sense of fascination. Talk about relationships and the mysterious, and use lots of humor as well as emotional and sensory descriptions. Enthusiasm is contagious.

5) Don't say anything to impress her, such as bragging about your job, girls, or friends. Instead, indirectly convey value via demonstration and incidental story details. If she can tell that you are trying to impress her, she will perceive you as lower value.

6) Don't act as if anything is a big deal. Be fun and playful. Vibe with her, but don't react to her. Act the same way you would act with your eight-year-old niece.

7) As you hang out with her, and she has an opportunity to win you over, *then* show her your increasing interest. She must recognize that she has genuinely won you over with her personality.

8) Balance indicators of interest with indicators of disinterest. Do this both in your conversation with her and also as you escalate with her physically. This has a great effect.

9) Wear one accessory that gives other people an excuse to initiate a conversation with you, such as a hat, or a certain ring or necklace. Have a good story prepared for when this happens.

10) Have a life. Go to the gym and stay in shape, and continually improve your wardrobe. Cultivate your circle of female friends. Throw parties. Put effort into your social circle. A girl should imagine herself being a part of your cool life.

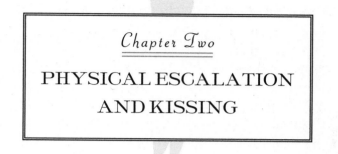

Chapter Two

PHYSICAL ESCALATION AND KISSING

WHEN IT CAME TIME TO WRITE THIS BOOK, it seemed fitting to me that we should make an official record of my knowledge and tactics regarding physical escalation and kissing.

It's amazing to me how applicable this chapter can be to every other aspect of your game. In fact, there are lessons in this chapter that will give you valuable insight on indicators of interest, the use of disinterest to preserve comfort levels, compliance and microcalibration, role-playing, inner game, and more. So much so, that I've decided to put this chapter here toward the beginning of this book.

Physical escalation is actually quite easy. Just read along with me and I will show you how. Just do what I say and it will work. Don't worry, it's easy, and the moves I'm going to teach you will not get you rejected. Trust me. It's fun and you can stop anytime. Now, let's get right into it . . .

Everyone's first question is, "How will I know when the time is right to kiss her?"

The easy answer is that a woman, any woman, will give off very specific signals when she is ready to be kissed. All you have to do is

---

Lesson One:

Women give off signals when they are attracted to you.

---

watch for these signals and you will know exactly when she is giving you the green light. I call these signals her indicators of interest. (See chart.)

If a woman touches you often during conversation—for example, if she touches your arm when saying something to you—then she is signaling her interest in you. Furthermore, this behavior is unconscious—she's probably not even aware that she's doing it. Women are hardwired to touch when they feel attracted.

If she giggles a lot, or asks you a lot of questions, or tries to joke with you a lot, then she is interested in you. These are also green lights.

Another example of a green light is when a woman continually turns to face you with her body. This means that even if you turn away from her a little, then she will also turn until she is facing you again. Women do this unconsciously when they are attracted to someone.

Another green light is self-grooming: For example, as she is talking with you, she will touch her hair more and start to toy with it. She'll toss her hair, drawing attention to it. She will touch her face and her neck, and the back of her hand. She will scratch her cheek, next to her nose, and between the lip and the nose. It's hardwired, designed into the circuit of our brain, to scratch these key points. It's a behavioral design.

If a girl is laughing at all your material (even stuff that really isn't all that funny), that is a signal.

If a girl grabs your arm and leans into you or puts her head on your shoulder, that's a signal.

If she leans in toward you for extended periods of time, or crosses her legs toward you, that is a signal.

INDICATORS OF . . .

INTEREST (IOIs)	DISINTEREST (IODs)
Proximity	Avoidance
Self-grooming	Impatience
Scratching face	Crosses arms
Toying with hair	Hand toss
Giving attention	Rolls off
Vibing with you	Disacknowledgment
Giggling	Breaking rapport
Offering value	Disinterested
Touching you	Pushes away
Showing appreciation	Disqualifiers, Negs
Asking questions	Drops conversation
Leaning in	Leans back
Facing you	Faces away
Trying to impress	Disallows frames
Allows escalation	Gives resistance

If she folds her arms or leans back or turns her crossed legs away from you, don't go for the kill until these things change. If it doesn't change, don't bother going in. Be willing to leave. These are all bad signals.

Here's the secret: If you see her do at least three of these indicators of interest (such as touching you, toying with her hair, asking you lots of questions, and giggling during conversation), then you can kiss her.

The easy way to interpret her signals is this: "The more, the better." A single green light may not really mean anything. But you can expect an entire flurry of green lights from a woman when she's really warming up toward you.

Here's the best part: With practice, over time, you will also develop kissing sensors. What I mean by this is that after you get enough practice going for the kiss, you will just *know* when the time is right. You will develop a feeling—an intuition, an inner sense of when she is ready for you to kiss her. This sense develops naturally through practice.

I remember one time when I explained this to my friend Dan. He was asking me how he would know when the time was right to go for the kiss.

I answered him by saying, "Of course, you already know that you can just watch for her signals, her green lights, and then kiss her. But even better than that, my advice is to just start a lot of conversations with girls, and then go for the kiss as often as possible, just for the sake of practice. By doing this, you will naturally develop sensors from the practice, and then your sensors will activate and notify you every time a girl is ready to kiss you. It's like having clairvoyant powers."

A few months later, Dan called me up to report on his progress, and he said, "Mystery, I've got to tell you, it worked! I went out and practiced your Kiss Gambit on as many different girls as I could, and before long I just started to get this eerie feeling whenever a girl was ready for me to kiss her. It's like an alarm bell going off in my head!"

I said, "Well, that's great, Dan! I'm glad to hear it worked!"

Dan continued: "It took some practice before it became perfectly accurate, but now, I've gotta tell you, I might be at work, selling a phone to a customer, and suddenly my sensors will activate and I know, absolutely know, that I could just kiss her right then and there, and I know I would get away with it.

"I mean, I wouldn't kiss a customer, but I use it a lot in the bar. I'll be out practicing my game, talking to some girl, and suddenly my sensors will activate, and know I can just kiss her. I used to use Mystery's Kiss Gambit when it happened, you know, to cover my

MYSTERY'S KISS GAMBIT

I designed a kissing exercise that you can practice in social situations whenever you think the time is right to kiss a girl. This gambit is designed so that you can go for the kiss smoothly, and deftly avoid any embarrassing rejection scenarios. Here's how it works:

As she is talking, hold up your finger to your lips and say:

"Shh . . . You talk a lot. Would you like to kiss me?"

Now there are only four things that can happen, and we have a way to handle them all:

- If she says *yes*, then kiss her!
- If she says *no*, then say, "I didn't say you could, you just looked like you had something on your mind." Then just continue talking and move on to the next part of your conversation—you have avoided rejection.
- If she says *maybe*, or *I don't know*, then it actually means *yes*! Often a woman wants to kiss you, but she just can't admit it out loud. It's okay, just say "Let's find out," and then *kiss her*.
- If she says *not here*, then she is actually saying, "I want to kiss you, but I can't do it in front of these people." Demonstrate your social intelligence by telling her, "I understand." Now you know you can kiss her the next time you are alone together.

ass in case I was wrong, but lately I don't even do that anymore, I just go straight for the kiss. It's that accurate!"

Trust me, if Dan can do it, then you can, too.

The best part about kissing a woman is that even if she refuses the first kiss, you can just try to kiss her again later, without losing your chance with her. You might have thought it was a rejection, but in my experience, women often refuse the first kiss as a matter of course, and usually the door is even more open for you to kiss her again than it was before you tried. We will talk about this more later on in the book.

What if I'm not sure? It can feel so awkward and nervous "making a move" at the end of the night. How can I ensure that things will go smoothly?

The first part of solving this problem is understanding where that awkward feeling comes from in the first place: The way that you interact with a woman, over time, is what begins to feel normal between the two of you.

When you are interacting with a woman, touching should be a normal part of that interaction from the very beginning. Even innocuous little social touches, such as gently pushing a woman's shoulder, or touching her forearm, or throwing your arm around her—you must be constantly doing this with her. That way, physical touch becomes a normal part of the way that the two of you behave together. It would feel weird not to touch.

Lesson Two:

Touching should be a normal and constant part of the way you interact with other people, from the very beginning. There should never be some *big moment,* but instead a series of tiny little moments, and they're always no big deal.

If you wait too long, if you don't start touching her and her friends when you first meet them, then even innocuous touches will seem weird later on.

So you see, the reason it feels so weird when you try to make a move at the end of the night is that you waited too long; you should have been touching her the whole time.

Lucky for you, this chapter is filled with all the moves you will need to know, in order to do exactly this. Let's get started with our first move, the Shoulder Tap:

As you are saying something to her, tap her shoulder with the back of your hand.

Now, this Shoulder Tap move might not seem like that big a deal, but that's the whole point! After all, if you want to become a more physical person, the easiest way to start is by using harmless little touches as you talk to people, which will seem normal and so-cial to the both of you, like it's *no big deal*.

How hard can it be to tap a woman on the shoulder as part of what you are saying to her? There's nothing to it. So there's no ex-

---

Lesson Three:

Force yourself to start using innocuous social touches as a normal part of your conversation with a woman, such as touching her shoulder as you say something to her. Just force yourself to use more touching during your social in-teractions.

cuse not to immediately start adding this piece into your conversations with women. Don't just do it once—do it all the time.

The secret is to touch her as if you yourself do not even notice your own touches. Your touches should seem as though they are automatic, beneath the rest of your conversation and below your conscious awareness.

Lesson Four:

Touch her absentmindedly, as though you yourself are *not even aware* that you are touching her.

Let's go to the next move in our arsenal, the Shoulder Grasp:

STEP 1: Look away from her with your eyes and grasp her shoulder with your hand at the same time as you say something to her.

STEP 2: Look back toward her as you let go of her shoulder.

That's all there is to it. Again, this is just a simple little move that you can start incorporating into your social interactions. It doesn't convey any sexual or romantic interest; there's nothing creepy about it at all. All it does is help condition people to feel that it is normal for you to touch them.

The important thing to notice about this move is that I am giving her mixed signals of interest and disinterest. In this example, I touch her shoulder with my hand, which signals that I am interested in her, but I also look away as I do it, which signals that I am disinterested in her.

This is important, because the use of disinterest here allows me to accomplish a level of touching that could otherwise appear to be too forward. In other words, the more disinterest that I use, the more touching I get away with. Much of the game itself is based around this principle of disinterest.

Lesson Five:

Whenever you do something that signals that you are interested in her, such as touching her shoulder, then soften the impact of that interest by also doing something to signal disinterest, such as looking away while you touch her. Of course, that is only an example — be sure to play around with various combinations.

By the way, the actual words that you say to her are not really important. All that matters is that you have something to say, so that your touch appears to be part of the bigger whole.

For example, I might touch her shoulder as I look out across the rest of the room and say, "Look at all of these people in here." Then I let go of her shoulder at the same time as I look back toward her, saying, "I love people watching." I continue talking from here, perhaps going into a people-watching game. See how my touch is un-

---

Lesson Six:

Your touches should appear as though they are a natural part of your words, even though they may be completely unrelated, logically, to whatever you are actually saying.

---

related logically to whatever I was actually saying, yet it was still a natural part of how I said it?

The next thing I want you to notice, from the previous example, is that I grabbed her shoulder, but then I let her go. This is also important. The longer you are touching someone, the more noticeable your touch can become. It's better to touch her and then release before things ever have a chance to get awkward.

Therefore, when you touch her, you should always be the one to push away first. You touch, and then you push away.

Lesson Seven:

Touch and release, touch and release. You are the one who makes the move, and you are also the one who pushes it away. She will never be in a position to "reject" you because you already pushed her away first.

Our next move is the Grab Both Shoulders bit.

Use both of your hands to grab both of her shoulders, move her a little, and then let go.

For example, as you are saying something to her, use both of your hands to grasp both of her shoulders, and physically move her, as you are talking, so that she is positioned slightly differently from how she started—even if you have only turned her a few inches. Then let go of her. You should continue talking through this entire process, as if you don't even notice the fact of your own touch.

Let's say that I am using a scripted routine and I want to incorporate this move. Here's how it might go, with words, using Lovedrop's *Honey I Shrunk the Kids* routine:

LOVEDROP: You know what? [He grasps her shoulders with both hands and turns her slightly.]

LOVEDROP: I'm gonna take you back to my place tonight, I've got a . . . [Now he releases her shoulders as he looks around conspiratorially, as if afraid that someone might overhear.]

LOVEDROP: . . . I've got a *Honey I Shrunk the Kids* machine . . .

[She starts laughing.]

LOVEDROP: . . . and I'm going to shrink us down, like Barbie and Ken dolls, and we're going to swim, and explore that fish tank, right there, and we'll find magical new lands, and have amazing adventures . . .

Notice how he grabs her shoulders while he does this routine, even though he could have just said the words without touching her at all. Thus he is actively incorporating physical touch into the way that he interacts with her.

Notice also how it seems as if he's not really even aware that he is touching her, but rather that he is entirely focused on the story that he is telling her.

He is also the one touching her, and then he is the one letting go, so that he is always the person leading the entire process, and she never has an opportunity to push him away.

The next move I want to show you is Thumb Wrestling.

As you are talking to her, hold up your right hand in front of you, so that it is flat and your palm is facing to the left. Say to her "Go like this," so that she will hold up her right hand in the same way.

Next, say, "Let me see," as you use your left hand to gently grasp her wrist and then bring her right hand so that it is palm to palm with your own right hand.

Next, say, "Okay, go like this," as you curl your fingers and bring both hands into thumb-wrestling position.

Thumb wrestle with her for a little bit, just for fun, and then push her away and continue on to the next topic of conversation. Act like it was just a bit of fun.

Lesson Eight:

Always use baby steps to get what you want. Never try to get too much at once.

Notice how I could have just said, "Let's thumb wrestle. Give me your hand." But then she probably would have said no. Why? Because that would be asking her for too much up front, which in our experience only pressures people to say no. Instead, I used baby steps: First I held up my hand, then I asked her to hold up her hand, then I touched her hand, then I began thumb wrestling with her. Step by step, I got my way!

By using baby steps in this way, and taking things one step at a time, I am able to get her to follow my lead much more easily. Always lead a woman one step at a time.

Here's another move that illustrates this principle. It's called the Handshake Routine:

YOU: Have you ever heard of the L.A. Handshake?

TARGET: No . . .

YOU: Here, go like this. [Holding up my hand as if to shake.]

TARGET: [She holds up her hand.]

YOU: [Taking her hand] Okay, it goes like this, and like this, then there's a snap at the end.

TARGET: [Playing along.]

YOU: Okay, try it again; that was pretty good. [We handshake again.]

YOU: Okay, now, have you ever heard of the San Diego Handshake?

TARGET: No, what is it?

YOU: Okay, let me see your hand . . . [Showing her another handshake.]

YOU: That's pretty good! Okay, now, have you ever seen this one? [Fluttering your fingers quickly over her forearm, while having her do the same to you, several times.]

TARGET: What is that one?

YOU: I don't know, some drunk girl showed me that! [Motioning dismissively toward her while turning slightly away with your body.]

TARGET: [Laughing.]

[You turn back and continue leading the conversation to the next topic.]

See how she played along because you were leading one step at a time? However, if you had asked for everything up front, for example, if you had said, "Here, gimme your hand, I want to show you two or three different handshakes," then she might have just said "No thanks"—because that would be too much to ask for at once. Get it?

While we're being fun and playful, I would be shirking my duty if I didn't mention the High-five.

Whenever something particularly cool happens, or she says something to impress you, or you just want to vibe with her, hold up your hand, fingers pointed up and palm facing out, toward her.

Exclaim, "High-five!"

If she high-fives you back, just smile and continue talking. This is almost always what will happen.

If she doesn't high-five you, then she is being rather rude. Hold up both your hands now and say, "Whoa . . . excuse me . . ." as if you are joking to yourself and having fun. Smile and continue talking, to her or to anyone else you prefer.

If a woman refuses your move, no big deal, you'll just chill back for a few moments and then make another move. That's the kind of guy you are. In fact, she will appreciate this carefree vibe that you bring.

Lesson Nine:

It's not about avoiding rejection; it's about responding to it attractively.

Even when a woman doesn't go along with your move, don't react in the slightest! Act completely normal. You're just the kind of guy who likes to have fun and who doesn't take anything too seriously. Act as if you didn't really even notice what happened. In fact, feel free to keep making moves on her as long as she remains in your proximity.

This "no big deal" vibe is very important! It's what allows you to get away with all this touching while other guys stand around helplessly. You know what every good Venusian artist knows: that women will normally refuse various moves, and that it's no big deal. The only question is whether you feel deflated and give up, or whether you relax and continue having fun, and continue making moves, and act like it's no big deal either way, because you're not needy. You're just having fun.

We've really made some progress! So far, it is now fun and normal for my hands to touch her hands, or for me to grab her by the shoulders and also for me to physically position her. It's fun and normal for us to be playfully physical with each other. These physical touches are a normal part of our experience as we interact with each other. And we're not done yet.

Here's our next move: the Arm-in-Arm:

ARM-IN-ARM

With the woman standing to your right, hold out your right elbow toward her, as though you are offering her your arm.

At the same time, using your left hand, take her left hand under your right elbow and rest the palm of her left hand on the top of your right forearm.

The result of this is that she is now "on your arm."

Because this move signals interest toward her, you must soften it by signaling disinterest as well. An easy way to do this is to point at her and say, "Now don't get any funny ideas; that's all you get!" and continue the conversation.

Keep your left hand on top of her left hand. Why? So that you can feel if she is about to pull her hand away from you, in which case you can preempt her by dropping her hand before she can drop yours. Do it in an absentminded, dismissive way.

Lesson Ten:

Disinterest creates feelings of comfort. If she is being resistant to your touch, then use more disinterest. For example, toss her hand away, turn your body away from her, or talk to someone else in the group. Do not do this as though you are trying to punish her, but rather as though it's no big deal.

HAND-ON-LEG

While sitting next to her, take her hand and rest it on your leg. Soften the move by saying, "Don't get any funny ideas." Continue talking to her about something unrelated.

If you feel her start to pull her hand away, then preempt her and toss it off your leg yourself. This toss should feel a little dismissive to her, but again, you act as if it's no big deal to you, as if you were focused on what you were saying.

Now, you might ask me, "Mystery, I don't get it. Why am I putting her hand on my leg?"

Good question. The answer is that you are testing to see where she is emotionally. You are testing for how much compliance she will give you. That's all we're doing with any of these moves—test to see how much compliance she will give and to condition her to be more and more compliant as a normal part of our interaction together.

Let's illustrate this with our next move, the Kino Test.

THE KINO TEST

As I am talking to a girl, I will hold out my hands, palms up. I continue talking—the conversational topic itself is unrelated. The implication is clear on my face that she is supposed to comply and put her hands into mine.

Does she give me her hands? This is a compliance test. If she puts her hands into mine, then she has complied. This will almost always happen, if delivered right.

Next, as I continue talking about something unrelated, I squeeze her hands a little bit. I am testing to see if she squeezes back.

I then push her left hand forward and pull her right hand back, and then I push her right hand forward and pull her left hand back. I reverse again, back and forth a few times as I continue talking to her, just testing to see how eager she is to follow along, or if there is any resistance in her touch.

I then slowly lower my hands as I continue talking. I am testing to see if she will follow.

Then I give her hands a dismissive toss, while our conversation itself continues unabated.

If at any time during the routine I had detected resistance from her, I would have immediately preempted her with a dismissive toss of her hands, thus ending the Kino Test with a physical signal of disinterest.

"Wait a sec," you might ask. "If she resists, then I toss her hands away. That makes sense. But you're saying that if she complies, I also end the gambit by tossing her hands away? So I am supposed to show disinterest either way?"

That's right, you're supposed to show disinterest either way. The disinterest is what keeps things comfortable and fun between the two of you, allowing you to keep making more and more moves.

Remember, you make a move, and then you push her away again. Do this over and over again; it should be a part of the vibe between the two of you. In fact, this should also be a part of the way you talk to her.

The next principle I want to talk about comes from dog training. The concept is very simple: Reward good behavior. Makes sense, right? If you want to encourage something, reward it. Now we all know women are not dogs, and it would be a stupid mistake to take this analogy too literally, but the basic principles of behavior still apply.

Let's say you are trying to train a dog to sit. First you say, "Sit!" If he sits, then you say, "Good boy! Good boy!" and you give him a doggy treat. Notice how you are rewarding him with a feeling of appreciation?

Doesn't that just make sense? You reward your dog for compliance—that's how he learns. And when you say "good boy," you aren't just saying the words. More than that, your tone of voice sounds all happy and excited. A dog can't understand the English language, but you know he can still feel that appreciation in your voice.

This gets down to one of the most basic mistakes that men make in the way that they relate to women. Most men are too eager to give a beautiful woman more attention and more appreciation, even when she hasn't earned it. They start a conversation by telling her how beautiful she is. They ask her if she has a boyfriend, and they offer to buy her a drink. They touch her but they fail to push her away. They give her green light after green light, when they don't even know who she is. This behavior only lowers their value in her eyes.

A Venusian artist knows better. Save your green lights, and make sure that when you give a woman your growing attention and appreciation, it's only when she has earned it.

When she complies, or tries to impress you, or to vibe with you, those are the times to smile more, to lean in more, to ask more questions. In this way you can condition her so that she will continue to be more and more compliant in the future.

Lesson Eleven:

Whenever a woman is compliant to one of your moves, reward her with your growing attention and appreciation. In other words, give her your green lights, but only when she feels like she has earned it. Get her to work for it.

The next move is a popular one in the pickup community; it's called the Spin Move.

The Spin Move, like all the other moves in this book, is something you should practice all the time. Find an excuse to throw it into your social interactions, just for the sake of practice.

Notice how the Spin Move incorporates lessons such as constantly making moves, rewarding good behavior, and showing oc-

THE SPIN MOVE

STEP 1: As you are talking with her, hold your hand up and look at it. Say to her, "Look at this." [This is a compliance test.]

STEP 2: When she looks at your hand, say, "Go like this." [Another test.]

STEP 3: When she puts her hand up like yours, take it and say, "Now do a little spin." [Yet another compliance test.]

STEP 4: Spin her around and say, "Very nice!" [Rewarding her.]

STEP 5: Toss her hand dismissively and continue the interaction.

[Showing disinterest, then repeating the cycle.]

casional disinterest—disinterest that makes it possible for you to repeat the process and test for compliance again.

Another way to look at this is with a fishing metaphor:

Lesson Twelve:

BAIT-HOOK-REEL-RELEASE

BAIT: The bait is any time that you test her for compliance. That is, any time that you "make a move."

HOOK: If she complies with your move, then you could say she has hooked. (If she doesn't hook, then immediately go to the Release step.)

REEL: This is where you signal her with green lights to reward her for compliance. As she senses your growing interest and appreciation of her, she begins to feel that she is slowly winning you over.

RELEASE: Next, push her away. This disinterest builds her attraction levels, and it is also what builds her comfort levels, allowing you to repeat the process and Bait-Hook-Reel-Release all over again!

Make no mistake: This metaphor is a piece of solid gold when it comes to gaming and picking up women. In fact, you can apply it to every aspect of your game; furthermore, I encourage you to apply it to every tactic in this book while you're out practicing.

Just for the hell of it, let's apply this metaphor to the simple hug:

BAIT: You are *such* a little *shit*! Get your ass over here! [Holding my arms open to motion for a hug.]
HOOK: [Target hugs me.]
REEL: [With both arms wrapped around her.] Oh my *God*, you are totally one of us! You're a character. I love you!
RELEASE: [Pushing her away.] All right, now get off me! [Smiling.]

I use Bait-Hook-Reel-Release over and over again in my game, gaining more and more compliance over time with each move that I make. I'm telling you, this metaphor has it all: repetitious compliance testing, rewarding good behavior with growing interest and appreciation, and adding elements of disinterest to build comfort and discourage resistance. What more could you want in a metaphor?

The next move I want to talk about is pretty simple . . .

ARM-AROUND-SHOULDER

Just throw your arm around her shoulder. You probably do this with your buddies all the time anyway. Do it with the girls as well, and in fact do it with all her friends. Do it with everybody! Just be sure to release.

I know it seems like just a single paragraph of this book, but the Arm-Around-Shoulder is so much more important than that. If you aren't doing this regularly while talking to girls and their friends, then something is definitely missing from your game, so start using it! The idea is to do it for short vibing moments, and not to make people feel imposed upon.

In fact, even more important is our next move:

THROW-BOTH-OF-YOUR-ARMS-AROUND-TWO-GIRLS'-SHOULDERS-AT-THE-SAME-TIME

This move looks exactly how it reads. Imagine that you come up behind two of your own friends. As you do, you throw an arm around each's shoulder while standing between them. You laugh with them for a moment and then you push off them again. Remember to always balance signals of interest with signals of disinterest.

If a move like this would be no big deal with your friends, then why would it be any different with your new friends—that is, the woman you are socializing with and her group of friends?

It wouldn't be for me, and that's why it's important to keep practicing moves like this, along with all the other moves in this book, until the same is true for you. A natural, smooth delivery of these moves requires practice.

Use this stuff! It's one thing to nod your head as you read along. It's another to actually practice doing this while talking with real, live people. These moves work great, trust me—it's easy, and you can stop anytime.

The next move I want to show you is called the TV Test:

TV TEST

STEP 1: [Bait—baby step.] As you are talking with her, put your hands on her shoulders.

STEP 2: [Bait—baby step.] Say to her, "Okay, check this out," as you turn her around and wrap your arms around her shoulders from behind. Her arms should be under yours, but in a comfortable way. You're hugging her from behind, over her arms.

STEP 3: [Bait.] Without missing a beat, say, "Okay, now imagine that we're watching TV. We've been hanging out for, say, about six months, so we've already had all our fights . . . and found all our boundaries . . . Now what's your favorite show?"

STEP 4: She'll say *Friends* or *Sex and the City*. [Hook!]

STEP 5: Say, "Okay, so we're watching *Sex and the City* . . ." [Reel: Holding her and rocking back and forth a little bit.]

STEP 6: [Release.] Suddenly push her away, saying, "All right, show's over!"

This is a great routine, one of my favorites. Of course, you wouldn't use the TV Test as your first gambit; you have to build up to this point. That's why we do all those shoulder claps and spin moves early on. Get it?

What if she mentions her boyfriend?

If at any time she mentions her boyfriend, that's a classic signal that you were showing her too much interest without making her work for it as a reward. Stop giving her so many green lights and instead practice Bait-Hook-Reel-Release.

Don't worry, the situation is recoverable—just keep practicing, and try to keep a lid on your interest levels from now on.

Oh, and whatever you do, don't start asking her all about her boyfriend. He may not even exist. Just be chill and go into your next story. It's no big deal.

What if she rejects me when I go for the kiss?

Now I want to tell you one of the biggest secrets about going for the kiss: Your chances of kissing her are actually *better* after the first time that she refuses a kiss than they were before.

How can this be? The concept isn't intuitive to men, because we either want to kiss a certain woman, or we don't. (In other words, when you refuse to kiss a certain woman, even once, it's usually because you have no intention of ever kissing her.)

But women aren't programmed like this. A woman needs to put up a little resistance at first, especially with something as intimate as kissing, or she'll feel easy. And you don't want to make her feel easy, do you?

Let's review Lesson Nine:

> It's not about avoiding rejection; it's about responding to it attractively.

When a woman refuses a kiss, she isn't actually rejecting you, and in fact she will be disappointed if you give up. Now is the critical time to respond appropriately . . .

She just needs to see how you respond in such situations; it's her way of testing your emotional programming to ensure that you are a suitable mate. She needs to see that it's *no big deal* to you, that you're just being fun and playful (as opposed to being all intense and romantic) and that you'll roll off her like it's no big deal, and you'll even come back in a few minutes and go for the kiss again.

When you respond to her in this way, it conditions her to feel safe around you, and it conditions her to relax and enjoy it when you make a move, since she knows that she can put a stop to things at any time, and that if she does, you'll be cool with it. She has nothing to worry about. Instead, she has something to enjoy.

The only way to lose a girl after she refuses your kiss is if you get frustrated or needy about it. But instead, if you respond like a high-value guy, then she will actually become more attracted to you than she was before. It's all up to you.

I know this sounds crazy if you haven't been out practicing your game. But if you actually go out and practice this stuff, you'll see what I mean. As long as she keeps giving you green lights, then you can keep going for the kiss—and soon she'll go for it as well!

The next move I'd like to introduce you to is Lovedrop's Kiss Gambit:

One way to get to the kiss is to work your way up to it with lots of little pecks. Do you know what a peck is? It's one of those innocent little kisses where you only use your lips. They are harmless and come off at first as if nothing is happening.

If you don't feel ready for the full-on kiss, just start pecking her—everywhere but her lips!

- Give her a hug and peck the top of her head.
- Hold her close and kiss her forehead.
- Lean over and kiss her on the shoulder.
- Kiss her on the back of the neck.
- Kiss her jawline.
- Kiss her cheek.
- Kiss her chin.
- Kiss her lips.

The whole time this is going on, you are using your fingers to rub her shoulder muscles, and also stroking your hands and fingertips across her shoulders, arms, back, and the outside of her hips.

Even if a woman is resisting your kiss, as long as she is still giving you green lights, then Lovedrop's Kiss Gambit will often still work.

Next thing you know, the two of you will be kissing with tongue. Don't be too aggressive—savor each embrace of the lips, use your

MYSTERY'S CALIBRATED KISS GAMBIT

This one is really simple. If she's giving you the green light, then lean in, and lean back—just enough to poke your face into her personal space for a moment and test for her response. If she doesn't flinch or move away, then go right in and kiss her.

tongue sparingly, and remember to push her away periodically. You can always go back and kiss her again.

A word of caution: When you are making out with a woman, remember not to let things get too hot and heavy, or you could give her feelings of buyer's remorse. If this happens, you could wake up the next day to discover that you can't even get her on the phone anymore.

All things in moderation—don't get her too aroused until the two of you are in a place, such as a bedroom, where you could actually make things happen.

MATADOR'S MICROCALIBRATED KISS GAMBIT

At a certain moment in the interaction, you should feel a genuine affinity, both from the girl toward you and from you toward the girl. This affinity should be the *current emotional state* of you both. Over time and through practice, you will be able to pinpoint whatever state another human being is in, and you will be able to shift their state by shifting your own. In your experience, this is accomplished emotionally. But in the physical world, all of this emotional communication is actually occurring through subtle signals. People constantly ping each other and calibrate to each other's emotions, unconsciously, via facial micro-expressions, body language IOIs and IODs, tone of voice, reactivity, and so on.

The time comes to initiate a kiss, a higher level of touching. During a certain point in the conversation, the expression of affection will become warranted. She may say something cute or funny, and you now have a "reason" to show affection.

What I'd like you to do next is look at her in a very endearing, sincere, affectionate way. Not too much. The ultimate goal is authenticity: a real perception on her part that you are feeling affection for her and that it's coming from a real, core place.

Use your hands to cup both sides of her face gently along her jawline; smooth, graceful, not choppy, not too masculine, something that a man of a romantic nature would do, and with an air of playfulness permeating throughout.

Then, with a current emotional state of playfulness displayed on your end, with happiness and affection, initiate in a very slow, graceful manner, a kiss toward the side of her cheek.

Then pull back, but just 10 percent, and look at her with a sincere smile. The most important thing is that it's perceived as coming from a real place. If she mirrors you back with a similar emotional state, with affinity, with warmth, then reinitiate the kiss, this time on the lips.

The moment you put your hands on your cheeks, you will be able to sense a change in her current emotional state, if she is not ready. It will feel like tension on your fingertips, a tendency for her body to want to turn away from you, a tendency for her face to turn from one side to the other. These are indicators that she's not ready yet. If she is acting like that, then do not go for the second round; she's not ready. Instead, do a roll-off as a nonverbal IOD, then continue the set and eventually try to kiss again.

If, after the cheek kiss, you pull back to look at her and she doesn't mirror back your current emotional state, then do not go for your second round, the kiss on the lips. It's a seamless exit point. If she wasn't ready, you will know it, two steps in advance—and you won't ever get caught in an awkward "trying to force the kiss" situation.

If she *is* ready, you will get a current emotional state of warmth, joy, and affinity, and it will come from both ends. The kiss on the lips will seem natural, beautiful, and pleasurable for both parties.

Chapter Three

THE HOUSE IN FULL SWING

WE HAD SET UP OUR OFFICE in Project Miami in what was meant to be the dining room. A large square table dominated the center of the room. I sat across from Lovedrop, and our business competitor and housemate Mehow sat directly across from James Matador, owner of the house and my soon-to-be co-star on VH1's *The Pickup Artist*. The table was a mess of papers, wires, and laptop computers, with a large speakerphone in the middle. Our employee Justin shuffled some papers behind me.

Along the wall behind Lovedrop were five identical atomic clocks, each one labeled for a different city: Sydney, Los Angeles, Chicago, New York, London. They ticked along in cadent synchronicity. Our new company was called Venusian Arts, and the three of us—myself, Matador, and Lovedrop—were business partners. We sold instructional videos on pickup, and we flew all around the world teaching seminars and doing live, in-field training. Mehow, on the other hand, ran a competing business doing exactly the same thing.

Mehow typed manically on his laptop, tufts of blond hair poking out the sides of his baseball cap. Of Polish descent (his name is Polish for Michael), he used to believe that his pale, skinny body and his ugly face, combined with his receding hairline, made him unsalvageable as a romantic prospect. But now look at him: a royal terror. Those same attributes were now what made him so impressive to new students when they saw him picking up girls.

Behind me, the room opened up toward the rest of the house. Crema Marfil marble steps swept down to the foyer and the big red front door on the left. Continuing, the landing sloped down a few more marble steps into the living room, with the white couch and the white rug. *Scarface* played on the projector.

The voice of Al Pacino echoed from the living room: "What I try to tell you? This country, you gotta make the money first. Then when you get the money, you get the power. Then when you get the power, then you get the women. That's why you gotta make your own moves."

"Oh Matador," I said suddenly. "What is this I hear about you having a threesome with my girl last night? The girl from New York."

Matador looked up from his laptop, where he was watching *Rambo: First Blood Part II.* "I thought you were giving her to me," he said, "'cause you asked me to take her home—"

"I said 'Hockey'! Do you know what hockey means? That means stay off my girl!" I pointed a black-painted fingernail in Matador's direction. "I said there was a *hockey* game on TV at the bar. I said my friend won his *hockey* game in Montreal. That means roll off of my set. Do not game my girls."

"But you were already leaving with another girl, right in front of her! And you said I could take her home!"

"I said take her home, don't *sleep* with her! Take her home."

Matador turned to Lovedrop. "This is how it is, bro. I did threesome Mystery's girl last night, but it was revenge because he stole my set last week, that girl Amber."

I said, incredulously, "I stole it by my existence on this earth . . ."

Matador said, "Lovedrop, do you see how he does it? He is rationalizing right now."

I continued talking over him, saying, "She was all starry-eyed, you know. I'm Mystery. I can't help it if your girls are coming over to my room trying to hide from you—"

"Mystery, bro." Matador was shaking his head. "You can't rewrite history. This is an exercise in sanity."

Mehow looked up from his computer. "You guys are hilarious. While you're fighting over girls from last year like high schoolers, I'm putting together my new microloop theory. It's gonna be *epic*."

"Micro-*loop* theory?" asked Lovedrop.

"Micro-*loop* theory," I said: "Is that anything like microcalibration, invented by yours truly?"

Lovedrop said, "Yeah. Is it, Mehow? Mister giant-ego inventor guy. If you're going to live here in this house you can't pull that 'Mehow Method' crap."

"My stuff is original," Mehow insisted. "Anyway, I'm not gonna keep renting a room here, not if my next deal falls through. It's been a great party but if I keep living like a king on both coasts, I'm gonna go broke."

"Now, Mehow come on, you don't mean that," said Matador. As much as he complained about Mehow, he always hated to lose a renter.

"Oh, Daddy means that," said Mehow. "The magic Miami cash machine is soaking up cash like a hungry hooker. My girlfriend is in San Diego, my people are in San Diego, my house is in San Diego—"

"Hey guys, by the way," interrupted Matador. "Did you hear about Mehow's One-Second Rule? From his book. It's kind of like Mystery's Three-Second Rule . . . except it's *two seconds faster!*"

Lovedrop snickered.

"Mehow," I said, "you have got to be joshing me with this. Can you at least pick another word besides *micro* when you 'invent' something straight from out of my book? I mean look at my diagram."

"Microloop theory is not the same thing as microcalibration!" said Mehow indignantly. "Nothing we analyze is new or unique;

only the models are. Any slight improvement that I can make to a model *is* an invention. It's something new. Remember, I am a professional inventor."

We all looked at one another in mock amazement and all slowly said "Whoa! Ooo!" as we raised our arms in the air, quivering in mock fear. We all burst out laughing.

"I'm serious!" said Mehow. "I spent my entire life inventing things and breaking into stuff like slot machines and voting machines—"

"You can't get around this one, Mehow," said Lovedrop. "It's in your book! The One-Second Rule!"

"I always give credit where credit is due," said Mehow. "I'm always bringing the value and bringing the value."

"Check this out," said Matador. "Hey, Mystery. You guys know what's better than eight-minute abs? Mehow's got this new thing. Check it out. It's called seven-minute abs!"

We all laughed.

"Ha ha ha," said Mehow. "Someday you'll all be working for me. I'll show you guys." He squinted, trying to pretend that he was suddenly engrossed in his laptop.

"Oh Mehow," said Matador, "that may be, but I think you should know that Justin sent out your latest invoice this morning. So right now, *you* are working for *me*. Expect something 'epic' in your in box soon."

Mehow snapped, "I know I'm the only one paying those invoices!"

"I pay mine," said Lovedrop.

"I pay mine," I said.

Mehow continued, "I've got the payment on the Bentley. The insurance on the Bentley. Matador's invoices. I'm not going to be able to get my boat. That next deal better pull through—"

"You can run, Mehow, but you can't hide!" Matador grinned. "I'll pop up from behind a rock when you least expect it and slap you with an invoice. You could be out in the middle of the Arizona desert, and I'll jump out of a fucking cactus and serve your ass."

"Oh, by the way, guys?" I said. "While we're all here, my candle wax girl from Halloween is coming over tonight. Stay off her. She is my set. She will come out with us tonight as well. Oh, and I need to get my nails done. So if you don't mind, I'd like to have Justin drive me into the Grove. It's Saturday, so the kitchen is broken,[1] and my humanity is making me feel hunger currently, and I don't have any cash on me, so I need to resolve these issues."

"Listen to Princess here," said Lovedrop.

"Hey Mystery," asked Mehow. "This candle girl, was she from the Bondage Ball that you guys went to on Halloween, with Johnny?"

"Yes, she was," I said with a smile.

Matador grinned. "The Bondage Ball . . ." He whistled. "That was a fun night."

"Ooo! Was it all a bunch of, you know," asked Justin, "whips and chains?" He was easily amused by the perverse. "People in leather gimp outfits? Guys getting spanked?"

Lovedrop said, "Let me just say, when you go to one of these things, you realize there is a whole other level. Holy shit."

"It was like some ancient Rome shit," said Matador. "I remember I hooked up with that one girl Vanessa, Johnny's friend."

Lovedrop said, "I don't remember her specifically, but I remember Johnny had a bunch of girls there. I remember we had the VIP table."

Matador said, "Do you know what one of those girls tried to do? She tried to ash her cigarette in my mouth. She says, 'Open your mouth and stick out your tongue.' So I said, 'What for?' And she says, 'I'm going to ash my cigarette in your mouth.' And you know, she said it so naturally dominant that I almost went along with it. I thought, *Gee, okay, sure, why not? Let's see where this goes.* But then wait a second, you know. There's that pride that kicks up, and you say 'Uh-uh, nope. Fuck that.'"

---

1. Our cook didn't work on weekends.

He started doing his Andrew Dice Clay voice. "No one fucks Dice. Dice. Does. The fucking."

We all laughed.

Lovedrop said, "You know that Bondage Ball made me realize I'm a pretty vanilla guy. That's the word they use for people like me. *Vanilla*."

"Do you notice," said Matador, "it's always the *white* people at those crazy things? There's no Indians in there, no Latinos, no black dudes walking around." He paused. "It's always the most *Brady Bunch*–looking motherfuckers." Matador, being Indian, always notices these types of things.

"I guess everyone's got their thing," said Lovedrop. "Well, what do you think, Mystery? You were making out with three or four chicks at a time in there. Is that your kind of scene or what?"

"Don't get me wrong," I said. "It was on Halloween. So that gives me the plausible deniability. It's not, you know, ordinarily my lifestyle; not that I'm surprised by it, and I suspect that others there were indulging in a new subculture. However, some of them, I'm sure, live for those balls. They're big. This thing was big. We're talking Miami, Bondage Ball, Halloween. It was incredible. It's an incredible sight; a spectacle that everybody is a participant in. I recall having my groove on. It just flowed."

"Mystery," asked Justin, "how did you pick up this candle wax girl?"

"She was having wax dripped on her," I replied. "They had a pool table covered in sheets of plastic, and she was lying there. She was the half-naked girl with wax being dripped on her. That was the novelty."

Lovedrop laughed, "I remember Mystery just walking around that pool table staring at her, while the guy was dripping wax on her, and she was writhing around on that pool table—"

"She did look pretty hot," said Matador. "I mean when she was on the table."

"I mind-warped her," I said. I frowned as I tried to recollect exactly what happened. "I must have opened her. I don't remember. As I recall, I had to do maneuvering, you know? Talk to several people, and merge. There was plotting taking place, in order to speak to her. Nice body."

Lovedrop said, "Mystery had the 'porn stare.' You should have seen him. He was enthralled."

"Speak for yourself, pal," I said. "It was just a snag, for shits and giggles, you know? I thought, which girl do I want? How about that one, the one with the wax? Let's talk to her; she seems sexual."

"It's impossible to get any work done in here with you guys chattering away," said Mehow, irritated.

"This is our office, Mehow," said Matador. "You're not supposed to be in here anyway."

"You guys aren't having one of your super-secret VA company Gestapo meetings, are you?" asked Mehow. "I thought it was okay for me to work in here otherwise. You are more 'alpha,' okay? Now can I get back to work?"

Matador started walking around the table. "Oh Mehow . . . you can't get anything past us, we're on to your new Microloop Razzle-Dazzle Theory and we—" He looked down at Mehow's laptop.

Mehow slammed his laptop shut.

Matador said slowly, "Was that 1-800-FLOWERS dot-com?"

"No, I . . ." Mehow was searching for words.

I sat up. "1-800-FLOWERS dot-com?" I rolled my eyes and started laughing.

"Oh Mehow!" Matador was gleeful.

"Come on guys it's nothing—"

"Then why'd you close your laptop?" asked Lovedrop.

"Mehow! 1-800-FLOWERS dot-com!" Matador danced around the table maniacally. "You're never gonna live this down!"

"Mehow," said Lovedrop. "Bro. Listen to me. Did I ever steer you wrong? You can't send flowers. Melissa doesn't want flowers, bro. You can't razzle-dazzle 'em with your microfizzle theory—"

"Oh come on," said Mehow. "Just 'cause I was buying some flowers for Mel—"

"Buying temperature is old-school now. You've got to *vibe* with the girls, Mehow. Trust me, bro. Say it with me: 'I am good enough. I am good enough.'"

"That's entirely beside the point—"

"Well, that's a sad cowboy song, Mehow," interrupted Matador. "But you know, Socrates once said every man"—he paused—"and I mean *every* man, has to go through his personal hell to find his salvation." He nodded seriously. "No one can escape it. Think about it, son."

"This is good for you, Mehow," said Lovedrop. "You need to grow a thick skin. It's all the benefits of a Texas high school education, without actually having to go there."

Just then the doorbell rang.

"Mystery, it's your one-on-one student," said Justin. "He's from New York. His name is Adam."

Since we started Venusian Arts, we occasionally have a student come and stay with us and learn one-on-one, for a price, of course.

Matador sat down, put on his headphones, and went back to his movie.

"I'm going to meet someone new," I said, suddenly feeling a little excited at the prospect. I stood up. "I'll get the door. Boy, do I have a weekend in store for him."

"Mystery. Nice to meet you." I nodded and smiled as I shook Adam's hand.

He looked like a good enough guy. Medium height and build, about mid-thirties, not unattractive, not horribly out of shape. He just needed someone to get him up to speed.

"Wow, this is a great house," said Adam. We stood in the foyer as he admired the architecture. "Look at this place. Modern. Wow."

"The house is of unique design, right?" I said.

"That's for sure," said Adam.

"And the spirit of the architect is present in so many locations throughout the house." I gazed around. "You really have to stand here inside the place before you can appreciate his vision. He really thought it through."

From the landing, we could see down a few marble steps into the living room, with the white couch and the white rug, and we could also see up a few marble steps into the office, with the clocks ticking away along the wall. The rest of the house was hidden from view by a white wall with a large red painting in the middle, a splash of color against white, the first thing you see upon walking through the front door.

But the house had a way of opening up to you progressively more and more as you approached the edges, with whole new spaces appearing before you.

As Adam and I walked to one end of the landing, suddenly we could see the rest of the house. A few steps up and to the right was the kitchen area, with its own adjacent living room and a pool table. A catwalk extended over the pool table and above the hallway to the three bedrooms.

Downstairs lay a room with vaulted ceilings, completely open before us, resembling a dance floor. Translucent white curtains, two stories tall, covered the left wall. Beyond them, we could just make out the backyard and the pool.

"You know," I said, "I've flown all around this area in Google Earth. And this house is the only one that is diagonal on its lot. *That* is metaphor! And of course this is the house that most enticed Matador. Which I find ironic, because he always needs things to be symmetrical." I chuckled. "Little did he know, his was the only house that just wasn't straight."

"Well," said Adam, "I brought my clothes for tonight, and a pad of paper, and I printed out those notes you sent me in the email." He lifted up a backpack. "Is there somewhere that I can put this for now?"

"Just put it down right here."

"Okay," said Adam, "I've got a question for you. It's just been bothering me on the flight down here so I have to ask."

"Shoot."

"Isn't it wrong to chase so many women?"

"That's an ethics question," I replied, as I continued to show Adam the rest of his home for the weekend. "My job as a teacher is to discuss the how, not the why. For whatever primal reason, men like to have sex with girls. We like to have sex with them. Some like many, others want to primarily filter through some options to choose one for some religious marriage thing. Fine, whatever; everyone has a reason."

"So your job is not to discuss ethics," said Adam, smiling.

"My job is not to discuss ethics." I chuckled. "That's right. I enjoy many women. And I get them. And all I have to do to get them is be playful, fun, have a good smile, make them laugh, allow them to feel connected to me, don't let them shit on me, and then we get to mutually pleasure each other. The entire process is fun. The catch is great fun. If it wasn't, I would just have one girl and marry her, and have sex with her only. Thing is, I want two women. And then I'll have a nice home with two girls. Till I find that, it's playtime for Mystery."

I slid open the door leading to the pool and the gorgeous day. There was a large patio with an outdoor kitchen, massive grill, and round table, where we sat.

"What if a girl's feelings are hurt?" asked Adam.

"I liked a girl a lot in grade six," I replied, "who was a good friend of mine, but who ended up kissing my best friend John. I was crushed. I cried and cried in the mirror. But you know what? I got over it! Obsessing over one girl sets you up for emotional failure and ego let-downs. She isn't *the one*. I know you wish she would be, but it's not going to happen. You will find better in the future. You need to practice two thousand times before you will land the girl you *really* will want in the future. Begin practicing."

"But what do you say to those guys who have been pining over the same girl for the past year? Maybe he gave her his number four times in the past year?"

"It's a lost cause," I answered. "I would tell those guys, 'You messed up. In a year, after you become a stud, she will find interest in you. You will not 'grow' on her. Move on. She's dead to you. Move on. It's *over*. Cry at home and then get out and find others. Until you get good, you will never get her. Four times giving your number? Pathetic, dude. I feel for you, though. I've been there. Drop it. Give her negs and brush her off from now on, when you see her. Tell her about all the other girls you are interested in. *Maybe* this will bring her around in six months. That's it. You flogged the horse dead, man. She is dead. Drop it. Move on. There. My advice as a concerned pickup artist. It's *not* going to happen with her. You blew it.'"

"Wow, so there is no hope?" asked Adam.

"That's not true," I said. "There's a lot of hope. But not with that specific one girl that you think you have a magical connection with. You can't get bitter when reality doesn't turn out to be what you thought it was. I have a friend back home in Toronto who is really bitter. The thing is, I was, too. I remember hating this shit. So I snapped. I had exhausted my excuses to *not* get good at the game. Well, I think my friend is reaching the boiling point himself. At some point you have to give up on failed excuses and pursue change."

"I'm ready to do that," said Adam. "That's why I'm here. I just want to start doing what works. I was a late bloomer, I guess."

"Man, I was a late bloomer," I said. "I didn't have sex until I was twenty. My first girl was a 6—and I was happy. I mean, she let me touch her breasts! I remember knowing her for two weeks and going to her cousin's birthday or something, and I met her family there. Later on, she and I went for a walk. We walked to my father's van, and I was so fucking scared. She held my hand, and my heart was beating like mad. She then sorta pinned me up against the van. My head was bursting with my heartbeat. She then—bang!— kissed me, and I was blown away. I couldn't think. She put her tongue in my mouth and I was shocked. I was a happy, happy, happy camper. I didn't think she'd French-kiss me right away. Re- member when we were young and we called it 'French-kissing'?"

"Oh yes, French-kissing. I vaguely remember that! *I* want to be able to take control with women," said Adam, "like how she took control of you."

I laughed. "I remember this one girl," I said. "She was a friend of my cousin, who brought her to stay for a weekend, and I had the chance to see some pictures of her before she arrived. So when she did, I jokingly said, 'Hi, you'll be sleeping in here with me and I'll take good care of you.' I grabbed her by the hand and took her into my room. It was just a joke. I then treated her normally for about twenty minutes and we all just shot the shit and then I came back to joking about how she was going to sleep in my room with me, and about ten minutes later, she and I were kissing. She slept with me that night. Crazy, eh?"

"Stop! That is great, but how do I get started?" asked Adam. "I'm ready to change my life."

"Ah yes, that is exactly what I wanted to hear. Let's go downstairs, cool down, relax, and get started," I said. And then I led Adam inside and down the stairs to the first floor of the house. From there we walked around behind those same stairs, down a smaller hallway, and down another flight of stairs, through a shattered door, and into the dark.

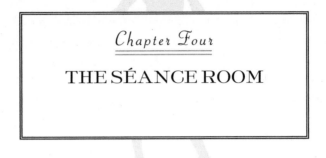

Chapter Four

THE SÉANCE ROOM

WE DESCENDED another five or six steps into a black-carpeted room, deep in the bowels of the house. Our eyes were just starting to adjust to the darkness when I flipped on the light switch.

Billows of black cloth covered the ceiling above, lit up from behind with the glow of red light. The wall to Adam's left was painted blood red, and the other three walls were covered in floor-to-ceiling mirrors. The infinity effect was pronounced. Symbols and other writings covered the mirrors in creative bursts of mad genius and black ink.

An imposing, four-poster bed made of dark wood dominated the room, with a crushed red velvet comforter and a big pile of dark pillows against the hand-carved headboard. Nearby, a red leather couch and a black leather sawhorse sat in the corners of the room. A single candelabra burned beside the bed, its nine bloodred candles twinkling into infinity across the mirrors.

Adam sank into the couch; he felt like he had snuck into Dracula's bedroom. "Wow," he said. "It's amazing how much the candles are multiplied by the mirrors. It's like a thousand candles burning in the dark."

I smiled. "Pretty cool, eh? I like to brainstorm down here. It's absolutely amazing the effect you can have over someone's state of mind, purely based on how you set up the room. The lighting, furniture, colors, and so on."

I gazed about. "Emotions are funny things. There are emotions involved, when playing this game of pickup, that we have to learn how to handle when practicing. I have, in the past, employed a video game metaphor. It's appropriate, actually, given that we are surrounded by billions of human beings on this planet. But emotions don't understand logical ideas like that. Emotions are pre-programmed behavioral modifiers hardwired into your brain through one hundred and twenty thousand years of natural selection in human evolution. It is in fact these built-in motivators (called emotions) that assisted millions of people before you to live long enough and motivated these ancestors to mate. In other words, look at emotions as indicators telling you what your body believes is most important to you."

Adam nodded and continued to listen.

"If your ancestors didn't have hunger," I continued, "they would have increased their chance of dying. And so the humans with the hunger gene would have an evolutionary advantage and replicate more, giving off more hungry babies. Hundreds of thousands of years of this have built a survival machine that, while not perfect, is pretty damned well calibrated to assist you with your survival and replicating. You are a DNA machine.

"So, when you are lonely, this is a strong indicator that something must change. We like to sometimes simply wish the emotions away because they don't feel good. Some people even try to do that. They will take drugs or meditate or talk themselves into thinking that they hate girls because you feel so bad when you think about them. Thing is, notice how this emotion will motivate you to get out of your house for a change? If you are lonely, this is a great sign that your body and your mind are functioning properly and it is telling you that you will increase your selfish gene's chance of survival by replicating if you get out and find a mate.

"Being horny is another feeling that we try to satiate by masturbating to Net porn. Thing is, imagine if you didn't masturbate again until you got a girlfriend. Can you imagine the motivation you would have to get laid? Your body would make you go out every day and try to get some.

"So how do we use these two emotions to motivate us in proper ways? Use your reasoning to prioritize what is important to you in a global lifelong perspective. I'm sure you will find that having a woman, or many women, to hold and love, and love you back, is very much a needed and desired thing. We are ants in a colony of six billion. Sure, an ant can live in a segregated ant farm all by itself. But it wasn't 'designed' to. The environment it's best suited for is within its social collective. See? Humans too are not designed to live in a lonesome environment. We weren't living in a box for the past hundred and twenty thousand years. Our environment included other humans, and we adapted motivators to deal with others. That's what emotions are. So when you get these emotions, reason on how you can satiate them properly and with focus instead of detours and denials. Disciplined focus. Lonely? Good. Build a plan.

"Plan to get out into the public four or five days a week. Go out alone if you can't bring a pickup buddy. You shouldn't go out with friends who do not want to pick up girls. No offense to them. Find a friend who wants to get a mate out there, too. If this friend is a girl, great. You will look even cooler. But if worst comes to worst, go out alone. When I went to a new city to live, I had to go out alone. There is nothing wrong with this. This isn't a loser thing, this is in fact a cool thing. A guy confident enough to get out alone and stir up some trouble is cool. While out there you will make some guy friends who hold the same goals as you. In fact every man, at some point in his life, will wish to sleep with a girl you know. It's not a bad thing. It's not a dirty thing. It's not a selfish thing. It's natural. It's behavioral. It's human nature.

"Go out four or five times a week and explore where girls are in a very systematic way. You will use your logic for this. Find out where they are. What's good on a Tuesday? Mondays? Friday and Saturday night is always good somewhere, but Tuesday night places are harder to find. Since you'll be going out four or five days a week and entering into the ant farm collective on a regular basis, this lonely feeling will dissipate a bit. A very good start and a needed Band-Aid. See, if too many of these emotional indicators are triggered, we call that stress. Your body has asked you to relieve your stress. Go out and approach women. The stress will begin to dissipate. This is where it gets tricky. There is another internal hardwired motivator circuit that 'seems' to get in the way. It seems to contradict the first emotion. Our internal motivator circuits are very well calibrated to the dynamics of social life—you are a fine-tuned engine—and these emotions will indicate to you what is most important whenever it gets in a situation it *knows* (through years of natural selection) is important to your genes' survival.

"So when you meet a girl that you are not attracted to, nothing happens. You can walk up and say something easily because you have nothing to lose. In fact, because this is so easy, I suggest meeting lots of ugly women to start your day because it gets you rolling and you can always make friends. They might have a sister or a party to invite you to.

"But when a beautiful girl is near, your brain will give you a *state change*. A state is an emotional state such as lonely or angry or horny. The horny state is really a painful bitch to deal with. This is what all the pickup artists talk about when they discuss state changes. When you watch *Titanic*, even though it's all fake, it can make you cry. That is a state change. And just by *seeing* a pretty girl you have a state change. Isn't that amazing?

"Now, this state isn't really horniness. Horny is when you have an erection. It's some other state and I'm not even sure what to call it. We could call it *acquired* or *locked-on*, or even better, *aware*. It's the aware state. When she is there and you want to talk to her, you are more than nervous, you are *aware*. Pulse quickens. I personally feel a wonderful sensation of butterflies in my stomach, still to this day, even yesterday when I met a girl, and your mind races for 'things to say.' Right?"

Adam nodded. "I definitely can relate to that feeling," he said.

"I am a pretty rational guy," I said. "I am guided by reason and humanity and not by mythical being or forces. I'm not a horny ass-hole player. I love life and care for people, and have close friends, and think things through. There was a time I *couldn't* get girls. I had such a low self-esteem and I was twenty, before I had my first kiss. Or was I twenty-one? Anyway, so I snapped. I thought, *Dude, you've got to get good at this. This is too stressful. This seems like a very important thing to solve.*"

Adam nodded. "Exactly."

"I hoped a relationship would drop in my lap," I said, "and I wouldn't ever have to deal with getting good at picking up girls. Does that sound familiar? I considered how if I already had a girl I'd be happy and wouldn't have to chase. But then I thought, *No! I have to master this for a lifetime. I'm not going to marry the first girl I meet. That isn't realistic. I'm young, I can't keep a girlfriend when I don't know anything about them.* You need to prioritize your needs and values. Put girls up there with sleep and food, and stop abstaining from things that should be in your life as matters of fact."

Adam was starting to understand. This was something missing in his life, something important, that he needed to get handled. These feelings weren't going to go away, and it needed to become a serious priority.

"This aware state," I continued, "like I said, is a bitch. You are lonely and so you go out and attempt to meet girls. Then when you see her, this invisible barrier in your head, this state change erects itself between you and her."

Adam nodded.

"Okay—what's the deal with the aware state? This nervousness when approaching a girl? This horniness. This importance? Well, if you succumb to it and approach her as if you are nervous and very aware, and act like she is so important, this indicates that you do not surround yourself with beautiful women. If on the other hand you don't take her shit and give her some negs, you will *seem* like you don't have this state change. See, if she is beautiful, she must deal every day with the fact that men snap into this aware state and they all act the same.

"You can't ignore the aware state because man, it's a strong state, but what you can do is hide it. Ever have a headache and you just didn't bother telling anyone? They didn't know what you felt, did they? Well, if you hide the fact that your aware state is in full-blown "on" position, and pretend like you don't have this with her—neg her in a fun way—she will see you as hard-to-get and different, and she will try to make you like all the rest. She will, in fact, chase you! That's it. That is the psychological switch that makes what I do work so well. It is in fact the biggest secret going in picking up girls. I did it yesterday to a girl. She begged for my number. In my mind I'm thinking, *Oh God I want her.* I approached *her.* She had me before hello. But I still made her work to get me. Only a man of quality would make that happen. In fact, I've been tricking this for so long that I'm starting to think that maybe I am a man of quality."

I paused as I heard the door jiggling.

Lovedrop entered the room behind us. "Oh," he said, "I see you're already down here."

I nodded and then continued, "Okay so . . . consider this. I met Leo DiCaprio at Villa. No, I was at Green Door. Anyway, he came up to me, and Matador was closer to him so he went to Matador (I guess he wanted to confirm it was us) and then came up to me, and we talked for a few minutes. He said he enjoyed the show, and really felt for the students, because he always viewed himself as a geek growing up, so he just felt a commonality with them. Interesting about that by the way: Commonality is a connection switch, so that is what caused him to feel more connected to them; that common experience.

"Anyway, what was notable to me was that Leo appeared to be nervous. In a similar manner that others who have seen my show are nervous to meet me. So that kind of threw me for a loop because he was nervous to meet Mystery."

"What do you mean?" asked Lovedrop. "Because he's such a big star?"

"Exactly." I nodded. "It was just interesting to note that, though I'm sure he gives that same feeling to so many other people, that doesn't mean he no longer succumbs to the same emotions. As if he were suddenly not human anymore, which, of course, is not true. He has the aware state too, sometimes, just like anyone else. He doesn't let it stop him from going after what interests him in life.

"Just like when I met Eric Stoltz," I continued. "I personally believe he is a great actor and I appreciate his work. So when I had chance to meet him in front of Poquito Mas, it was brief, but I had to go say hi and tell him I live in the neighborhood. I just remember reviewing how nervous and excited I was to meet Eric Stoltz."

Lovedrop interjected: "The thing is, though, that people can tell when you are that nervous. We come off reactive, and we must train ourselves to come off as unreactive—until it becomes our actual vibe."

I said, "Look at it this way. Have you ever been having sex with a girl and you think to yourself, 'Why is she letting me do this? Me! Why!?' Well, they do. So stop asking yourself that. Just enjoy it. The same is true when you are conversing with a girl. Don't bother thinking, *Why is she letting me talk to her?!* It's insecure of you and that doesn't look good. People can feel it. Just relax. It's a Zen thing."

Lovedrop said, "Think about it. There must be an 'ideal' vibe for social interactions. So what is it? We know that relaxed is better than nervous. We know that fun is better than boring. And that is it, in a nutshell. But let's explore it a little further. I would like to direct your attention to these notes written on the mirror to your right."

He pointed, and Adam followed with his eyes and looked.

Written on the mirror in black letters were these words:

YIN / THE GHOST	YANG / THE FLAME
Comfortable	Happy, smiling
Relaxed, chill	Having fun, laughing
Disinterested	Expressive
Not needy	Always adding value
Unaffected	Playful
Unreactive	Positive
Cool, calm	Talkative
Carefree	Curious
No agenda	Makes things happen
Not trying to impress	Warm, friendly
Not trying at all	Competent, a winner
No big deal	Enthusiastic
Nonjudgmental	Appreciative
Dependable, solid	Exciting, crazy

Lovedrop continued: "The list that you see on the mirror represents the ideal vibe for interacting socially, and for being attractive to women. The Ghost and the Flame. We like to call this 'the Zen of Cool.' I believe that once you get this right, you don't need any other game. Go ahead and write the list down in your notes.

"I cannot exactly put the Ghost or the Flame into words, but I can give you many examples of different words, approaching from different angles, so that you can begin to have an intuitive sense of the vibe I am trying to describe to you. Each word is a slightly different variation on the same concept.

"Now of course, by looking at the list, it may seem to you that each item is the diametric opposite of the item beside it. And the correct vibe includes both sides of the chart, *simultaneously*. This is a paradox, to be sure, and may at first seem counterintuitive. I admit we cannot prove that our model is true, per se, but nevertheless we have determined that it certainly is what gets results. And that is why you are here, is it not? Results?"

Adam nodded.

Lovedrop said, "Soak up our vibe from us as much as you can while you are here with us this weekend. That's really the key. You will always have the time when you get home to practice the different routines, and practice the delivery, and practice logistics, and practice microcalibration and escalation, and so on. But you only have these few days to soak up our presence, just being with us, here in this house, and going out with us. Try to get in as much by osmosis as you can while you are still here with us. Do you understand?"

Lovedrop continued, "We look at the proper attitude as a yin/yang symbol. Why? Because that symbol describes two things in one. The proper vibe is two vibes, *combined* into one. Now let's clarify those two vibes.

"The yin is like being a ghost who is unaffected by anything thrown its way. Nothing can touch you or shake your emotions. So when someone says, 'Nice shirt, I had one of those back in high school,' you reply with, 'Oh man, you got me,' and then smile. And when someone says, 'Your jokes aren't that great,' you reply with, 'Why do you have to call it out like it is?' Just roll with the punches, no big deal. Nothing can touch you.

"Remember, people react more to those of higher value, and by reacting, they lose value in comparison. Do the opposite. React less, and you will come across as higher value. Be 'cool.' People can sense this vibe and they will find you attractive. When you react less to them, it causes other people to react more to you. This is why it's so important to speak slowly, with pauses, and to move slowly, avoiding fidgeting, and to lean back instead of leaning in, and to open over your shoulder, and so on.

"As for the Flame, what is the best way for me to describe it? The way that most people look at this pickup game is wrong. They think of the woman as a beautiful butterfly and they hope to catch her with their gambits and their killer routines. It's as if they are holding a butterfly net, and they are swinging it around, trying to catch her. That is how most guys picture the game. Like they are trying to 'catch' her.

"But that is entirely the wrong way to look at the situation. The more useful view is that the woman is not a beautiful butterfly at all, but rather that she is an ugly moth. And furthermore, that there are many moths flying about, not just her. And if you want to catch a moth, all you do is turn on a bright light. A moth is attracted to the light. It circles in the proximity of the light.

"*You* are meant to be that light. The fun and warmth of your presence is precisely the light that draws the women to *you*. It is you they are drawn to. You are not trying to 'catch' anyone—this is about attraction. They must be drawn by your display of value and your presence. When that happens, the women will start giving you their green lights, their indicators of interest, and you will know to start escalating.

"So you see, the yang is like being a flame who shines with such fun and positive emotion that people are drawn in by their own desire for its warmth. This is why it's so important to be expressive with your face and with your voice, to be emotionally compelling and enthusiastic.

"Do you understand?

"Another way that I describe it is, the Flame is like the Care Bears. Do you remember that cartoon? They are these cute, fuzzy teddy bears. Each one of them has a different symbol on its chest, like a heart, or a four-leafed clover, or a rainbow. And when someone is particularly mean or nasty, then the Care Bears all shout 'Care Bear Stare!' and they point their chest toward the bad guy,

ON BEING PLAYFUL

Funny can be cold.

Playful is warm.

Be *playful*. Be . . . full of play.

Today, be full of play.

Add playful into your game over the next four nights. Integrate playful into your game. Be playful.

Pillow fight. Bite an ankle. Flick a girl's shoulder. Yodel. Buy some finger puppets.

Funny makes people laugh, but sometimes doesn't help get you the girl. Playful always helps get you the girl. Know the distinction. Cocky and funny is okay. Cocky and playful is the way.

and this glowing light shines from their chest and strikes him full force, and he is showered in good feelings, and he starts to sprout flowers, rainbows, and butterflies, and he turns happy and good. That is like when you shine the warmth of your light and playfulness to everyone as you vibe with them, and draw them in with those good feelings. You are just that kind of guy. A giver to everyone. That's just how you are. Get it?

"The last point that I want to make is that you must always cultivate this vibe inside. It is not reserved, brought out only for certain people, for those girls that you want to sleep with. Rather, you must always practice this vibe in *all* of your interactions, so that it grows strong within you, so that when you are finally in the presence of a 'creature unlike any other,' you will be ready for her.

"I want to elaborate on this Ghost/Flame concept. When I meet up with a good friend, I am not nervous. Girl or guy, they are my buddy and I feel at ease. Think about how you feel, and act, around close friends. Ever leave one friend and go to another and you still feel at ease? You just start talking about stuff, 'Hey what's up? I just got back from the gym. Get this, there was this guy there who had no freaking neck! You should have seen how he . . .' and off I'm yakking. It's no big deal."

Lovedrop interjected, "Notice how the Ghost and the Flame are really the same thing? Being comfortable and normal with people means being conversational with people. They are two sides of the same coin. Each implies the other."

"Exactly," I said. "Well, I noticed that when I had three girl-friends—yes I cheated, sue me—I would yak with one then leave and meet another and then later go to the other. It was just matter-of-fact and I treated them all the same. In fact, sometimes it would get confusing because I would hear a story about a friend from one and later recall that the story came from the wrong girlfriend. Oops, shit happens." I shook my head.

"Thing is, I would treat the girls like they were the same girl. Just different face. 'I' was still the same. Over time I noticed that when I treated strangers this way and just treated them like I knew them all my life and didn't hit on them or have any visible motives, I would connect more quickly. That is the Ghost again.

"So, suggestion: Walk up to strangers and behave in your mind as if you know them. Just start talking to strangers about what's on your mind. I do this and it really helps.

"I will elaborate more about this 'Just Start Talking' concept, but for now, know that there is something profound here."

I started picking at one of my fingernails, then continued: "The Ghost is about being unaffected by things. In part, it's about not getting caught up in a wave of negative emotion, even and especially when someone is out of line.

"Thing is, the best-looking girls are the ones I prefer, so by *assuming* they will have attitudes, and by not getting emotionally charged by the girls' replies, you can start to work on getting good at removing their shield. Getting a ten isn't harder, it's just different. It takes the same amount of time to get a ten as it does to get a six."

Adam said, "Sometimes girls are rude whether they are a six or a ten. I opened a set two nights ago, and they acted like I was a jerk for saying hi. So I said to them, 'There are people here trying to have a good time and meet people. You obviously want neither. If you can't handle the consequences of being in a public place dressed as you are, then you really need to go someplace where you won't be bothered by anyone trying to talk to you. Good day.'"

"Too reactive," said Lovedrop.

"Shouldn't I call them on their bullshit?" asked Adam.

I answered, "You were attempting to educate them here. That is not your job. Don't bother educating people when they are stupid. Just leave. Once you go into damage control, just leave. Move on. It's more mature and more efficient. Be an artist, not a guy."

"Okay," said Adam. "I guess I see what you mean. So then, is it useful in any way to imply to the girls that I have money?"

"You can include it as an incidental detail during conversation," said Lovedrop. "We call that an embedded DHV. You can convey that you have money. But you can't outright brag, or you will look really bad."

"Forget money," I said. "The real game isn't played with money. Why? Because the girl doesn't know you have a great car. And by telling her this, you look like a fool talking about it. She won't see the car until after you have pulled her. *That's* when you will have value in her mind for your car—value that you will squander if she catches you bragging about it."

"Like you care to brag anyway," said Lovedrop.

"By caring," I continued, "you pay too much attention to her and therefore aren't able to neg her properly. Well, you can lie to yourself for a bit by thinking you are the best man in the world with ten girls at home and this girl just wants you for your body. Behave this way and she will consider you a man of quality.

"Acting normal around beautiful women is a way of conveying preselection. That is, conveying that there are other beautiful women in our lives. Women are women everywhere. Behaviors are preprogrammed by a woman's genes. Her genes are selfish and wish to replicate with the help of the best males. Show you are the best by acting like you get *lots* of girls. Not by saying this—you could be lying—but by behaving *as if* you get them. Act normal around beautiful girls and this will indicate that you're used to being around them."

"Whereas if you just brag about how many women are in your life," said Lovedrop, "you just come off like you are lying. And that's not how a ladies' man would act anyway, 'cause he wouldn't care to. He wouldn't brag, but he wouldn't be shy, either."

I said, "Girls generally dislike a shy guy. They want a man who is outgoing. Once you have agreed with this statement, it becomes your job to play outgoing. You can be shy, but you hide that fact. It is a must to be outgoing. I don't think acting shy helps you out. Now, if the girl is shy, be outgoing still, just not so outgoing that you blow her out. Does that make sense?

"I forced myself to overcome the social conditioning that normally guides my behavior without my even thinking about it. A totally confident man can easily talk with strangers in a playful and fun way and it won't seem intrusive. People will merely think you are one of those outgoing people. It's just a matter of fact.

"You know the lead singer from the band the Verve? 'Bitter Sweet Symphony'? He is butt-ugly and I bet he gets laid. It's attitude, baby. I am not a bad boy. I am not the typical player guy that you might imagine. Thing is, I wanted to have women so I began donning a bad-boy attitude. Now I am a player. So when geeks—like I was—want to get a woman they look to me as an example of a player to role-model. This is an entertaining notion. Not all bad boys are geeks in disguise, though, because many bad boys are really idiots in my opinion and know nothing about why they get the girls they get. Even the wise man dwells in the fool's paradise.

"Let us kindly differentiate between a nice guy and a gentleman. Like Satan himself, a womanizer or pickup artist is a gentleman, but not a nice guy. A gentleman will open the door for a lady, but won't for a bitch. But he will smile as the door closes on her—see

Rhett Butler. A nice guy will open doors for all the bitches in the world and get no thank-yous and will still do it.

"This difficulty you have, Nice Guy, to tell someone to fuck off when you need to, tells me you have a problem with self-esteem. You need to set your rules and live by them. And when people break the rules, they pay the price. *That* is the type of man a ten wants. The man with the plan. Take charge. When you don't know the answer, get in there anyway. Attitude beats knowledge. Don't worry about what others think. Girls want a man in charge.

"Watch some daytime soap operas. Learn what girls think romance really is. Then watch *Gone with the Wind* and study the attitude of Rhett Butler, seriously. And then notice Richard Gere's little attitude adjusters in *Pretty Woman*. For example, when Vivian sits on the table, he tells her there are four chairs to choose from.

"Here is one of the most critical pieces in the entire game: I noticed whenever I was not only in a good mood but rather in an *awesome* mood, girls would flock my way. My mood was usually due to something external like a new career opportunity or meeting someone I really admired or something cool like that. I would then be on cloud nine for the next couple of hours, all enthusiastic about life, and whenever I would meet a girl while I was in that mood I would tell her about my great experience. I almost always got the girl when I conveyed this vibrant positivity. It got me thinking. So I tried to fake this mood. I'm talking I actually lied to a girl and told her about my awesome day as if it just happened when in fact it occurred weeks ago, and it worked. To tell a girl that her presence in your life is just the icing to your cake makes her feel good to be part of your great day. In fact, I think a great opener would be to walk up to a girl and say, 'I just had the most awesome day.' And smile. Then tell her what happened. Recite something very cool—and detailed. Involve her. Tell her about your brush with greatness. Nothing boring like you just got an A in gym class, though. After a ten-minute chat of how great your life is lately, you then cap it with, 'and now I meet you. It can't get any better.' Even though she may have not said a word, she will be excited by your emotional state. Be more into yourself and your great day than into her."

I smiled. "My axiom for the day: Enthusiasm is contagious."

"But what if I can't lower my standards?" asked Adam. "I don't want to approach anyone lower than an eight, and there aren't enough girls to practice on."

"That's acceptable," I replied, "but are you sure this isn't sour grapes to avoid opening? Consider beginning a night by approaching a seven. Don't expect to get her. It just gets you into gear. Then when she is interested in you, move on. Makes you feel good for the next girl who will be much better looking. Soon you'll get into that talkative state.

"When you open, show her a smile, confidence, coyness, charm, be well dressed, and be friendly. Don't pick her up. Don't hit on her. Don't compliment her. Just be. Like when you are with a good friend. Then tell her you intend on bringing her with you to a get-together."

Adam asked, "What do you say to this: 'Everything happens in its own time'?"

"That is more of a female type of view," I replied. "I would say, there is no evidence to support destiny. This philosophy is known as determinism and I don't buy into it. I *make* my destiny."

"What if things go wrong?" asked Adam.

"Find a new girl instead of fixing things," I replied. "Thing is, I noticed it's easier to just find a new girl than to work on damage control issues."[1]

Adam said, "Okay, here's another one. How will I know if I've been standing around too long?"

"Here is yet another subtlety about the game," I replied. "You must work fast. Really work the room. Mingle. Keep busy. If the room just isn't keeping you busy, you are in the wrong room. You must change your location then. Busy isn't looking for your next

---

1. When I'm in a rut, though, I chase ex-girlfriends. It's bad, eh?

girl but rather when you are talking to one, or her circle of friends. Working the room not only satisfies the 'the more doors you knock on, the more will open' axiom, but also you're striving to appear very social. Other women will notice you with many women, though you are not hitting on these women. They will wonder if you are taken or not. Let them wonder this when you next approach them. You will convey your wonderful personality to them through interesting and humorous thoughts and anecdotes and it isn't until they show positive body language signs that you move in closer and tell them the other girls are just 'interests.' It shouldn't take more than twenty minutes, tops, to bring a girl in this way. When women see you surrounded by other women, it makes them see you in a sexual light. What is it that all these other women find attractive about you? they will ask themselves. And, if they start to hit on you within the first ten minutes you can neg them gently. 'My, you come on strong' is something you can say if she happens to fix her bra strap in front of you. 'That isn't until we're alone.' Then immediately change the subject back to something nonsexual.

"I like to think that having gotten good at the game in clubs in the city, I am now capable of getting women anywhere. All you need to do is point out the girl to me and I can approach her and make her think I'm a cool guy. I can't promise I'll have sex with her but I can promise she will think I'm very cool and a man of quality.

"This is the issue in a nutshell: If you go for one girl a year, you get zero. If you go for one hundred girls in a year, you get ten. Left side or right side of the road. None, or a lot. If you try to just get one, you lose.

"I'm on the planet for some seventeen thousand, four hundred more days. Assuming I die at eighty, then I want to enjoy women. I love the difference. Otherwise I'd stick with only one. I love the adventure, the different cultures—I love wasabi green mustard and *futo-maki* but I also love pierogies. Enjoy the variety."

Adam said, "The other night, a woman didn't want to talk when I opened her set. She said, 'I just get tired of talking to so many guys. I meet so many guys that I just get tired of it.' To which I say, 'Well, that's no fault of mine, but maybe you should've considered staying in tonight if you were in such a bad mood.'"

I shook my head. "Don't you get it? Can't you see her side of it? I'm telling you, I've been with quite a few tens in my life and they have later become some of my best friends. This is a real issue for them. They have men hitting on them *everywhere*. In fact, it's so bad, many of these girls *don't* have boyfriends because of it. Nobody to them is considered quality if you just go to her and tell her, 'Hi. How ya doin'?' They will group you in with the rest of the schmucks. In order to win, you must not approach them directly. You have to enter into her group and ignore her. When she notices that her friends like you a lot, this will get her thinking that you are quality. And then when you pleasantly neg her three times, she will discover you to be a challenge. You aren't like the rest—in fact, the best way to show her you are of quality is to behave as if you have the same problems as her. If I wish to obtain a ten, I'll make all her friends think I'm awesome only after I've done the same to another group of less attractive girls nearby. They will come by at some point when I'm in the target's group and this means from the ten's perspective, lots of girls are coming to me vying for my attention. I also check my text messages at least three times, as if I'm getting texts, and I act annoyed and say, 'Some girl keeps texting me!' Notice how I act annoyed about all this attention? Suddenly she and I have a similarity and she assumes I'm a man of quality. She now finds me interesting, a man of quality, and a huge challenge. We know that a ten wants to be with a man who is a ten, too. Well, since looks don't matter with guys, if you behave like you are a ten and the people around you treat you the same, then to the target *you* are a ten and she will now pursue you. Don't be easy to get, either."

Adam said, "I was out the other night with a friend who stutters. It was brutal. How will women ever like him?"

"Hmm," I said. "Like all insecurities, if it doesn't bother him, then there is no real problem. If a fat guy meets a girl and openly attempts to hide his fat by slouching or wearing pure black—merely a psychological trick—or makes excuses like 'I'm on a diet,' then he looks insecure. On the other hand, if he is fat but dresses very nicely and never mentions it and acts as if he were a stud and a ten, then he will have much better probabilities with women. Notice the fat guys with gorgeous girls. Other lowly fat guys think, 'What does he have that I don't have?' The answer: self-security.

"So if you st-st-stutter, you st-st-st-stutter. Don't be shy. You aren't weak genetically because of it. It's only a stutter, not a third arm. If you were to say to them, 'Yeah I st-st-stutter. That's me. Get used to it. Can't handle that, then f-f-f-fuck off,' then you've more got the right idea.

"Make jokes about it. Fake some of the stuttering in ways that show you really are comfortable with it. If *you* are comfortable, they will be more comfortable. If they make a joke, analyze whether they were giving you good-natured ribbing or really messing with you. If it's good-natured ribbing, you could say, 'In my w-w-world, everyone talks like this. You should hear how wack you s-s-sound to me!' And smile. If they are truly messing with you, shrug it off. So much more composure that way.

"I'm tall and slender so sometimes people call me Stretch. It used to bother me but now I simply smile and call them Shrimp. I smile, though, and this makes it worse because I make it seem like they didn't get to me. I'm too valuable to care about what they think. Some say, 'Boy, are you tall!' I always answer, 'Thank you.'

"Maybe this is a bad example because being tall has been more advantageous than a hindrance for me, but I hope you see my thought. Fuck 'em. You stutter. But you are more valuable than they are. Give them smiling negs."

"What if I got a girl's phone number, but she isn't calling me back?" asked Adam. "Is there a 'killer line' that I can use when I get her number, so that she will call me back later?"

"Truth is," I said, "once you have conveyed your personality, and put all the talk into her, and left her to come see you, and she doesn't . . . you did everything you could. The problem must have been in your talking somewhere—maybe you didn't build enough connection, or win over her friends. For whatever reason, when you closed her, you didn't do a good enough job. She is not there to fix now. You did what you did and have to live with the result. The result being she didn't see you. All you can do is move on and do it fast. That is in fact the best revenge. No time to call her all pissed; that's not the style of a pickup artist. They are too busy to care. The only reason you ask this is that you are trying to control the damage. Drop it. Move on.

"Girls are like tomatoes. You run around the field looking for good ones and when you find one you try to pluck it off the plant without bruising the tomato. If it is bruised accidentally, though, you don't try to fix it; you throw it out and pluck another one."

"What if I don't want to move on to a different girl?" asked Adam. "What if I want to get into a relationship?"

"I suggest hunting with the sex in mind first," I replied, "and then, the relationship is an option afterward. To hunt for a relationship first keeps you from having sex, keeps you from learning, scares many girls away, and prolongs the relationship from becoming deep. Get things sexual first, then choose how far you want the relationship to go from there. It's more logical, more efficient, more reliable to getting long-term relationships, and, well, more fun. Why chase only for relationships when you can do that and see many girls until the right relationship girl comes along?"

I cocked my head. "Is it because you are lonely?"

Adam paused, and then he said, "Yes. I mean, of course I feel lonely without companionship."

"Well," I said, "if you ever find yourself feeling alone when you wanted to go out, imagine that I am there, encouraging you to just go for it and try. I am there *with* you. You'll be telling me what happened later, anyway, right?"

"Sure!" said Adam.

"Okay," I continued. "When you are there in the aware state, when your heart is beating strong and you are hating that horrible feeling, know that everyone reading your field report is also there, feeling the exact same mind-numbing pain and sharing the experience. I went through this yesterday again myself. And it *is* mind-numbing. And we share this. When you get into this aware state tomorrow, we will be there for you. All of us."

"I just don't want to screw it up with someone who I can naturally connect with while I'm just learning the game," Adam said.

"Look," I replied. "I decided years ago to get good at this art. I was fed up with the failure. So I challenged the failure. And yes, I did fail, more than I succeeded. But something came out of it. I can now seduce, effectively, nines and tens.

"One of my guy friends back home in Toronto was with me for almost my entire learning curve phase, but he chose not to try and fail. He and I spent the same amount of time in the public gatherings. Only I tried and failed. He didn't try at all. He is now kicking himself because years have passed and I'm getting profound attention and he is still stuck in his rut.

"I told him, 'Start to fail. That way you will be good by the time that dream girl comes along.' But there is little chance of him getting a dream girl with his current skills. I feel I may just be ready now.

"Think longer term and try the new way I will show you. You will internalize the programming, the methods, the rules, and the routines. They will then be there in a couple of years when your dream girl comes along. Otherwise you'll be using the same old technique everyone else uses and that means you get nothing."

"This past weekend," said Adam, "while I was waiting for my date to arrive at the club, I was just too shy to initiate a conversation with some of the ladies there. I felt bad about it because I have spent a lot of time reading how to do this, but I think I learn best by observation."

"Your logic is self-sabotaging you," I replied. "Learning by watching is not acceptable. You know that, man. You have to get out there. You can't learn how to drive a car by watching someone do it. You have to get behind the wheel. Others can tell you the basics, but you need to really drive to learn. Do you have your license? It's exactly the same learning curve, buddy. One hundred percent the same thing.

"Everyone tells a pickup story. I once French-kissed seven girls all at once. I had the balls to just ask, seeing as they were all into me. I was twenty-two at the time.

"I once had a threesome with these two girls—one was an exotic dancer, the other a dancer. I knew them very well and went out with both separately before getting together with both. I went out with one for two years. The other less, but we were still 'friends.'"

Adam said, "Another problem I have is finding motivation to go out and practice."

"When I don't feel like going out," I replied, "I have my friends force me. When I don't feel like getting dressed I have my friends say, 'Dude, get dressed.' When I am in the car not wanting to go in because I'm tired, I say to myself, 'Just take a look inside.' When I get in and I don't want to enter a set I think, *If I don't, I'll stale the room and blow my cover.* If I have a bad set, I say, 'Recover soldier,' and press on. If it's five minutes from closing and my night was shit, I think, *Maybe my dream girl is to be found in the last five minutes.* My night may change to a great night! I've had that happen before.

"My goal is to live with two girls. For real. Look, I'm not the greatest of all time. Fuck, who knows, maybe I am! I just don't have a reference. How good is good? I don't know. All I can do is be honest about how good or bad I'm doing and let you judge. I'm not out to be a guru here. I wish to impart knowledge to those who are already artists. The exchange of subtleties is what I'm looking for.

"Now, tonight is a Saturday night. Get out there. Try and fail and tell me what happened. Plan it. Think about where they are. Find. Then work tonight on the Meet phase. Approach and say hi. Then talk about how Elvis died his hair black and his hair was naturally blond and how that just seems weird to you. Then if she doesn't join in the conversation, say, "Well, nice meeting you," and walk off with a smile. No harm done in chatting about Elvis. Never give a line. Never show signs of your hitting on her. Make her guess. If she starts talking, use a small neg. If she has gorgeous long hair, and it's fair to say that it may be an extension, then say, 'Very nice hair. Is it real?' Smile and be honest in saying this. She will say no and you will say, 'Oh. Well, it's still very nice.' Smile. You are actually not hitting on her. You are making her feel self-conscious and therefore thinking about how she can change your impression of her. She will try to impress you. But you are so matter-of-fact that she finds it difficult. Stay playful. If she isn't, be like Rhett Butler: The girl says, 'You, sir, are no gentleman!' And he says with a smile, 'And you, ma'am, are no lady!' So be playful and confident at the same time.

"When we go out tonight, get numbers! Go for four of them tonight. That's about one per hour. How hard is that? You have an hour to meet three women and do it up. One out of three should like you if you act like Rhett. That's only twelve girls to chat with. Not rocket science. The first is hard; the rest get easy for the day. Tell me how many girls you chatted with. If you say, 'Only two,' and didn't get any numbers, then we know where your problem lies already. If there weren't girls worthy of getting, you went to the wrong place. So much for the use of your intellect. If you didn't go for sevens and eights, you messed up. They were practice for you. They could have friends that you do like. They could be friends and join you in your future days of hunting!

"See, being around women attracts women. For example, a guy standing with three girls who know him. They may not be hot girls, but they like him and laugh with him. Then there's another guy who is surrounded by three guys. See the difference in impression? Clothes make the man, but ladies make the ladies' man.

"Is it possible, even remotely, that of the seven billion humans on this small planet, some are men capable of obtaining their desires? Could some of these guys even have sex with beautiful women? Someone has to, right? Who are these guys? They are out on the planet's surface somewhere, right? Some may even be in America, right?

"See that beautiful woman? Is it possible she had sex before? Could that man she had sex with be on the planet still? In America? Could he even be a man in my city? Why is it impossible to believe that I'm that particular man? She's very real and so am I. She isn't the most beautiful girl in the world. She isn't famous. She's a real girl who used to be a shooter girl at a club I met her in and we hit it off and I went out with her on and off for three months. That's not too unbelievable, is it? What part makes you think I couldn't get a girl like her? I'm six foot five. I'm healthy. And I exude charm. I'm playful and confident toward women.

"Sex is something everybody does. *Everybody.* Some have sex with thousands of women in a lifetime, others with one in a lifetime. Then there are the weird stragglers who get nothing. But if I got nothing, I certainly wouldn't be spouting off such good info. If I could give info like this, you'd figure I must be able to use at least some of it, right? It's not *that* hard to get laid, is it? I've had hundreds of girls so far. Some were ugly. But some were beautiful. And yes, that girl, I'm the one who slept with her, not you. In fact, I thoroughly debauched her.

"I was hanging with a guy once who was into picking up girls and he called them all bitches. 'Let's go get some bitches.' I never told him I felt offended, but I truly did, you know? Even using the word *chicks* is to denote an irreverence to class and style, though those can be needed when presenting yourself to a woman.

"Consider using *women* or *ladies*, but not *broads* or *honeys*, since it brings the image of Casanova to the gutter. When speaking to women, I actually prefer to call them 'guys,' since it is completely nonsexual. By consistently using the words we would use in front of women while behind the scenes, we prepare ourselves to be better equipped to present the proper classy attitude.

"Don't get me wrong. In bed, I can swear and fuck like a mink. I'm not offended by words, but in order to create a more classy image of our art, we must at some point remove the stereotypical stuff. A true artist doesn't use pickup lines. He uses intro scripting. His intros are polished and nonsexist. His routines are natural, humorous, and fun. His attitude toward the subject is that of a professional. He systematically finds the best places and works the rooms.

He treats everyone with respect and dignity. Even the other guys. All is fair in love and war, but this war is merely a game. So let's not kill or hurt anyone on this game of love.

"Think of this as like a paintball game. You know the game will be a four-hour session going in. You prepare yourself with cologne and your gum and your lighter and off you go into the field. It's not a battle, it's a game. Paintball is fun to play and while you get a couple of bruises, you never die. See, in paintball, when I shoot someone, I don't yell out 'Die motherfucker die!!' It's a game and not real war. It's fun. So when you find yourself getting all gung-ho about the game, fall back and realize it is only a four-hour game session and you won't die.

"I think that the Venusian Arts is a gentlemen's sport. It's fun to socialize and enjoy the chat even if you don't get laid. At least you learn for the next scenario. However, calling it a conquest is empowering when you get the girls, so I will continue to enjoy my conquests. It's relativity. Those not yet proficient in the pickup arts will feel like shit and think they can call the girls bitches to feel bigger. But the ones who consistently get the girls prefer to call them ladies because they realize the worth of them, because it took years of work to get good enough to consistently get the girls. I *love* women. They are so wonderful. I don't work this hard for just anything.

"Let's seize this evening and get into some adventure. What do you say?"

Chapter Five

STORM COMING IN

"IS MYSTERY AROUND?" asked Matador. An unlit cigarette dangled from the corner of his mouth.

"Downstairs," said Lovedrop. "With the one-on-one student, Adam." Lovedrop wore a T-shirt and jeans, with a pair of sandals, his curly hair in a ponytail, and a pair of dark sunglasses.

They basked in the sunlight on wicker chairs, on a large redbrick patio in front of the Project Miami mansion, surrounded on all sides by expensive gardening and the jungle vegetation of South Florida.

Across the street, a neighbor opened his mailbox and waved.

"I guess you heard about my threesome last night," Matador bragged, grinning. "That chick from Skybar from last Saturday. Oh and the New York girl." He lit his cigarette; the cherry burned red as he took a drag.

The neighbor across the street called out in a French accent, "You guys must get up pretty early over there. I wake up at six and you guys are already moving. I see lights on." He waved again and walked back toward his house.

Lovedrop's eyes followed a giant locust as it walked by on the bricks. He thought, *The insects here are unreal.* He admired the view. The house had been built diagonally on a corner lot, and the lawn sloped down away from them in all directions toward several large, gated estates across the street.

Matador continued, "What did I tell you? Dude—Miami is wide open. They haven't seen guys like us down here." He started doing his Scarface impression, his lips curling down at the ends: "What I tell you? This town's just one . . . big . . . pussy . . . just waiting to get *fucked.*" His voice twisted into a perfect Al Pacino–style imitation Cuban accent.

"Mehow is going to move out," said Lovedrop, adjusting his ponytail. "His last deal fell through; he can't afford to maintain two households forever. Your invoices take a bite."

"Hey bro, I can't pay the full mortgage on this house by myself," said Matador. "I need to get some rent from everyone, and also split the expenses like the maid, the cook, the pool guy, the electric bill—"

"I know, I know, I'm just saying, he's doing his Beavis thing right now. He's down there with a spreadsheet open," Lovedrop said, and then he did his impression of Mehow on a calculator, with a Beavis voice, "Add the six, carry the three . . ." They both snickered.

Matador blew a slow stream of smoke into the warm winter air. "I don't want him to move out, but someone else will take the room, worst case." The top of his black-with-white-stripes Adidas tracksuit was tied around his waist, and he wore a gray tank-top, showcasing his physique.

"Do you think this lawsuit is going to be an issue?" Matador asked. He lifted a mug with one of his massive arms and took a sip of coffee.

"I don't know," Lovedrop said. The Rat's whiny laugh echoed in his head: *By the way, you guys are all getting sued.* He thought about it for a moment.

"It's all psychological," he said. "A lawsuit. It's about grinding someone down, to run them out of money, out of morale . . ."

"Right," said Matador, who stood up, taking another drag from his cigarette. "I'd like to meet this guy in a dark alley. I can just imagine the surprise on his face." He relished the thought. "Motherfuckers better hope I never get cancer."

"I'm not too worried about it, actually," said Lovedrop. "Not in this case. The suit was filed by some Mystery copycat from Scranton who runs a fan site. He has a history of filing frivolous lawsuits. Our VH1 lawyers are going to take care of it."

Matador nodded. "Speaking of VH1," he said, grinning broadly, "it looks like I'm going to be on the show."

Lovedrop smiled. "Congratulations. Mystery said you beat out all the other contenders. He said you were the best."

"Hey man," said Matador, doing his impression of a postgame interview of a basketball player, "I'm just trying to win some games. I'm beautiful, my sperm is beautiful . . ."

Lovedrop chuckled. "Well, I'm going to make some calls," he said. "It's possible the bills could get heavy. The time has probably come to ration supplies and stop dumping five grand at Tantra on Monday nights."

"Think about it, brother," said Matador. "To live at the very high end, we don't need more than twenty-five thousand a month. A nice place, worst case, that's ten or fifteen grand a month for all of us. A Ferrari. You can get a Ferrari for a couple grand a month. Plus insurance. Even with limos, bottles, restaurants, bodyguards, personal trainer, assistant—I'm telling you, you cannot piss away more than twenty-five grand in a month. You cannot do it!" He gleamed triumphantly.

Lovedrop said, "We've got that student downstairs. Are you coming out with us tonight or what?"

Matador took a long drag on his cigarette and stared pensively into the distance. He didn't seem to hear anything.

"Matador?"

Matador exhaled slowly.

"Matador!"

"Yeah, yeah, I'll take care of it, I'll take care of it," Matador said as he put out his cigarette.

"I'm gonna go inside," said Lovedrop, and he stood up abruptly. "One more thing: You can't pick on Mehow so much, or the Rat. They bitch about it. You make enemies; they fantasize about getting back at you. We have enough enemies."

"Understood, understood," said Matador. He took another sip of his coffee. "Hey brother, you know I'm a little rough around the edges; I'm not political like you. People like you. But I'm trying to change, I'm trying to listen. You know I'm making an effort."

"I know, you're doing good," said Lovedrop. "You're just such a brute."

Matador laughed. "Hey brother, you know if you ever need me to handle things Matador style, you just say the word. You know I've always got your back."

"I know," said Lovedrop, and he walked inside the house, closing the big red door behind him.

Chapter Six

STATISTICS AND BEAUTIFUL WOMEN

AS THE HOUSE GOT READY for our night out with Adam, I continued to help him with his barrage of pickup questions. He was smart and motivated—the two critical factors to success in this game.

"Let me ask you this," said Adam. "Where can I go to find the most beautiful women?"

"Finding true beauties is something that most men think is easy," I replied. "I find this to in fact be the most difficult phase of the game. I enjoy the company of particularly beautiful women, and these are, for technical reasons such as ratio to population, hard to come by. I have gone out with models, singers, exotic dancers, bartenders, even a private eye. I must admit I have been with a few not-so-good-looking girls, too. My first girlfriend, in retrospect, was a six!

"'Finding' issues include: increasing your chance of meeting beautiful women, available women, and a high enough ratio of women in a given area to increase your statistical chances of success. Hence the first of my rules: The more doors you knock on, the more will open.

"Think public gatherings, wherever humans bunch up in groups: malls, restaurants, coffee shops, festivals, clubs, bars, galleries, attractions. Think, where else?

"Meeting women is the same no matter where. The location has little to do with the differences in the girl situations. The difference lies in how many girls, or guys even, are in the group and whether they are sitting, or talking or reading and such. I will devote time to the different scenarios sometime soon. I've been through enough to know the dos and don'ts of almost every scenario.

"My number-one annoyance is when I decide to go out and play the game. I know that the game lasts roughly four hours a session. Say, a club from ten P.M. to two A.M. It annoys me when I have to waste that valuable time parking the car or waiting in line or having to deal with my friends behaving strangely.

"RULE: Plan your strategy for finding women. Know exactly where you intend to go. Know your city. Know the day. Minimize waste of time by getting there a bit early so you can settle in.

"RULE: Never buy a girl a drink. This makes you seem like every other guy. She may, however, buy *you* a drink. I used to get on average two or three drinks bought for me in a given four-hour session. Now that I am famous I have to turn down drinks, or I will end up puking in the bushes out back before the night is over.

"RULE: Avoid drinking too much alcohol when playing the game. Alcohol is an excuse to alter your feeling of 'fear.' You decrease your statistical chances of success. Sober people have more reaction time with which to process information.

"For example: Two girls, one guy, sitting at a table, guy is sitting closer to the one you want. What do you do?"

Adam talked really slowly, pulling a pair of old jeans out of his luggage. "Okay, I have no idea. What?"

"The answer is, approach the other girl," I said. "Why? She is an obstacle to the first one. If the other girl *is* single, then her 'friend' must approve of you first. Do not hit on her, of course. *Never* hit on a girl, actually. Why? Because you may have theoretically assessed the situation wrong and the less good-looking girl may be going out with the guy. Be attractive, but don't hit on anyone. Talk to them and exude charm and confidence and humor and allow her the opportunity to use her innate powers of seduction on you. Talk to the guy too. Now that you have this girl laughing—although you are not showing direct interest through any form of sexual innuendo—talk to the guy. Make the guy your friend. See, from his point of view, you are just a cool guy. You are charming and funny and have much to say about his areas of interest. This means that now, from the girl's point of view, the guy thinks you are cool, so you have his approval. The friend gave you her approval through laughter. And in the process you found out by asking 'So, how do you all know each other?—From work?' all the details you needed to know. If she is in fact free for the taking; you disarmed the potential bombs already. By this time, the others are paying attention to you, so the girl you secretly want will begin to feel neglected. Depending on her rating, you begin the attack. Eights and under are played out differently than nines and tens. They are two entirely different strategies in my opinion. But there are always exceptions.

"Eights enjoy the attention you give them. Nines and tens are so used to this attention you must give them three negs first, such as, 'Those are very nice nails you have; are they real?' If she admits they aren't, you say, 'Oh. Well, they're still nice,' and then turn away.

"See, what happens in their mind is this: 'Most guys think I'm the bomb. I'm used to that. But this guy doesn't think that. I must have screwed up my first-impression image. No worries, I'll just fix that.' She now thinks that she can bat her eyes and fix the little smear in her image. You weren't an asshole about it; you just showed her you noticed a flaw but were polite about it. She will try to impress you now. She is chasing you. Do it again; another neg. 'Ha! Your nose moves when you talk. It's so funny. No, really, it's so cute. Ha ha.'

"Nines and tens don't get treated this way. How? Like a normal friend. Like someone you can joke around with. That's all they want. To be accepted and this is what you are doing. But she is now even more into fixing the not-so-pristine image she is accustomed to having. So she tries to solve this little issue. And what happens while she's busy solving the issue? She's talking to you. Conversing. She's interested in making you like *her*.

"You can never ask a ten, 'Can I have your number?' Why? Because every guy in the world and his father asks. You are different. You say, 'Well, it was really nice meeting you.' As you start walking away, you then say, 'For an outgoing girl, you are pretty shy after all.' If she is interested in you by now, she will say, 'Why?' This is the beginning to flirting. You say, 'Because I'm leaving, silly.' This word, *silly*, is never used in front of a nine or ten from a stranger. So this shows your confidence and coyness. And, this is the third neg. Notice none of these negs are really bad. They are just not the usual flattery she gets from guys. You are now waiting for her to say something—just staring at her. She is on the spot. She is a ten and she knows it. She has an ego. You never really hit on her. You were coy. You were about to leave without asking her for her number. She knows you aren't like the rest. You must have girls chasing you, from the attitude you are displaying. If she doesn't say anything with regard to her giving you her phone number, walk away with a smile. However, this isn't likely, because she has an ego. In this case you have played on her ego to actually want to make you like her and she will now be open to getting together again. See, being on the spot, she has to come up with something very smooth to say to keep her ego bloated. She is now having to prove her social abilities to you. She is trying to impress you still anyway. Anything she says will come out flirtatiously but you accept it with open arms. She wants to show you she isn't shy so she will be bold and ask for *your* number. When she does, say, 'No . . . but we can exchange numbers. Fair?'

"RULE: Never give your number to a girl unless there is an exchange. If you get around to asking for her number and she says, 'I'll call you,' just say, 'No, I'll call you.' If she doesn't give her number, she wouldn't call you anyway, so just say, 'Nice meeting you,' and leave. After a girl does give her number to you, you may then write yours for her as you say, 'We'll trade . . . fair?' She will smile and say, 'Fair.'

" 'Nice meeting you.'

" 'Nice meeting *you*.'

" 'I'll call you this weekend.'

" 'Bye.'

"You have just picked up a ten! And she chased you! And you made her ask for your number. You were hard to catch. She won't forget that. You aren't an easy guy. You aren't like the others. You were a challenge. But she finally won. Well, hopefully—she still has to call you." I grinned. "By the way," I said, "the scenario I just told you about happened to me exactly as is, and the girl was a ten! The best-looking girl in the club! Secretly, though I showed this coyness and reserve, inside I'm thinking, *Oh God! Oh God oh God oh God!* I hid it well. I have her number. She will hopefully call me on Saturday. If not, I'll wait until Sunday to call her."

"Let me ask you this," said Adam. "How many girls can I expect to meet if I get really good at this stuff?"

"Hmm," I said. "If you approach one girl per month, and some people actually do that, then it is unlikely you will sleep with a girl in the next six months. If you speed up the pace, things become much better for you.

"Here are my general statistics when I'm into the game. I go out three or four times a week, as I'm very social and I really love the attention I get being surrounded by women. It's actually a fun thing to do, better than TV or a video game in my opinion. But let's say conservatively that I go out only three times a week. I go for four-hour sessions—ten P.M. to two A.M. usually—at three days per week is twelve hours per week of really fun seducing time. I will approach about three girls per hour—that's one every twenty minutes on average. That's twelve girls total for the night. Not bad. Twelve girls approached in a club, or that could be divided by two clubs— I usually bounce to another club once in a night—a realistic number. I'm sure you can easily find six girls in a club that are worthy of you. I usually start with the best-rating girl in the place, unless that situation is hard. Heck, she could be in a group of guys. Then what I do is go for lower-rated girls but I get them to surround me in front of the one I want. This way she *sees* that I'm a ladies' man; it triggers the preselection attraction switch in my target's emotional programming. The positive testimonial she receives silently from these women allows me to enter into her world. She will know I'm a fun guy and will be intrigued to find out why all these women flocked around me. This is a consistent approach of mine for the last decade, from before I became famous.

"I used to average a new approach every twenty minutes. Of these, in my first few years of practice, one out of three per hour didn't go past the opener and I good-naturedly aborted with dignity. There is really no such thing as failure—there is zero pain in aborting, as this is a well-rehearsed contingency plan. So those approaches take up little time at all.

"This left me more time per hour to chat with the remaining two approaches that went past the opener. However, on average one of these girls per hour would lead to an abort, whether she just didn't like me, or the situation went down not all that great. Again, I left with dignity. I'm just a guy chatting and having fun. I'm not *hitting* on anyone.

"However, one out of three per hour ended up panning out to my getting a phone number or more. This means I got on average four phone numbers per night. These days my numbers are much better than that. But even when I was starting out, I got realistically anywhere from three to five numbers in a night.

"Now, just because you have the number doesn't mean you are gonna sleep with them. My numbers grow stale quickly. Things happen to reduce the chance of sleeping with her, too. So, out of twelve girls approached in a night—six girls at each of two clubs—only eight go past the opening and only four become options with numbers. Of the four, maybe two will pan out to our getting together. That is six to eight get-togethers with women in a week. Yes,

I've done that, but what I've also done lately is qualify the girls more and only call the girls I really want. I had thirty-four numbers on my pending list about three weeks ago and now I've rounded it down to less than eight. I just tore it apart. Called them all and if I get a voice mail and I leave a message and they don't call back if I left a message two times, I drop the number 'cause I don't have time for that. They would call if they really liked me. So anyway, when it's all said and done, I end up with three girls who want to sleep with me per week and I round that down to making two friends who want me but I play hard to get—I invite them out to clubs so I look like a ladies' man or just chat on the phone or hang out with them—and I then can sleep with one new girl a week. I may not even have sex with them. Again, this is an average based on my going out three times per week. With this much fun and excitement, sometimes I go out more.

"Guys think that unattractive women are easier to get, when the truth is they are just different. You have different obstacles to contend with. If you are going to practice getting good at something, why not practice getting good at tens? You have a greater reward to boot.

"Going for fives is just a self-esteem thing, not a skills thing. If you decide to chase nines and tens and only them, then that will be the skill set you get good at. They aren't harder to get, only different.

"This week, thanks to a car issue, I only went out two times. On the first of these two sessions, I spent time with one girl only, but she was a ten so it was worth it, and I got out late, ten P.M., and left early, one A.M. So I was happy for the amount of time I played. The other time I was late out, too, but stayed until two A.M., therefore for a three-hour session, and I attracted two girls, one of whom I let go 'cause her new 'boyfriend' was so lame and I couldn't do it to him—he didn't see me coming. I was holding her hands and she was so into me and he just sat there all pouting so I said whatever, have her. The other girl I got the number, though. I could have gotten more but we went to three new places that day. One of them sucked, one was dead, and the one where I did get action was just not quality enough to seduce six worthy women. So I only got two numbers this week. Not bad for two short nights out, though. I also expected less because we were researching new territory.

"Girls overlap, too. I mean, I could have two girlfriends who are very close to me and go out only two times a week for only an extra roll in the hay every couple of weeks. Over the course of the last few years, I've had sex with many girls and the monthly average is definitely better than one. But one's good enough for most guys, per month, right? Of course some months I got no new girls because of long-term relationships that only allow two girlfriends and no extra nookie. But you get the idea. It's an average.

"My point to all this? The more doors you knock on the more will open. If you are wondering why you don't have a girl, it's because you stay at home too much. Go out three times a week and meet twelve girls a session. Of that, get four numbers. If you only get one number a week, you may be a month or two away from having sex. But if you get twelve numbers a week, you get to have sex with the best of the best and get a good few up-and-running into relationships to spread your valuable time between. Have three girlfriends. I have done that before.

"If morals get in your way with sleeping around this way and you want to have only one permanent girlfriend, I still suggest working hard in the getting-numbers phase 'cause many won't turn into rich relationships, due to stupid things like: she lives too far, her job gets in the way, school, or what have you. So get the numbers and kiss the girls. You don't have to sleep with them. Just obtain options for the future."

I opened my closet, picking out an outfit for the evening. I love being noticed, so it ended up being a straw cowboy hat with Harry Potter Quidditch goggles, jeans, a black T-shirt that says "Mystery," and a full-length faux fur coat. For a finishing touch, a large, heart-shaped locket hung from my neck.

Adam asked, "Are nightclubs really the only place you can go to meet women?"

"I suppose nightclubs only is not exactly accurate," I replied, "though you can't deny clubs hold the highest density of hotties in a given area. Where are they? Grocery stores are not realistically a good place to hunt. Sure, I can approach a girl in a grocery store but of all the girls I've gotten, none came from a grocery store — hotties don't crowd grocery stores. Maybe clothing stores on a Saturday are more interesting."

"Any ideas?" I asked, and then we started listing possibilities.

"Singles bars."

"Nightclubs."

"College pubs."

"Private parties."

"Clothing stores."

"Food courts in malls."

"Restaurants — but it's hard to meet a girl eating at a table."

"Where else?" I asked.

Adam thought about it for a moment.

I continued. "Looks like clubs are the statistical best bet. If I'm wrong, tell me a better place. I care only about results. Nightclubs are the most difficult place to pick up. If I go to a small town, I fucking rock, thanks to my experience as a club hunter. I go in clubs because there is population, and it's the hardest to hunt in. Every other place is easier but there is no population.

"Tell me," I said, "where there is a place with at least twenty girls in a given area for me to approach. I will approach the most impossible situations. I will hit on a girl in a fucking wedding dress."

Adam chuckled.

"I am not an authority on seduction," I said. "But I do believe I am an expert. Well, I get by. Point is, I was at the grocery store thinking about all this talk about meeting girls at the grocery store. I have considered the scene and come to a conclusion. Again, this is after much consideration.

"You don't go to a grocery store to pick up girls. It's lame. Grocery store attempts are the lamest way to get girls. It's not right. It's not even an option.

"While I won't say it's an impossible place to meet a girl, it's highly unlikely. Even an experienced artist would find it a challenge. You don't have to waste your time there.

"Oh, and don't bother going to movie theaters thinking you are going to pick up girls there. You will only get frustrated looking at all the girls there with dates. Don't waste your time, nor mine having to read your failures when you go to these places.

"I care only about results. Can a man meet a woman at a grocery store? Yes. What is the likelihood? Small."

"Why?" asked Adam.

"Because even if you were there all day, I'm sure you wouldn't see a slew of hotties. One or two or even three a day? What is a newbie to do? Wait around all day for the hungry girls? I suggest putting one's efforts into more statistically rich venues. There are exceptions to every rule and by all means, when at the grocery store, if you see a babe, approach her. But don't hang there all day expecting to get lots of action. Is it possible to meet a girl walking by your porch? Sure it's possible, just improbable. I would suggest getting off your porch to increase your odds.

"If you ask girls where they would like to meet their next boyfriend, I doubt they will say at the grocery store or at the Laundromat. I'm not actually sure what they would say, but I can wager on what they wouldn't say. Could you meet a girl on an elevator in your building? Sure. But are you going to stand in the elevator all day waiting for the one lady to come by?

"Nightclubs are where it's at. And by nightclubs, I mean fun bars with dancing, too. There isn't much choice for a girl in a club actually. Most of the guys open with such bad pickup lines, like 'Excuse me, I don't mean to bother you, but I really like the way you look and . . .' It isn't even a competition. I swear to you, I've been doing it for some time now and I no longer care how many guys are there. They are not part of the equation. They all hold beers in their hands to feel secure. I *never* hold a beer. Girls are picky. And they pick the best guy of a particular group. And the group around are lame, beer-holding guys so when you come along and make her laugh and don't hit on her and give a couple negs, you are in like nobody else could be.

"There are anywhere from thirty to forty girls rated 8.5-plus in a single club. I approach twelve of the best in an evening, coming home with three to four numbers a night, minimum. If the place isn't great, you can move on to another. The women expect conversation and many are single, looking for you to come help them escape their boring lives. You can show you are a social leader by the number of people around you paying attention to you. This is a demonstration of higher value we call 'Leader of Men' and it activates attraction in women. Learn about social hierarchy and why the female prefers a male with higher 'standing.' Why run around searching for one woman at a time when you can wait in a valley where all the animals will come to drink from the water hole? They also dress up and look good. They also are very cautious about men there. Sure. And, when you get good at the art, you will not even notice the defenses they have because you will be very good at working in a club. You get good because you meet so many in a night and have so much approaching experience. You learn from every one of them. How many guys in there meet a girl and then act interested in the girl's thoughts and not just her body? Put me and you in the room and I'll clean up! Why? Am I better looking? Who knows. Who cares. Am I studlier than thou? Maybe, but then maybe not. The difference is that I understand statistics. I understand what most men do not. I know what women are looking for. I give it to them. Oh, and one more thing. I don't make excuses why I shouldn't go and meet girls where they are the most plentiful.

"Society has its mating rituals. When a woman wants to find a mate, she will get emotions driving her to seek social situations. She doesn't bother getting dressed and looking good just to dance. Dancing is even a way of showing the health of the body for a suitor—you! She is seeking a mate. And yes, she will go to a place where there are possible mates. Granted, she will only pick the best. But girls don't put body and looks high on the priority list. The top three traits are a good smile, a sense of humor, and confidence. The fourth is connection, by the way. So there you go."

"To be honest," said Adam, "I think clubs suck. The main reason I don't like clubs is the noise. I feel that there's so much info conveyed through speech tone, volume, and rhythm that it's all lost if you have to scream at someone standing two feet in front of you. I also like my conversation and my routines to go off smoothly, without having to repeat myself. How do I get around this in clubs?"

"The problem is," I replied, "people don't go to public gatherings without music. When there is no music, many people are too scared to chat with strangers so they feel uncomfortable and don't go to that place. Thing is, most people aren't players. A club is actually very logical. You are thinking about only your intentions. See, for a girl, the main reason to be there is to meet a guy. But, they have to do something to look busy while in there. Some need an alternative excuse, like coming to drink with friends, which is utterly absurd. Who the hell really wants to pay five dollars just to get into a noisy place to talk with friends? Then you've got the old-style mating ritual: dancing. This shows off your health, vitality, and physique. Everyone has a different way of meeting others. Thing is, players should know the most efficient way. This doesn't mean the rest of the world does, too. So it looks like noisy clubs are the way. They attract lots of people. What other thing does that without actually taking the people's attention totally, as a play or concert does? The entire club industry is designed to make money off people wanting to meet a mate.

"You don't like the current mating ritual? Okay, agreed. It's not the most efficient. But then what is better? I'm talking not better in an exceptional way, such as meeting a single girl in a park. I'm talking about the masses. How do the masses meet mates? What is your alternative to clubs for all the masses? How about getting with the program and getting good at the real mating scene instead of perpetual wishful thinking?! Meeting girls while rock climbing is possible but we aren't concerned with what is possible, rather with what is probable. Do you foresee the masses going rock climbing as a ritual to meeting their potential mates? I don't see that happening. Clubs are the mass ceremony events for mating. Join in and get good rather than coming up with excuses left, right, and center."

"Well," said Adam, "you know a lot of people say, 'I went out tonight, just for a drink and some music.'"

"Notice the excuse used here?" I said. "It's an excuse women use, too. Imagine a place that didn't serve alcohol, or play music. Sure, the perfect pickup place, but then the girls wouldn't have an excuse for being there, other than to get picked up.

"Do you really think this dude got all dressed up and went out to actually listen to music and drink? Drinking at home is cheaper and home stereo systems play the music you want. Why pay the cover, too?

"This is why clubs have loud music. It's a thinly veiled excuse to look for mates.

"Isn't it funny how the number-one reason guys don't have girlfriends is that they simply don't get out of the house enough and into public gatherings? Time and again, *finding* the girls is the hardest part to getting girls. You have so much more chance of having sex with a beautiful girl if you could just find her. It's Tuesday and my bud wants to shake the feeling of rejection from a girl he tried closing on today, so we are going to a café tonight at nine. Thing is, it's Tuesday. Where do you go on a Tuesday? This place will be dead like any typical café. Hoping some talent will come our way . . . hoping. We aren't smart about this. We don't know really where to go. But we are getting out, so that's better than not, right?

"In addition to working the clubs, of course I'm still going to practice pickup wherever possible outside of them. But I must say again, I have found nothing that is comparable to clubs. I mean, of the girls in my past, a good seventy-five percent were from clubs. Others were from school, friends of friends at parties, once walking the main street in my city. None in a store, none in a coffee shop, although coffee shops are great to bring someone you've already found. Girls have got to be in mating mode."

"I went around one time," said Adam, "smiling and saying hi at every single good-looking girl I saw. I got lots of favorable responses."

"It's a good first step," I replied, "but how many numbers do you get from this? I have put my skills to the test everywhere. Malls, banks, the street, stores, food courts, restaurants, bars, clubs, concerts, fairs and festivals . . . everywhere. Clubs are the place. You can get girls in other places but why work on the edge of the real game? There are tons of types of clubs. Bars and social restaurants are included. Steak houses and dance halls and parties are possible. Sure, if I meet a girl in a bookstore I'll be ready. But I'm only ready because of all the practice I've had in clubs.

The benefit of being in a club is *quantity*. There simply are more opportunities to see women of beauty. With that benefit comes a series of shitty things. Noise, crowds, dark, alcohol, male competition, raised bitch shields are just some, never mind cover charges. But the benefit outweighs all the shit. The solution is to minimize the shit. Here is how:

"Noise: Don't approach girls in the loud areas. There are always a couple of areas of a club that are the least noisy. That is the field. Around the dance floor? That is the trap. You can't initiate a chat there so why be there? I know, to look at the girls you can't approach. Fuck that. Stay out of the trap. It's a trap. Dance floors are not a pickup field.

"Crowds: Go early. Approach the bartenders and hostesses early. Get in early. Ten P.M. Get there at nine-thirty P.M. if you have to. This usually saves you money on the cover, too. Solve crowd issues by *working* crowds. Don't approach a single girl. Approach a group of people. This allows you the ability to display social proof. At midnight, bail out to another club—it keeps the crowd fresh for you and offers the opportunity to instant-date girls as they join you to the next club.

"Dark: Stay in the lit areas. Usually they are the most quiet and least crowded. See, pickup is like fishing. Having a fish on the line is the exception to the general rule. Wait and wait and wait is the general rule. Then a woman comes in from the dance floor and, bam, you yank the line. Hook them. Three-Second Rule it and address the target's entire group. So in a way, the fishing pole is changed into a net.

"Alcohol: It's hard enough when *they're* drunk. A pickup artist's game is always better when he's not drunk. Don't drink, and keep the sharpness—trust me, pal, you're gonna need it when a girl is in front of you.[1]

"Male competition: Yes, there are more guys. But they don't smile. They don't surround themselves with people and talk talk talk and laugh. They don't walk around holding the smile on their face. They hold a beer on their chest and lean in and 'look cool.' A pickup artist realizes that the only obstacle with regards to other males is that the more faces exist in there, the more busy the vibe will be. Like MTV rather than C-SPAN. Solution: Be MTV yourself! That is why gimmicks are useful.

"Bitch shields: Yes, they are higher. But the solution is not to punch through it, but to trick her to lower the shield. How? Group theory and negs. Approach the group while ignoring the target and using negs on her. Disarm the friends with stories and humor, and when they all love you, you can finally turn to the target. By this time the negs sank in and lowered her self-esteem. Her shield down, she wants attention from you, the life of the party—the guy who sort of pushed her out of the spotlight of her own circle of friends. And there you have it. Add more groups so that the next group will have noticed you in a previous group (social proof) and the closes come caving in like a nuclear reaction.

"*This* is group theory. Use fun conversation to entertain and convey personality to both the obstacles and the target. If you don't have enough practice to just riff it, then use routines. That way you

1. I break this rule all the time.

can practice the talk talk talk that makes you the center of attention. There are many routines that have worked for others. Photo routine, question game, teach the target mnemonics, recite a pattern. It's all about conveying personality. And while you are ignoring the target and entertaining her friends, she perceives you as you are, but amplified by the smiles of her own peer group. This is the mechanism I am teaching you now."

DIGITAL VOICE RECORDER EXERCISE

I challenge each and every one of you to go out four nights this week, for a minimum of four hours per night, and make this task an important project. Bring a digital voice recorder (or at least a small notebook) and record every attempt. At the end of the four days we will figure out the details of probability. The more doors you knock on, the more will open. Look at a map of your area and select the best places for the best nights. *Prepare.* Consider the proper attire for each place. Know your openers. Be a detective. Do this like it means money to you. Like it means sex. Love. Go out alone if you must; don't go out with more than one other person (preferably a girl to make you look cooler). Be inconvenienced by this project a bit . . . use this challenge as the excuse to focus on what is important.

At the end of this week, after your four days of four-hour sets, reassess your success.

Recorders on.

Chapter Seven

THE STRIP CLUB
IN VEGAS

A COUPLE OF YEARS AGO, when Lovedrop was still fat, the boot camp instructor staff sat in our own roped-off area at the hottest strip club in Las Vegas. I had been doing these boot camps in different cities for a few years now; students come for a class and then we take them out at night for some in-field practice. It was a tradition on Sunday night to take all of the instructors out to celebrate the end of another successful boot camp and practice stripper game, which I taught to all of them.

The club was a dimly lit cornucopia of flesh in red velvet. It was intoxicating—all of these hot women, perky, ripe, young, and sometimes naked, bouncing around, serving, just available, approaching, touching, and constantly in a controlled sexual frame—but, of course, you can't really sleep with them all. In fact, you can't sleep with even one of them, if you are like most guys. Yet being there still puts you in that mood, doesn't it? It sure would be nice to sleep with just one of them.

It's just a fantasy.

That's what they sell, after all. *Fantasy.*

Still, though, she is hot; she is beautiful; and here she is in front of you. She wants to have a drink with you. Yes, of course, you know she is working, but she did pick you to approach, out of the whole room, and she's very cute. After a while, as you talk to her, she actually seems to be a pretty cool person; she's not bad at all. And she's beautiful.

You open up to her a little bit. She giggles when you make a joke. She touches you, on the arm, the leg. And then, at some point as she smiles, you suddenly think: *She likes me.* It happens, from time to time, doesn't it? She snuggles against your side and says that you turn her on. She wants to know: *Would you like a lap dance?*

And why not? When in Rome . . .

You're starting to feel a little excited, from the anticipation. Of course you're not supposed to touch the girls during a lap dance, but that's okay. *Just sit back and relax.*

Her hair cascades down around your face as she straddles you. She smells so good. She brushes against you and begins to rock her hips back and forth. She inhales sharply; the rest of the room becomes lost in her rhythmic motion and fades into a velvety haze of smoke and flesh. This is what all girls should be like! Her breasts are in your face; her breath is hot on your neck as she rides you, her voice moaning in your ear, her wet lips, her tongue—

Sorry . . . the song's over. Would you like another dance? It's twenty dollars by the way.

"God, I am horny," I said as I sat down. "I feel like sexing an entire cheerleading team."

Lovedrop and I reclined in soft opulence. Style, now a good friend of mine after he studied me for his book *The Game*, sat close by, deep in comfort building with his girl; he was in town to party and hang out at our seminar.

A business associate of mine at the time, George Wu, sat across the way, gaming a stripper the way I taught him. George used to run one of my websites. He's probably still out there somewhere running a website based on me. Lots of people do that, actually. There are an endless string of wannabes out there, trying to look as affiliated with me and the Venusian Arts as possible.

Wu's redheaded lieutenant, Biff, sat in a circle to the right with his crew, joking and horsing around. They were just close enough for us to hear Biff's loud, abrasive voice, braying like an ass in the night.

Throughout our roped-off area, exotic dancers sat in and among us, working their game on the various pickup instructors, who in turn practiced their stripper game.

Biff's group of friends burst out laughing.

We heard Biff say loudly, "What's twelve inches long, and white?"

"I give up," said one of his cronies.

"Nothing," said Biff, "except for my huge cock!" The group of them exploded in another fit of hyena-like laughter.

"Jeez," said fat Lovedrop. "The 'huge cock' gaff never gets old with these guys." Lovedrop had a double chin and his face was covered with tiny beads of sweat. He wiped it with the back of his hand.

Style looked over. "He's been making some rather derogatory comments about his students from this weekend." He shrugged uncomfortably, wincing. Then he turned back to his girl and they continued their conversation.

We heard Biff say, "I had the worst group of students last night. They were a bunch of mutants." He really did bray like an ass. "There was Fat Mutant, Short Mutant, Gay Mutant, Drunk Mutant, and Troll Mutant. Troll Mutant was my favorite. He looked like a troll. He asked me what the trouble is with his game. Meanwhile, I wanted to ask him 'Why don't you just whip out your X-Men superhuman powers, since you're a fucking *mutant!*'" Biff laughed his hyena laugh. It was horrific, like a cross between a repeating, uncontrolled hiccup and someone being stabbed in the stomach.

I looked over at Lovedrop and said, "Biff is offensive to me. Why is he still with this company, again?"

"He's George's boy," said Lovedrop with a shrug. "You gotta take that up with George."

"Fuck that guy," said Matador, sitting down to join us. "He's a punk. You know what that motherfucker did in New York? He supposedly came out to help me out on my boot camp. But the real reason he volunteered was so he could deliberately try to sink the program."

"What?" I asked. "What do you mean?"

"Biff came out to my program, offering to help, and then tried to sink it, *on purpose*. He got drunk, and he was a complete dick to my students. He didn't even go by the name of 'Biff' because he didn't want to get bad reviews. He wanted *me* to get bad reviews. And he got into a big fight with one of my students! A fight! I got refund requests because of him."

"Sheesh," I said. "That's unacceptable behavior."

"He was trying to destroy me as a viable entity. And then to make matters worse, when I went to George about it, George takes his side!" Matador was fuming. "George said he thinks I can 'try harder' to get along with Biff!"

"Well, you are a bull in a china shop," I said.

"That's not the point, you crazy magician! He tried to sink me!"

Across the way, we heard Biff saying loudly, "Fuck Mehow. He uses buying-temperature game. People who use buying-temperature game are tools."

Lovedrop said, "Matador, maybe you're just being paranoid."

"Paranoid, huh?" Matador replied. "Missile Tits, do you know what kind of shit Biff talks about you, when you aren't around?"

"What?" said Lovedrop, rolling his eyes. "I'm dying to know."

"He talks shit on your game, fat boy. He talks shit about your buddy Mehow, he says you're a spy—"

I laughed. "A spy?"

"That's crazy talk," said Lovedrop.

"That may be," said Matador, "but it makes you wonder how George and Biff are talking about you when you're not around, doesn't it? They are close."

Lovedrop shrugged. "They probably talk about what a jerk-off you look like for buying the exact same leather jacket that I wear."

"Dude, that has nothing to do with this," said Matador, exasperated. "I told you before that I'm sorry I bought your jacket. I won't wear it on the same night as you—"

"You just don't do that shit, bro." Lovedrop was still at the overornamental phase of his fashion development. He wore fake earrings, a necklace chain, a thumb ring on each thumb, and black rubber bracelets from Hot Topic; his fingernails were painted black and he was wearing eye shadow. Over the years, he would come to discard most of these ornaments and masculinize his look.

"You can't even take Biff out in public," said Matador, "or introduce him to your friends. He made a complete drunken idiot out of himself in New York."

"What happened?" I asked.

"He was about to get his ass kicked," said Matador, "mouthing off like usual to these two guys in the bar. The one guy goes 'Hey,' and pushes Biff in the face. So then he acts like he's about to get into it with these guys—you should've seen these guys by the way, they were huge—and they were about to jump him, so I went 'Whoa, whoa, whoa, one second!' and I picked him up, and put him over my shoulder and carried him out of there."

"It's the old 'get-drunk-and-pick-fights-with-two-huge-guys' gambit," I joked.

"Yeah, no shit. So at the end of the night, the students go home, and Biff and I go to a strip club. And we're having trouble getting in 'cause the bouncer thinks he's too drunk."

"Go figure."

"Yeah. So right when I'm trying to convince them that he's cool, he pukes all over the bouncer's shoe!"

Lovedrop snickered.

"Imagine being there, bro," said Matador. "He literally pukes on the bouncer's shoe while we're trying to get in the bar. So I had to carry him back and put him in the car. Hoping he'll sober up. But then we go to the next place, same problem. Bouncer says he's too drunk. I'm trying to convince the bouncer, then I turn around, and there's Biff sleeping on the ground behind me."

Lovedrop and I burst out laughing.

"It's not funny," said Matador, shaking his head. "I can't believe George even keeps him around."

"Wait a second. What do you mean, 'George keeps him around'?" I said indignantly. "I . . . am Mystery. I don't have any say in the matter?"

"O-kay," said fat Lovedrop, rolling his eyes. Lovedrop was six foot two, and he weighed two hundred and twenty pounds back then, all of it fat—not an ounce of muscle anywhere on his lanky frame. He hid it pretty well under his black leather jacket. He also wore an undershirt to minimize the effect of having man-boobs, but it didn't help much.

"Why don't you talk to George?" asked Matador.

"I will," I said. "*I'm* Mystery."

Across the way, we heard Biff say loudly, "Fuck Style. Did you guys read *The Game*?"

"Hello," said Lovedrop. "Style is sitting right here."

"He can't hear you," said Style.

Lovedrop looked over toward George, and he later told me that he noticed in that moment that George was watching me from across the way. After a moment, he started to feel vaguely uneasy at the sight. What was that look on George's face? Discomfort? Resentment? It was hard to tell through his Asian features.

Just then, Biff and two of his cronies jumped up, and the three of them lurched in the general direction of the bar, making funny faces, hobbling with an uneven gait and bent over like hunchbacks.

Style was aghast. "That's their mutant impression," he said. "They were doing that before."

"What a bunch of clowns," said Matador, standing up. "I have to take a piss," he said, and walked off.

Lovedrop looked back toward George, who was now watching Matador walk to the bathroom. He remembered something a friend had once told him: *You know that feeling you get when a woman is lying to you? That slight fake feeling, like something's just not right? Well, when a man lies to you, it's like that same feeling, but it's only about 30 percent as strong. It's very faint, but it's still there. After a while, you can tell. You can feel it.*

Lovedrop followed Matador with his eyes for a moment, and then he looked back at George again.

George was staring right back at him.

Lovedrop raised his glass and smiled. After a slight delay, George mirrored the gesture.

A smiling, dark-haired stripper suddenly walked up. "Hi," she said. "Do you mind if I sit down?"

"Be my guest," joked Lovedrop with a friendly smile, and he gestured for her to take a seat.

It almost seemed to her that he was being sarcastic, but she wasn't quite sure, since he added just enough friendliness with his smile, calibrating the delivery. He did seem genuinely friendly.

She sat down and started her routine, which you should never let happen. If you don't control the frame, then she will.

Picking up a stripper is like picking up a normal girl, but much more extreme. It's like speed chess. During a normal pickup, you of course want to steer the ship. You want to be the one setting the tone, the authority who determines the meaning of what is said, leading the interaction to where you want it to go.

With a stripper, it's even more pronounced, because she is also doing the *same thing*. She is trying to lead the interaction to a place where you are giving her money. Everything that she says is meant to bring you further down that road, in her direction, until your money is going into her hands. No matter how you answer her, no matter what you say, she has run this script a thousand times before, she has practiced it on a thousand approaches, and now she is practicing it on you. She wants to get your money.

Meanwhile, the pickup artist is trying to lead the interaction to a place where the girl gives up her body to him. Everything he says is designed to set the frame in his favor for accomplishing that goal. Everything he does is meant to lead her further down that road.

But as soon as the stripper starts talking, she is back on her script. And you can't let her lead you down that road. Hell, she's bored by it herself! Always remember, just because she started a thread doesn't mean you have to bite. Craftily cut her thread and start one of your own. If it's more stimulating, or higher value, it will win. Take over.

"Are you guys in a band or something?" she asked. "Are you guys famous?" She was fishing for information on our income.

Lovedrop joked, "We're just working on our look." He wasn't sure if George's eyes were still on him and he felt strange at the thought. He turned his head away for a moment, then he turned back to her and smiled warmly. "Who cares anyway? We're all gonna be dead in a hundred years, right?" He was careful to balance the nihilism with a warm, friendly vibe.

"I guess . . ." She hadn't encountered this response before. Then she got back on track. "Where are you from? You guys look like you're from L.A." She put her hand on his knee.

He smiled engagingly and then flashed her a weird expression with his eyebrows. He pointed to his head, "Turn that off, that program you're running," he said. "I used to live with a dancer." It wasn't true. He stole the line from me. I was proud.

She stumbled. "What?"

He raised an eyebrow, slowly dropped his gaze to her hand on his knee, then looked her in the eye expectantly. The vibe he conveyed was clear: *Are you kidding me? Your hand is on my knee. I can smell an agenda.* She sheepishly removed her hand, but she smiled. "Wow," she said.

He continued, with pauses: "We just finished our weekend here. And now we're celebrating. Like the end of *Ocean's Eleven*. It's our tradition. To chill out on Sunday night. In a place like this. Where no one will bother us. And we can just drink and relax."

"Do you want to get us a drink?" she asked.

Cutting her thread like it didn't even exist, he suddenly said, "The dynamic is all off in here, isn't it?"

"What do you mean?" she asked.

"Look around you. Look at all these people in here, right now." He gestured around. "No one respects anyone else. The dancers see so many losers come in. And the customers feel excited about the dancers, but that's because they see her as a stripper, when that's not who she really is. Her job is entertainment."

"That is so true," she said, nodding.

"Yet the customers still want to hook up with the dancer," he said. "Like make her their girlfriend, or whatever fantasy they have, but meanwhile the dancer could never do that because she knows the customer doesn't respect her. Yet there they both are, trying to get something from each other."

She shrugged.

He angled his body away from her, then leaned back. "I feel like a vampire sometimes," he said conspiratorially.

"What do you mean?" she asked, and cocked her head, applying some lip liner.

"Because of my lifestyle," he said. "My reality." He paused. "When the sun is going down, that's when I am waking up. And when the sun starts to come up, that's when I am going down to sleep." Conveying commonality and similarity. Lovedrop seemed to know what he was doing.

She leaned forward slightly. "Tell me more," she said.

"I go all over the earth," he said. "London, New York, Miami. I go to the clubs, I mix with everyone else, but I'm not really the same as them. They wouldn't understand. They drive their commute and they work for the man, and meanwhile I can manifest anything that I want."

He thought, *So much of this is in the delivery. I've flopped this routine before. The flying-around-the-world routine can sometimes come off as bragging, rather than demonstrating higher value, but it seems to be working.*

She asked, "What do you mean, 'manifest'?"

"You just . . . focus your thoughts, and you make it real. You manifest reality." He rubbed his thumb and fingers and opened his hand like a butterfly. She smiled.

He grinned. "I want to show you something," he whispered.

"What?" she asked.

"I'm going to take you back to my friend's place tonight, and show you," he said. "I've got a, uh"—he looked around surreptitiously—"I've got a *Honey I Shrunk the Kids* machine." He grinned playfully.

She burst out laughing.

He continued: "And I'm gonna shrink us down to the size of Barbie and Ken dolls, so we can swim in that aquarium right there, and find magical new lands, and have amazing adventures."[1] As he said it, he turned momentarily, as if looking for someone, or exploring a sudden thought, and then turned back to her again and smiled warmly.

She furrowed her brow, responding to his distracted rock star persona. "You are really funny," she said. "You are really different. What's your name? I'm Ashley." (IOI. But can you trust an IOI from a stripper?)

"I'm Chris," he said.

"You don't have one of those funny names like all these other guys?"

"That's just for logging into forums on the Internet. You're not supposed to use those names in real life."

"Oh, right."

"Here, hold this." He handed her his drink and stretched out his hands on either side of it like a sorcerer conjuring visions from a crystal ball. He said, "I don't know, if you can remember the last

1. Notice that she is actually imagining the sensations and emotions of this fun adventure as you describe it to her. So, although you cannot physically take her on the adventure, you can still lead her through the *experience* of it, via her imagination, which is all that matters anyway. Remember, most guys out there aren't stimulating a woman's imagination and feelings—instead they are boring her by asking what she does for a living, and whether she has a boyfriend.

time you were able to feel an incredible connection with someone . . ."

She nodded, and watched.

He continued, with pausing, "When you feel that, it's almost
like you can imagine a cord of light, extending from you to this person. And as you begin to glow, with the warmth of that connection,
you can imagine a time in the future, still feeling that amazing
sense of connection, and looking back on today as having been the
start of it."[2]

His hands became tense as he gestured above the drink she
held. He said, "The more you are able to picture that feeling, your
favorite color, and feel the glow of it in your stomach. And then it
swirls upward, glowing, and fills your chest, and it moves down
your arms, and through your hands." His attention focused on the
drink in front of him. "Give me the glass now."

As she handed it to him, he pulled his hands away from the glass
and it began to float in midair. Someone else gasped nearby.

"Oh, my God!" shrieked the stripper. Her hands were shaking.

Without milking it too much, he grasped the glass again and
then took a drink.

The magic trick was courtesy, again, of me. He used my 'Power-
Lev Principle.' I have always preferred magic that appears *real*. The
worst thing, to me, is when someone pulls out a deck of cards in
the club. That just makes him look like a trickster. But when I perform magic, I use mentalism and telekinesis effects, allowing my
target to interpret that something really magical happened. As for
Lovedrop, he later dropped the use of magic, because he said it
made him feel like a dancing monkey.

"Let me ask you something," he said, going into a cold read,
with pauses. "Did you have an experience, when you were really
young, that made you have to grow up, before you were ready?"

She put her hand over her mouth for a moment and her eyes
began to well up.

2. The infamous Incredible Connection pattern from Ross Jeffries.

Just then, we heard Biff bray loudly, "I've got a new joke for you guys."

He must have gotten back from the bar. His whole group of cronies were all sitting back in their original spot.

He asked, "What does a stripper do with her asshole before she goes to work?"

"I give up, what?" asked one of them.

"She drops him off at band practice!"

The pack exploded into a fit of guffaws and hyena laughter.

"I have to go for a minute," said the dark-haired stripper suddenly, jerked back to reality. "But I'm coming back. I want to talk to you more. Will you be here?"

"Sure," said Lovedrop. "This is our area. We're here until we leave."

"Okay, do *not* leave," she said. "I want to talk to you, but there's some stuff I have to take care of real quick. I'll be back." She squeezed his arm, stood up, and walked off.

"Not bad," I said, as soon as she was gone. "Not bad at all. Don't worry, she's just got to do her rounds, I think she'll be back."

"Good," said Lovedrop. "That's exactly what I was going to ask you."

Just then, Biff walked up to us.

"Hey," he said, as he sat down across from Lovedrop.

"What's up, bro?" said Lovedrop. "How's your night?"

"I saw you in that set," said Biff. "You had that stripper for sure. What did you use on her?"

"Well, let's see," said Lovedrop. "I cut her threads. I used harsh negs. I DHV'd up the wazoo. I did the vampire lifestyle stuff and the whole create-your-own-reality thing. I used some buying-temperature stuff to make her giggle. I did some speed seduction—the incredible connection pattern—"

"That incredible connection shit doesn't work on strippers."

"Yeah, I know. I threw everything at her but the kitchen sink. I even did a fucking magic trick, and then I used Toecutter's cold read from his palm reading routine. You know, the Steve Celeste book—"

"Why did she leave?"

"She said she had to take care of something and she'd be back."

"Well, you don't want to be just waiting for her when she gets back. I've made that mistake before." Biff shook his head with absolute certainty. "I'd be like, waiting for the girl and dude, like, as much as I want to show her my huge cock, I wouldn't get the chance because I look like a loser waiting for her."

"Yeah," I said, "plus it bleeds 'expensive time.' You at least want to be in another set, not sitting by yourself."

"So what would you suggest?" asked Lovedrop.

"When she comes back," said Biff, "make her wait for a minute while you talk to me, and then call her over. Let her sweat it out a little."

"I disagree," I said. "My advice? Don't play games. Go for the pull. Strippers can have anyone in that club. That is why, once they decide they want you, they don't think about games and instead just—bam! They go for your throat."

"Go for the pull?" said Biff. He shook his head. "You're basically calling her a slut. That's not something you want to do. I know what I'm talking about." Just then, he put his foot down wrong and fell flat on his face in front of everybody.

He quickly jumped back to his feet, trying to act as if nothing had happened. For a split second, everyone in our roped-off area paused, then resumed.

I cleared my throat, a faint smile on my lips, and then addressed Lovedrop. "I'm Mystery," I said. "I'll never steer you wrong. This is typical of all strippers and tens. She doesn't want a coffee shop date. She wants to actually hang with you. Don't make steps backward. Invite her back to the hotel now. Our energy is more potent there, away from the energy of the club."

"Hey," said Style, standing up with his sweet Asian girl. "Mystery, do you want to join us at the bar?"

"Oh boy, do I," I said, smiling gaily. "Good luck with all of this," I said, and the three of us walked off.

"By the way," said Biff as soon as he was alone with Lovedrop, "I heard about that problem you had with George."

"What problem?" asked Lovedrop.

"Don't worry about it. George said those things happen sometimes."

"What are you talking about?" asked Lovedrop.

Biff swayed a little bit. "Dude," he said, "I'm really feeling those tequila shots."

"I'm having a good time myself," smirked Lovedrop. "That's what it's all about."

"You seem to be hanging out with Matador a lot lately," said Biff. He hiccupped. "It seems like you're aligning with him."

"Aligning?" said Lovedrop. "You should have friendly relations with everyone if possible." He thought, *Biff has the political skills of a high schooler.* "It's just good policy," he continued. "You can't be burning bridges; it comes back to haunt you later in unpredictable ways."

Biff's eyes twitched back and forth. "But Matador is such a tool! He's weird, and robotic. His game sucks." He was really getting worked up.

"You say that about everyone," said Lovedrop.

Biff frowned. "I just feel like, he's, like, an angry, insecure dude, and he makes up for it by turning up everything alpha that he does to eleven. He's always got to be the most alpha. And he takes himself so seriously, it's like you can't relax around the guy 'cause everything is a clash of frames."

Lovedrop shrugged. "But what's your goal?"

"He threatened to break my neck one time," said Biff. "He's violent. He grabbed my neck in New York." His eyes continued to twitch rapidly.

"I make friends with people," said Lovedrop, "and they want to align with me, whereas you burn your bridges, and people want to break your neck. Is that it?"

"I don't care, like . . ." Biff trailed off. "Whatever. Matador's on his way out. And you don't want to be on the wrong side."

Lovedrop paused. "What's that?" he said.

Biff looked around to make sure no one was listening. He was swaying now, and he kept spilling bits of his drink as his arm swung around wildly. "George told me something," he said. He was starting to slur. He suddenly broke out into a big grin.

"Yeah?"

"He—" Biff broke off giggling.

"He what?" *This ought to be good.*

"George told me something."

"What'd he tell you?" *Let's hear it, you drunken idiot.*

Biff finally revealed: "George made out with a dude."

Lovedrop was taken aback. "What?"

"He made out with a dude," Biff said again, slurring. "He likes it."

"He made out with . . ." Lovedrop repeated the words and frowned. "A *dude.* That's it?"

Biff said, "To see what it was like." He hiccupped.

" 'To see what it was like,' " repeated Lovedrop.

Biff nodded earnestly. "Yeah." He shook his head, then closed his eyes for a moment. He slowly swayed back and forth.

"How often does he do this?"

"I don't know." Biff grinned proudly, as if he had just solved world hunger.

"Wow," said Lovedrop.

"I know," said Biff. "Don't tell anyone." Then he squinted. "Hey," he said suddenly. "Here comes your stripper."

Sure enough, there she was. She walked into our roped-off area and went right back to the spot where she had been sitting with Lovedrop.

"Act like you don't notice her yet," whispered Biff. "Then go back and talk to her in, like, a few minutes. Make her wait."

"Okay," said Lovedrop. He waited a moment. "Wow," he said. "It's funny how strong the urge is, to just go running right over there as fast as I can and talk to her. I'm really fighting it right now."

"By the way," said Biff. "You know Mystery has stolen two girls from me. I won't even bring girls around him anymore. And I know he stole that one girl from you in San Diego."

"Yeah," said Lovedrop, "that motherfucker is shameless."

"I won't even let myself hang out with him anymore," said Biff, "because he steals girls."

"Yeah," said Lovedrop, "but then again, in my case, it's not like she was my girlfriend. I hadn't really gotten more than ten minutes into the set—"

"But it was still your set, not his, right?"

"Oh, don't get me wrong," said Lovedrop. "I was pissed. And check this out: He had even promised that he wouldn't try anything. I told him I had a girl coming over, and he said, 'I understand, bro. Your set, hands off.' But then, as soon as she came in the front door, he was all over her. Google Earth routine, the works. You know the drill."

"Yeah." Biff nodded. "It hurt my feelings when he did it to me, because it's like he's willing to lose the friendship over a girl."

"He definitely owes me one," said Lovedrop. "He admitted that much."

Suddenly behind him, something snapped inside Lovedrop's stripper. She stood up quickly and walked out of our area, looking pissed off.

"Shit," said Biff. "She just left."

Damn it, thought Lovedrop, feeling a sinking feeling in his stomach. *I should have listened to Mystery.*

"I told you," I said to Lovedrop as Style and I returned from the bar. "You can't impress a stripper by time. You've got to pack a 'way-too-cool for this place' punch, and then close. I either get them to leave with me, or meet me somewhere later."

"So it really happens that fast then?"

"Yes," I said. "To get a stripper, you must create an impression within three minutes, tops. You have to go for a really subtle close in which you convince her to meet you somewhere. It's a three-minute interactive game to get a stripper. Everything after that is comfort building only."

"Okay," said Biff, rolling his eyes.

"I remember one time," said Lovedrop, "I saw a couple of strippers fighting over Mystery. It was at Crazy Girls in Hollywood. So the first girl had to get up and go dance onstage. So another one sat down and took her spot. He ran the exact same routine on the second one that he did on the first. Later on, the first stripper comes back and she wants her seat back! It was funny. She literally tried to pull the other girl out of her seat."

Just then, a smiling blond dancer approached us.

"Hi," she said.

I'm game. "What's your plan?" I said.

She frowned. "My plan for what?"

"I know you're working," I said, pacing her reality. "I want you to take your exotic dancer social program—your game plan—and turn it off." I touched her nose. "Beep."

She laughed.

"Now it's off. You're you. I will tell you when I turn it back on, but for now it's off. Now you're normal." I smiled.

"You're not a customer," she said. (That's acceptance of my frame, an IOI.)

"Customer?" I chuckled. "I'm not even here for a customer. I'm a good friend of DJ Dave. Do you know him? Are you good friends with him?"

"Yes I know him very well." I was busted; I only knew him by name!

"I'm very curious about you." (IOI.) I switched threads. "Forgive me for not being in the sexual mind-set." (IOD.) "I'm just not here today. Just so that you and I are on the same page, real quick"—false time constraint—"before I get to my question"—multiple threading—"I'm from Toronto, but I live in Vegas now."

"Toronto?"

"Toronto, Canada." I nodded. "And my last long-term relationship, it was almost four years, she was an exotic dancer, so the last thing I want to hear from you is talk about the problems of your job. It bores the shit out of me." (IOD.)

She giggled.

"So we are on the same page," I said. "You know, stripper boyfriend kinda thing."

She laughed. "Right."

"We're like a type," I said. "I have noticed that."

"Stripper boyfriends are a type?" She said it with a slight questioning tone.

"Perhaps, but exotic dancers have gravitated toward me. I think it's because I am a performing artist as well." I was reframing her as a performing artist, instead of as a stripper—and showing an understanding of her reality. "You know what I find really curious and interesting is, don't you sometimes . . . you get paid and you wonder what the fuck are these people paying me for?" (More pacing.)

She nodded. "I wonder that every day."

"And this is what I wonder, too." I nodded with her. "I am an illusionist, a stage performer. And when I get up onstage, I mean honestly, all I do is I talk, and it's just me, and then they pay me for it. And they're *happy*. That's even more crazy."

I stopped and crossed my arms. "You know, you're very pretty, but this is Vegas. Beauty is very common. I mean in here you're one of, what, forty girls? And around town you're one of how many?"

"Millions."

"Exactly."

"Well, I don't try to sing, I don't try to act."

"Well, what would you want to be if a magician could come along, and go *bink*, and you could be anything in the world? And don't say princess—I know it's on your mind." (Verbal compliance test.)

Just as she started to answer, I cut her off. "Before you answer"—

multiple threading—"did you notice when you started this job, you thought to yourself, *I'm not shy of my body. I'll show off my body and I'll get to make some good coin.* But then you discovered, it was work, actually; you had to learn how to speak. Eighty-five percent of this game is—"

"Hustle," she said.

"Exactly." I smiled. "And I bet you ten to one, you're still looking at it like a hobby and not like a business."

"Not like a what?"

"A business."

"No." She shook her head. "Now I have to look at it as a business. It's my only source of income. It's not a hobby. When I started out, oh yeah, I was partying; it was cool." (Disagreeing, an IOD, but then bringing it back to agreement at the end. IOI.)

"Then let me ask you," I said. "When you answer the boring, stereotypical stupid questions that every mark asks you, and they are marks, just look around"—pacing her reality, as well as drawing a distinction between myself and customers—"do you give them the same answers you gave them when you started out? Because those are the ones you began with. What you should do is swap those out and embed new answers that will arouse. That way it will separate you."

"I have pretty good answers for marks."

"You still didn't answer."

"What would I do if I could be anything? I'd probably want to teach, even though teachers don't make much money." (IOI. Compliance.)

"What about, okay, how's this: You have a skill set; how long have you been doing this?"

"Two years."

"So the skill set that you're most likely not appreciating that you have is—"

She reached out to me as I spoke, and touched me on the arm.

"Hey," I said, looking down at her touch, "this shit ain't for free." (IOD.) "You know what? Your program is still off, and you're attracted to me. I find that interesting. I'll tell you when to turn it back on. Wanna try a quick experiment?"

"Why?" (IOD.)

"It's a fun little psychological experiment," I said. "I'm gonna show you something that I normally don't show a lot of people. When I show this to you and—no, not that. Get your head out of the gutter."

"I wasn't even thinking that." She smiled, flirting. (IOI.)

"I'll try an experiment with you and if you are frightened by it, then go run along and go make some money before you piss your boss off. But if you are excited by it then we'll have something in common but only then, all right? Makeshift experiment here. I need something nonmagnetic. Could you kindly hand me those matches on the table there."

She picked the matches up and handed them to me.

"Okay, now give me your hand," I said. "The time constraints you think you have are merely an illusion."

"You're not going to light me on fire, are you?" she asked. (Playful. IOI.)

"No. Here, grab a match," I commanded. "Give me one, and grab one more. They're nonmagnetic, so this will do. I'm going to find out what you believe. Don't get me wrong: I love magic, I love illusion—when I was a little boy I wanted to grow up to be a magician. But there is another type of magic; it's the type that makes you say, 'Is it even an illusion; is it real?' That's called natural magic; that's the type that has really fascinated me. Hold these matches like this."

"They're not gonna light on fire, are they?" she asked.

"No, it's very subtle. Something I've discovered. I don't know if you believe in it but you've heard that people only use ten percent of their brains? I use eleven. From the top of your head to the bottom of your feet. How tall are you?" (Multiple threading.)

"Five three," she said.

"Five three," I repeated. "You know, my mom used to point out tall girls to me when I was a teenager and she'd say, 'Oh look, Erik, she'd be perfect for you!' and I'd be like, 'Eww, it's my mom, pointing out girls for me!' "

She giggled.

I pointed out another exotic dancer. "That's my friend, by the way. I mean my out-of-the-club friend." (Preselection, social proof.) "Okay, so anyway, there's an electrical potential inside your body between the top of your head and the bottom of your feet of about five hundred volts and it's because of salt water, natural electrolytes. If there is an energy that can be stored up over time, don't you think that evolution would have come up with a way to harness that valuable resource? You know, whether to heat the body or for your mind or—right? Tense your stomach. Good." By asking her this question, I was building compliance momentum; it's an example of Bait when using Bait-Hook-Reel-Release.

"What are you looking for?" she asked.

"Is there more to you than meets the eye?" I asked, trying to get her jumping into my hoops. "I mean you're very pretty" (IOI), "but beauty really is common." (IOD.) "What's really rare is a great outlook, energy. What would make me want to get to know you more?" (Hoop.) "Name one thing before I do this. One thing."

"What would make you want to get to know me?" She shrugged. "I don't know, my car?"

I squinted. "Your car?"

"I don't know, I don't know, I don't know," she said. "My cheery outlook on life." (IOI.)

"Tense your stomach," I ordered. "Imagine energy coming up. I'll tense mine. But still breathe. Now don't stop breathing, either."

At this point, the matches moved as if by telekinesis. (DHV.) She gasped in surprise. "Oh, my God!" she exclaimed.

"Isn't it crazy that the laws of physics permit that to exist?" I was enthusiastic.

"That was hot," she said. "That was hot. I mean, I like that." (IOI.)

"It's just crazy. It completely jazzes me. I want to hear your stories." (IOI.) "In fact I have a story . . ."

"Well, I would love to hear your stories but I am at work," she said. (IOD.)

"I understand—"

"So I really would but—"

"You have to run around and make your money before you piss your boss off. But wait, you're your own boss. Then by standing here and talking to me, you are exercising your freedom to be your own boss. I like that; that's powerful." I nodded.

"I forgot to ask you if you wanted a dance," she said. (Hoop.)

"You're such a shithead," I replied. (IOD.) "Do you know why you and I will never get along?" (IOD.) "We're too similar." (IOI.)

"Too similar?" (IOI.)

"We are. You won't take my shit, I won't take your shit. What fun is that? If I was in a room with myself too long I'd pull my own hair out. Hanging out with you, I'd be bald." (IOD.) "But I'm curious about you . . ." (IOI.)

Sitting nearby, Biff and Lovedrop were closely watching the interaction.

A few moments went by. "Dude!" said Biff, leaning over to Lovedrop. "Now he's got her sitting in his lap! Do you think she's just playing or does he have her hooked? These strippers are all full of fake IOIs."

"Well, now they're making out," said Lovedrop. "Is she allowed to do that in the club? I thought that wasn't allowed."

"By the way," said Biff, "do you notice your stripper has been systematically giving lap dances at all the tables in a circle around us?"

"Yeah, I noticed that." Lovedrop grimaced. "She's punishing me."

"Sorry about that," said Biff. He suddenly jumped up. "Matador is coming over here," he said. "I'm going to get out of here before he breaks my neck or something." He hurriedly made his way back to his pack of cronies as Matador approached.

"What'd that fucking guy want?" asked Matador as he walked up.

"Just giving me a few tips on stripper game," said Lovedrop. "He's got a hard-on for you, though, I'll tell you that."

"Yeah," said Matador. "He's got a man-crush on me. Kinda flattering, really."

"Weird," said Lovedrop.

"Hey, let's go," said Matador. "I've got the limo pulled up around back."

As everyone stood up to leave, I was still snuggling with my dancer. I rubbed noses with her. "Baby," I said, "we're gonna go to the hotel now for the after party. Run in the back and get dressed so we can get out of here."

"Okay," she said sweetly, and she jumped up and ran in the back to change.

Adam was rapt with attention as I told him all about our escapades and stripper game. I know it's advanced stuff, but the kid seemed to be learning quickly.

Adam asked, "She just went in the back, got her clothes on, and left the club with you?"

"Coming off a big boot camp," I replied, "having just successfully completed that caper, when the challenge was before me, I was like, 'Are you fucking kidding me?' Bam, got her. Just mind-warped her and she came with us back to the hotel."

"Then what happened?" asked Adam.

"Style was there," I said. "He ended up snagging a girl that weekend as well. Everyone had a blast; all the girls had a blast. When we got to the hotel, my girl wanted to try on Matador's hat, and he wouldn't let her take it off. She was really frustrated but he was just really adamant that he's keeping his hat on. She's an exotic dancer so she has to show how awesomely defiant she is; she tried to take off his hat, and he pulled back quickly, and she got pissed and punched him in the face! She ended up crying. So much drama. It's funny how a girl seems so hot at the club, but then when you get her back to the hotel, she's this crazy pain in the ass, punching people in the face. Still though, how fun is that? Good times."

THE STRIPPER RULES

RULE: She doesn't like the word *stripper*. Use *dancer*, or *exotic dancer*.

RULE: Don't assume that just because a woman makes money by peeling off her clothes, she is stupid. On the contrary, they are brighter than most of the men in there. Remember, if she can trick guys into thinking that she likes them, she makes more money.

RULE: The minute they dance for you for money, you are a customer and they don't sleep with customers. So don't let her dance for you—unless it's for free. They suffer from low self-esteem but hide it very well. They are dealing with a lot of issues emotionally in their head while they dance for you and because they generally think you don't respect them after a dance, you can't get in. Plus now she sees you as a customer.

RULE: Don't stay there long—thirty minutes, max, and only if you are into a chat with one. I initiate chat faster standing than sitting, so I go into a two-set of sitting girls and become more exciting with my conversation than any guy during the entire day.

RULE: Enthusiasm is contagious. Act enthused about something that happened to you and so will they.

RULE: Convey that your day has been incredible and then proceed to explain why. As if meeting her is completely secondary. Nothing can wreck this day! When a girl comes to sit, I talk my ass off, conveying my personality. I take over.

RULE: Don't buy her a drink, or anything, for that matter. And don't expect to actually land a stripper you've tipped. Sure, tip a girl onstage but that won't help get her. In fact it will hurt. Keep the money in your pocket—you are there for getting girls, not for the entertainment of only looking at them. You are not a customer, you are a pickup artist.

RULE: Have a performer image—appeal to the performer in them. This is where the stereotype comes from that strippers date losers in a rock band, because they are attracted to fellow performers. Use photos because they are so bored in there; a little look at some pics on your cellphone is a welcome escape. Let the photos convey you to be fucking cool. Talk about the excitement onstage. Get them to think outside the club. When leading their imagination, lead them into daylight, not night. Most guys think night only, and convey only this. The fellow performer approach together with the 'I am the Stripper Boyfriend Type' has worked for me.

RULE: Be the Stripper Boyfriend Type. Stripper boyfriends are different. Once a stripper knows you had a stripper for a girlfriend, she knows your caliber. It was easier to get another stripper once I had already had one. And peacock—wear what you want to attract. Your image needs to back up your game. Trust me, getting a stripper is not harder, only different. Some are very nice girls. It's just a job, remember. There is a way to get them. I've gone out with several dancers, one for two years, so I know the scene. I lived with her. I was one of those stripper boyfriends.

Experiment with this line and use it in the clubs with an air of cockiness, yet in a humorous way: 'Do you know my ex-girlfriend Vanessa? She used to work here. I forget her stage names 'cause she changed them as often as she did her underwear—once every two weeks. And now you know why she is my ex.' Use the name Vanessa, too.

RULE: Explain that you are well aware that all this is bullshit (the whole concept of stripping). It's just an entertainment form—good money. No big deal. Then drop the subject and don't talk about her world again. Bring her to your daylight world. Once she is out to the café or food place after, then you go vampire world on her. Strippers generally love the vampire romance stuff.

RULE: Use humor and don't hit on her, or compliment her.

RULE: Treat all strippers as 10s and use negs, because they are in a mental state of control while in their own territory. They hate sniveling losers. Negs work well.

RULE: Be slick on the close. Don't ask for the number. Make them ask you! Better yet, tell her you don't want to pick her up in the club even though you aren't a customer. Tell her to meet you outside but also tell her, "Don't expect much from me—I'm just hungry, okay?"

RULE: Most strippers are open-minded—they believe in stupid shit like ESP. Use that. Ghosts, too. Very interesting conversational threads stem from these supernatural beliefs. Many are in fact Wiccan and wear a pentacle—most strippers like rock music and long hair but some like dance music and short hair. Know which type you want, of the two types.

Some good conversational topics are God, the soul, UFOs, ESP, telekinesis, mind over matter, ghosts, poltergeist, crop circles, Atlantis, acupuncture, psychoanalysis, parapsychology, Sasquatch, the Loch Ness Monster, heaven, hell, Buddha, aromatherapy, psi powers, psychics, spells, Jesus as anything more than a magician, out-of-body experiences, levitation, twins having a psychic bond, witchcraft, demons, hauntings, exorcisms, Reiki, monogamy as a natural human behavior, and prayer. I'm just throwing it out there.

RULE: Be *big*. Be the center of attention. Don't think that the quiet seduction will work in the strip club. No sexual shit in the club. Once you have intrigued her enough to join you, she already decided she likes you.

RULE: Get to know the DJ—become his buddy. Hang out with him. Go for beers afterward. Seduce him in a way. He will lead you to all the women.

RULE: Make her think that you think she wants you. Be a challenge.

RULE: Connect using "I live my life one day at a time" frames.

RULE: Connect using "So many people are so judgmental about things. You seem really open and fun . . ."

Good luck.

Chapter Eight

THE ELVIS SCRIPT

IN THE BOWELS OF THE HOUSE, Adam and I were resuming our seminar after a short break.

"Okay," I said, "I want to talk about the approach. You know, opening the set."

"Well, what's the most powerful opener?" asked Adam.

"Actually, it's important that you learn how to use mundane material on the approach."

Adam frowned. "Mundane material? I don't get it. Why wouldn't I want to blast her with the most powerful material?"

"Because that's not how it goes down. Our goal when opening is merely to start the microcalibration process, and you only need a bit of mundane material to do that effectively, as long as your delivery is good. Let's talk about the Elvis Script for a moment.

"Although it's an old script, I developed it a few years back," I said. "This is actually a lesson in our brand-new theory, which we call microcalibration."

"Microcalibration?" asked Adam.

"Yes," I said. "I'll explain. Most guys, they approach asking ques-

THE ELVIS SCRIPT

YOU: Did you know that Elvis dyed . . . his hair?
HER: No.
YOU: Guess what was his natural hair color?
HER: Blond?
YOU: Yes, dirty blond. Isn't that nuts? Could you imagine Elvis as a dirty blond just like the Beach Boys? I think that if he didn't dye his hair, he would actually not have become famous. After all, he was doing the 'Rebel Without a Clue' thing—he was America's bad boy with those gyrating hips. Simply sinful! Priscilla also dyed her hair, obviously. Don't ask me what her original hair color was; I'm not Cliff Claven. But can you imagine what it was like to see them sharing the same sink, dying their hair black to appease the masses? See this? All natural! Yours?

1) You can eject anytime with "That's my thought for the day," then turn away. If they were entertained by your pacing, energy, enthusiasm, smile, or sense of humor, they may give you an IOI.
2) You turn your back to test them and if they say "So . . ." and try to reinitiate the conversation, it's a positive IOI and you may continue with your next routine or just say "Pleasure meeting you" and bail out.
3) Once you have consistently gotten your targets laughing with the Elvis Script, you will have learned timing and pacing and such. You will have already begun to see the repeating patterns in all the approaches. Voilà! Now you are free from any need of "killer material"—your delivery is what will hook the set. After that all you need is what we call "the absurd," which I will teach you soon.

tions, they approach trying to impress, trying to get something. They are all about *taking* value. But if you're a pickup artist, you are there to *add* value, not to take it away. Yet, as you can see, the Elvis Script is not some amazing, mind-blowing routine. Instead, it's just little bits that keep coming out, piece by piece. New students often have confidence issues and they fantasize about overcoming those issues via super powerful routines, so that the outcome is assured and they don't have to face rejection.

"But in the real world, that is simply not how you want to open. The point isn't to have some amazing opener that blows everyone away and makes them fawn all over you. Once you understand how things work, you realize that sort of opener is really not what you want at all. Rather, what you want to do is just toss out a little piece of value. It's actually better that it's only a little piece of value, rather than some mind-blowing routine. It's easier for the set to hook to.

"For example, say, 'Did you know that Elvis dyed his hair?' If your delivery is tight, then she will hook. And when she does that, you can reward her by tossing out the next piece of value, and then the next piece. If she responds with any sort of reaction, then you say the next piece: 'Guess what was his natural hair color.'

"Make sure you say the words slowly, with pauses, and enthusiasm. This is what causes her to respond again, perhaps by smiling, or feigning ignorance ('I don't know?' 'Huh?') You just continue with 'He was actually dirty blond. Isn't that nuts?'

"And then do a roll-off, then the next piece, and the next IOI from her. So if you are thinking about it properly, opening isn't about reciting some magic spell. It's just about tossing that first piece, and the next piece, and so on.

"Now let's say that she doesn't hook. Well, in that case, you just need to use more disinterest, and then you toss out another piece of value. Of course, we will teach you the negs, the body rocking, the delivery, and so on.

"You see, the cycle of Bait-Hook-Reel-Release starts in the very beginning, at the opener. And it just continues to cycle outward from there, escalating as she complies first to your approach, and then she complies to vibing with you, and then as you continue to flip her attraction switches, she will comply to jump through your conversational hoops. Eventually she will comply with your physical escalation more and more, as you qualify her and flip her connection switches. Game is really about building compliance, and microcalibration is the process for doing that. Bait-Hook-Reel-Release. And it all starts with the opener.

"So let's stop looking at the opener as a magic spell, and start looking at the opener as the beginning of a microcalibration process. Fair?

"Notice how I described the Elvis Script—as I actually use it— as part of a process of testing for compliance, and not merely as a piece of canned material to be recited like a magic spell.

"Compliance means that she accepts my value offerings as I say each bit. She should be responding with IOIs. Notice that what really hooks the set is not the line itself, but the 'energy, enthusiasm, smile, and sense of humor.' And, when you are able to get consistent laughs, 'you will have learned timing and pacing.' So to practice the Flame, we must work on our energy, enthusiasm, smile, sense of humor, timing, and pacing, until we are able to consistently hook sets and get them laughing *by delivery alone*, using mundane scripts such as the Elvis Script. By searching for a mind-blowing routine, you are missing the point: the delivery and the microcalibration process.

"It's also clear now that I am throwing out a piece of value as a way of testing for my target's response; I'm trying to get an IOI from her. I also use roll-offs and back-turns as part of my delivery, as a way of testing for a response. By giving her a back-turn as an indicator of disinterest, I am provoking her to reinitiate the conversation—and preserving her comfort levels in the meantime.

"When she invests, showing interest, I then give her the next little piece of value, and then the next piece, and so on. This understanding is crucial. Microcalibration is about tossing out value bit by bit, and then calibrating her responses by giving her IODs when she gives you IODs, and by giving her compliance tests when she gives you IOIs.

"It's really much simpler than you might think, but over time, things will crystallize in your mind. When I start talking, I start microcalibrating. My words are only a value offering to facilitate that process. The whole time I am talking, I am body rocking, as well as tossing out negs or IOIs based on signals coming from the target. To illustrate this, let's take a look at some of my openers. Be sure to notice where I pause. It's all about the delivery.

> When I was a kid, I went to a convenience store. Becker's. With my brother and my sister. I found a cracker jack box for twenty-five cents, and discovered that I was eating it, and I was outside, still with the quarter in my pocket, knowing that I hadn't paid for it.
>
> So I turned to my siblings, and I said, "Hey, I have to go back in." And they said, "Are you fucking *nuts?* You already got away with it, you're already outside, come on, let's go."
>
> And that was the first time, I ever stole, anything, from anyone.

> [*Pulling a seashell from my pocket and holding it out in my open palm*] Hey look at this. Isn't this awesome? Isn't it pretty? Yeah my friends and I, we went down to Santa Monica Pier, and we found *this.* And it's a keepsake. Isn't it pretty?

> Have you ever heard of Google Earth? I checked out this location—this very spot, where we are standing right now—on Google Earth. I zoomed in to this location and I saw that building there, and that building right there. It's like I have already visited this place . . . Isn't it cool? But now here I am, and it's so much better in 3-D.

[*Holding up my necklace pendant, a key*] I got this from a girl. She gave it to me. My *dream girl*. And I lost her number, and I have to live with this pendant.

Are you left- or right-handed?
    Target: I'm right-handed.
    I'm left-handed, you're right-handed. I'm special, you're not.

What can we notice about these openers?

(A) I DON'T TRIGGER HER AUTOPILOT RESPONSES. Women are constantly being approached by men, and there are certain weird themes that repeat over and over in those approaches.

For example, some men open with a massive display of interest. They'll say, "You are so beautiful. Can I buy you a drink?" Other men open by making explanations or excuses for themselves: "Hi. I came over here because . . ." Other men open by trying to impress: "I'm in town on business, I'm a lawyer, and my friends and I have a table over there . . ."

Over the years, as she rejects so many men, the repetition causes her to develop autopilot responses for filtering them out more quickly. The typical lines men use have become a trigger in her mind. But I don't trigger any of her rejection circuits, because I speak to her as one friend to another.

(B) I IMMEDIATELY LEAD HER INTO AN EXPERIENCE. I say things like "I was flying all around here in Google Earth . . ." and "Look at this seashell. I was walking with some friends . . ." and "When I was a kid, I went . . ." Notice how my words focus on stimulating the listener and creating an *experience*, rather than trying to win approval or get something.

(C) I AM MORE INTERESTED IN WHAT I HAVE TO SAY THAN I AM IN THE GIRL. A chump would be more interested in the girl, not in his own small talk. In fact, he would probably be worried that he is saying the wrong thing. The chump's interest in her makes her suspicious, while his lack of confidence in his own value offering makes her also feel disinterested in it. In fact, she finds him boring altogether.

But I do the opposite of this—I show disinterest toward the target, disarming her, but I show great interest in what *I* am saying. My excitement about my words causes her to also feel excited about my words. She begins to find me intriguing.

(D) I USE EMBEDDED DHVS. For example, by saying, "I got this necklace from a girl, my dream girl . . ." I flip the preselection attraction switch, as well as the willingness-to-commit connection switch. By saying, "My friends and I were walking down at Santa Monica Pier . . ." I flip the social alignments attraction switch.

(E) I AM MICROCALIBRATING. The opener is not merely a script to be recited from the page, but it is fluid, shifting as I calibrate in real time to my target's IOIs and IODs. In the pauses between my words, I am leaning forward or back, smiling or crossing my arms, facing in or turning away, showing more suspicion or more appreciation, or offering more or less value, all based on whatever would be appropriate to the signals she is sending. The opener must be viewed as an interactive process, rather than as a collection of words.

(F) I DON'T IMPOSE UPON THE GROUP, I ENTICE THEM. They don't feel pressured to commit to some long discussion or pushy sales pitch. There is no implied demand for a certain level of participation. They don't have to defend themselves from some needy agenda. They feel safe to respond freely, without fear of provoking anger or encouraging neediness.

When approaching a group, you might feel pressure to prove yourself—to impress them or get them to like you. No one wants to feel embarrassed or rejected. But this is unnecessary pressure.

When I open a set, I don't need to impress them, or win their approval, or prove myself to anyone. I just offer the tiniest bit of conversational value—just being friendly—and all I need is for someone to bite just enough so that I can toss them the next bit, and the next bit.

APPROACH GUIDELINES

- The best way is to open sets that are already in your proximity, so that you don't have to approach them in the first place. Just turn your head and *open them over your shoulder*. I often just say hi. If you are conveying value properly in the venue, this is all you will ever need to do.
- If you must approach a set in order to get close enough to open them, draw near to them at a 45-degree angle. *Walk very slowly* and comfortably, as though you are in your own world. Don't walk straight toward them or come from directly behind them. Do all these things for the same reason that you would avoid spooking an animal.
- Move in a circular fashion, not in a straight line, and with natural movements. Your trajectory should not point directly toward the group. Rather, it should curve near to them and then curve away again.
- As you walk along that curve and get closer to the group, you then "notice" them out of the corner of your eye, and then you "spontaneously" think to open them. That is when you turn your head naturally, and open them over your shoulder.
- To disarm any suspicions, use false time constraints and body rocking. It is very disarming when you come across as carefree and unaffected.
- *Do not turn your body to face toward the group until they are turning toward you in the same way*. If you appear eager, you could get blown out. Be aware of how the value differential is affected by your physical positioning.

- After disinterest, the biggest key to the approach is stim- ulation. Shine the warmth of your Flame onto the vibe. Use humor, curiosity, intrigue, stories, and fun to pump their buying temperature. Remember, if you do not *add value*, then you are just another guy who's only here to *get something*.
- The energy level of your personality should be cali- brated to be high enough to *stimulate the set*, but with- out spooking them. The reason I say to calibrate energy levels is that it will spook the set if you come in too en- ergetically. Anyone who has approached a thousand sets will already know this intuitively, so get a feel for it.
- *Stack forward.* A common mistake for new students is to get stuck on the opener, relying on it for far too long and getting mired in drawn-out conversations based upon it. *Don't milk the opener*—just take control of the conversation and practice stacking forward to your next piece of material. Better yet, vibe with them and prac- tice getting into a fun, humorous mood, which is more important than using canned routines. Routines are only training wheels to get you started.

Opening the set is merely about getting that process started.

"Let's continue meditating on the opening phase," I said. "Stu- dents have many questions in this area. The objective of the open- ing phase is to do just that: open. It should disarm the peer group so that you can begin the attract phase with its demonstrations of higher value.

"Stack the openers and yes, if an opener doesn't work, don't fin- ish it. Just cut yourself off and open with another one (stacking) just like a comedian does if a joke starts to stall the audience. He just drops it and moves on to another bit from scratch. You've got to be super ready for this. And, if you finally open the set, you can—but only if you want—go back and finish up open threads during the pickup."

"Maybe a 'pickup' is the wrong way to go about it," said Adam. "What if I want to take things slow? Won't we grow on each other over time?"

"There is no such thing as a second first impression," I replied. "It's a 'one time at bat' sort of thing. A girl will decide, based on the first five minutes of knowing you, whether or not she is interested. Make your presentation a good one. If she isn't interested, then she won't close you. That means when you come around a second time she already doesn't want you, so what can you do to change that? Grow on her? That's stupid. You're trying to excuse yourself from getting good at conveying a good first impression is all. Slow sucks. Slow is not a luxury. Passion is not something that builds over weeks but instead ignites instantly. The best relationships come from beginning passionately.

"Here is the most effective plan: Get good at approaching. That is step one. Not closing, not attracting. Go to where there are a lot of beautiful women and then approach twelve girls that night. Simple. Go out and when you see a group of girls, even though it will feel wrong, go up and chat. Then move on. Keep doing this until you feel better about it.

"That is the plan. Train as if every girl is merely practice for the next one and you won't get nervous to mess up, because nothing important is on the line. Once you start playing, it's more fun. The first three approaches are always the hardest of the night.

"*Play the game.* Go out four times per week for four hours each night. Bring a digital voice recorder. Press record before you approach a girl and stop when done—or just record your whole night. Approach twelve girls in a night, which averages out to one every twenty minutes while in the club. Twelve girls in a single club isn't hard. Or split that between two clubs. Don't waste time drinking, holding a beer, or sitting. Stay standing and the moment you see a girl you want, enter the situation. Going home, comment into the recorder about what you think you did right and wrong. Did you approach twelve girls? Did you get out four times this week? If not, you are screwing up and you shouldn't expect to get laid. The more doors you knock on, the more will open. If you want to get four numbers, meet twelve girls. You should kiss one or two girls a night. You should be having fun out there."

"Sometimes it's hard to view practicing pickup as fun!" exclaimed Adam.

"Personally," I said, "I think it's a blast. If, after all the stress and fear, you aren't having fun practicing pickup, you need to get yourself another hobby. Work outside in. Start with structure, then gambits to fill the structure, then practice in-field to internalize the routines so they naturally come out at the right time. Inner game improves with success. Think of this as like riding a motorcycle. Inner game comes after a month on your own bike and a course under your belt.

- Go out *alone*. All the best Venusian artists do it. It's fun to explore by yourself.
- Approach everyone. Become a social guy.
- Fake your smile. It will biofeedback and make you feel better.
- Crash and burn. Experiment!
- Open hotties with "So . . . who the hell are you?"
- Talk to strangers. Don't *try* to make them like you. Instead, make them think you are from the future.

"Think of this as surfing," I said. "It's like you're surfing people and every potential approach is the next wave. And you have to take them all on. Or think of it as a video game."

"What do you think of this opener?" asked Adam. "Excuse me, miss. You were just so pretty, I just felt compelled to give you a rose . . ."

"Well," I said, "first of all, consider removing redundant sentences from your intro. How are you? Excuse me. How's it going? How are you tonight? How are you today? Can I ask you a question?

"I also suggest never ever calling a woman 'miss.' You will never create a connection if you say this 'miss' shit. Don't use the word *ma'am*, either. Or *madam*. Also, you never ever compliment a woman you just met on her looks. We are artists. Let's put the art back into this art. At one time it's very possible that opener was somewhat acceptable but this has now become such stock, stereotypical crap."

"How about this one," said Adam. "First I say, 'Excuse me, ma'am, do you have a cellphone?' and then she says, 'Yeah, why?' and I say, 'Good, 'cause I was wondering if I can borrow it so I can phone God and tell him I found one of his missing angels.' Last time I did this, she totally smiled at me and laughed. After that I said, 'I am so glad you laughed because I was totally willing to make a complete fool out of myself just to get the chance to meet you. My name is . . . '"

"This sucks big-time," I said bluntly. "You look like a guy who has to fight the fear of possible rejection. But a real ladies' man wouldn't get this fear in the first place, seeing as he's comfortable around women. Also, it's a shitty pickup line. And now she knows why you want to meet her! In that case, she may have talked with you momentarily, but I doubt that you got her. Just because she laughed doesn't mean you gave a good impression. Nothing personal, by the way; it's just that this intro is lame and not very effective."

"Okay then, what do you think about asking her for directions?"

"Starting the conversation by asking for directions is bad, because it will cause an uncomfortable transition when you change the thread to something more conversational. Use an opening script that will allow you to smoothly transition the conversation from asking about directions to just enjoying the chat. For example, with the Elvis Script, you can continue onto some completely different chat thread. Also, it's not asking directions. Girls know that is a possible line. They are cautious and you haven't disarmed them. The Elvis Script disarms the 'he's hitting on me' emotion."

Adam asked, "Why is it so obvious to people how nervous I am?"

"Consider how you conduct yourself when you are nervous, versus when you are comfortable," I said. "For example, pickup artists hold their drink down by their leg," I said, "but nervous guys hold it really high up by their chest. That is what I look for in profiling the males in a group. I also look for this to see how comfortable a woman is with me. If her drink is held high up, she is still defensive. Just look around sometime and notice that most guys hold their drinks up high—higher than heart level even. Those are the scared ones. I wonder if you can remember where you had your drink all this time. If it's high up, it's time to change, 'cause you are conveying fear. Leave the drink at the bar!"

"One time," said Adam, "I went up to a woman I found attractive, and I gave her my number on a piece of paper. I didn't really say anything to her, though. I just walked away. What do you think?"

"No offense," I replied, "but she will never call you. She would feel uncomfortable to call you and talk with a stranger. In fact, she would be pretty lonely to call you just because you gave her your number. She will never call. You blew the entire image. You went

---

SMILE

Smile 100 percent of the time. Smile at *everyone*! Eye contact to all in the group. Don't wait for a smile back. Say hi. Pause and then use your opener. Don't be a smart-ass. Don't annoy. Be genuine.

against every rule we players have worked hard through trial and error to devise."

SMILE AND SAY HI

"Always smile when you first meet a girl," I said. "The aware state makes one forget to do this. I like to use a 'hi' followed by a pleasant smile and a pause for them to say something. When they do, pause and then with the same pleasant disposition, go into the Elvis Script. Consider not using the 'Hi, how are you' intro. Go directly from 'Hi' into your script. The 'How are you' thing is long-winded and shows you are trying to think of something to say.

"'Hi' is a good beginning to an opener. It isn't the opener itself, but it's a good beginning. After all, 'Hi' does not actually break the ice. It merely initiates the chat. You still have to remove the bitch shield.

"I can't believe that so many people hit up against the bitch shield and they actually think she is really like that. They leave thinking, 'Oh man, I'm glad I didn't get her; she's such a bitch.' Well, by giving you the attitude, she got rid of you, yes? This is a typical tactic of particularly beautiful women. They learned this through years of men hitting on them to the point of annoyance. So you have to be different and *not* hit on them. That is what negs are all about.

"Don't use lines. You don't hit on her, you just talk. Imagine opening a door for a girl and saying, 'The knob is dirty. Ew, gross.' Is this a line? No, it's a comment. Did I hit on the girl by commenting on the knob being dirty? No.

"Notice how it's just chat. Comments, not lines. Use nothing that suggests you are sexually interested. So when you comment on a spoon, you are initiating chat as if you were talking to a friend you knew. Again, they aren't lines, but comments.

"Keep going. You will get natural with this. Did you remember to smile? Did you exude disinterest? I mean, did you look like you were more interested in her or what you were talking about? Be more into yourself than her when you speak."

"How about this opener," asked Adam. "Excuse me, forgive me for interrupting, but I just wanted to tell you that I think you're absolutely stunning, and I really wanted to meet you. My name is . . ."

"Ouch," I said. "Consider rather noncomplimentary opening scripts like the Elvis Script or a similar thing. This above line has broken so many rules . . .

" 'Excuse me'—never say that.

" 'Forgive me for interrupting'—nope.

" 'You're absolutely stunning'—*never*.

" 'I really wanted to meet you' is honest, though you should not get to this until *after* you have initiated a brief chat for about forty-five seconds or more.

"Let me put it this way," I said. "Giving your name before you get hers is good, but not until you have sparked a conversation. I'm nitpicking a bit, but these subtleties will save you lots of time.

" 'Excuse me' sucks. It just doesn't work. I wish it would but we all know it doesn't. She doesn't care. 'Excuse me what? Fuck off. I've got better things to do than get hit on by some guy in a doorway, buddy.' Never use 'excuse me' as an opener. *Ever*.

"Don't worry about getting laid; that puts too much stress on you. We are proud of bombing. Go out and try. Do some crash and burns."

"How about this," asked Adam. "Can I introduce myself, 'Hi my name is Adam, and I thought you were the type of girl with a good sense of humor . . .' "

"Ouch," I said, making a face. "Nope. Please don't introduce yourself and give an excuse as to why you approached, as this shows a low self-esteem. Don't give reasons. Just talk. The only reason you should have is 'I'm entertaining myself.' Go in really fun. I mean point to things and say 'Bam! Killed it!' Don't try to pick her up. Instead merely convey an amazing personality and let her close you.

"I prefer less routined openings now, because of my experience, and build openers on the fly. Here's the sort of random thing I might spout off as an opener: 'I think Angelina Jolie, while truly a beautiful woman, is getting a little old, don't you think? She's got this new movie out and her eyes are soooo blue and the whites are sooo white. A woman that old has got to have yellow old-fogey eyes by now!'

"Notice, I haven't hit on the girl. I'm smiling, I'm confident, I'm pleasant. I'm not making her feel like I'm wanting to have sex with her. I'm not excusing my presence. I'm just neutral. This sense of the normal is so important.

"Adam, take that pen out and jot these down—they are good starting points to a new conversation:

"'Welcome to my world.'

"'I thought you'd like to join the party.'

"'I'm here.'

"'You traverse the stairs with such poise.'

"'What's your name? Oh, may I call you Sally? You can call me Mr. Poopee Pants.'

"'Hello, Suzy. Your mommy couldn't make it this afternoon. She asked me to pick you up and take you home. My that's a pretty dress. Would you like some candy?'

"'You have an interesting figure.'

"'Shh! People can see us!'

"'You drank too much last night, didn't you?'

"(Waiting for the subway.) 'Don't fall onto the tracks. You'll make me late for work.'

"'Do I have a tan?' And then: 'I really like tan lines. They are sexy to me. Not a farmer's tan, now. I don't think seeing a beautiful woman with beautiful pale skin and red arms is sexy. For a lobster maybe.'

"'I prefer a cold Pepsi over a warm one.' And then: 'I once put a Pepsi in the microwave thinking that I would drink a bubbly hot drink; well, all the bubbles dissipated from the drink and it tasted like sugary muddy water. Don't do it! You'll start growing hair in places you would prefer remained hairless . . . like your tongue.'"

"I'm tall," I continued, "so if a woman is sitting down, I approach her and show her my palm and say, 'Press my elevator button.' She presses my hand and I bend down saying, 'Going down . . . buzzzzzz' until I'm crouched at her level. I then say, 'My six-year-old niece *loves* that. Wait a sec, how, old, are you?' (Notice the pauses.)

"Try this: 'Hi. Can you hold this for a sec?' (Give her an ice-cream cone.) Then tie your shoe and say 'Now don't take a lick. I know you want to but you can't. That's not til later in the relationship.' Take it back. 'Your favorite flavor is' — pause — 'raspberry! No? Um, vanilla! No? Um, don't say.' (Pause.) 'Banana?' Then say, guess my flavor. She will pick the flavor you had in your hand. And you will go, 'Holy shit. Who are you, Jojo the psychic?'"

"Okay," said Adam, "I think I get it. It's a certain type of playful interaction you are starting with her, without overtly showing interest right away."

"Exactly," I said. "All that would do is make her uncomfortable. In my opinion the direct style — overtly showing interest — is workable for sevens and eights but indirect is best for nines and especially tens."

"I have friends who say the 'direct' style of game is better," said Adam. "What do you think about that?"

"I'm not trying to discourage you from experimenting with any specific style of game," I said. "I'm just trying to save you some time. Are your friends approaching groups? If they aren't doing group theory, they're cutting themselves off at the knees. There are women in the bar who went out by themselves, but they are few and far between. Most hotties are found in groups, plain and simple. And if you don't go indirect, you'll creep out the friends and possibly alienate them. It is a group, after all.

"I don't see this being about one's style. I'm all about winning — and indirect for groups is the way to win in this game. I'm not steering you wrong. I will save you a great deal of anguish."

"Understood," said Adam.

"And since I can tell you need to stockpile some openers, write these in your notes and try them out in the field."

PRIMORDIAL DWARF OPENER

"I just saw a special on TV about primordial dwarfs." (Pause.) "I want one!" (And then stack forward.)

THE GANDHI OPENER

"How's your history?"

"Well, did you know Gandhi was a lawyer?" (I had just spotted a guy on the Venice boardwalk who was dressed exactly like Gandhi, so I was free-associating based on that.)

"Did you know he was from England?"

"Did you know he was hung like a racehorse?" (Laughing.) (And then stack forward.)

THE *DIRTY DANCING* OPENER

"Hey guys, what movie is this from?"
(Imitating Patrick Swayze) "Nobody puts Baby in a corner."
(They will undoubtably say *Dirty Dancing*. Then stack forward.)

CHICLETS OPENER

"I swallowed my gum. Do you think I'll grow a Chiclet tree in my stomach?" (Stack forward.)

SPELLS OPENER

"You think spells work?"

She responds. Then you say: "I was having a rather spirited debate with some friends and I'm still thinking about it."

She responds again. Then agree with her beliefs. And listen.

Then say either "How the hell can people still believe in witch-craft in this day and age? I mean, what do I tell my best friend?" or "Have you ever cast a spell on someone? Have you ever had a spell cast on you? Then why do you believe it? What evidence?"

Don't be a "yes man"—actually hold your own ground, but be tactful so you don't begin an argument.

Be ready to move the conversation to some interesting anecdote, such as the time you and friends at a party were trying to conjure ghosts with a Ouija board but nothing happened but one of you faked some thread around a trophy that someone pulled and freaked everyone out. It was a blast.

After three minutes of chat, if you were able to capture her interest, you can introduce yourself formally.

You: "I wish we had a mutual friend so she could properly introduce us, but I'm Adam."

The opener may come out different each time you use it.

Do not say anything stereotypical since that will trigger her shield.

You: (opening) "You think spells work?"

(Don't introduce yourself—don't say your name for the first two minutes.)

Her: "Not really."

You: "I myself hold a great deal of skepticism about it, but thing is, I was having a rather spirited debate with my friend Sarah about this. She believes that love spells work, and I said, 'We are in the twenty-first century, for crying out loud,' but how do you use reason to convince a girl she is irrational, if she can't understand reason in the first place? Are you reasonable?"

Her: "I think so, yes."

(Stack forward.)

"What's another good routine?" asked Adam.

"Have some photographs," I said, "that you have taken previously, in an envelope. Keep them in your pocket. Then when you see a girl or a group of girls, go up while looking through your pictures and say, 'Look at this. Is that a thumb?' and then critique your pictures as if the girl is merely someone to talk to—you aren't *hitting* on them. You are just being pleasant. 'Notice how the landscape pics are boring, but pics with people in them are interesting and grab your attention. See this one? Boring. But this one has three people in it, and I notice how my mind goes to processing the situation by looking at expressions of the faces and stuff. Oh, and I hate the ones where the guy in the photo is just standing there looking in the camera. *Boring!* How 'bout this one though? See? Three people are not looking in the camera and they are talking— doesn't that look more candid? I like those the most.'

"You have a choice from here. Bail out with a 'Pleasure meeting you' or wing it for the rest of the set, 'cause by now you are in. As long as you don't hit on them in this first minute or two of talk and you convey confidence, charisma, a good sense of humor, smile, are well-dressed and groomed, and humorously neg the beauty of the group, you are money! Be the man they want. *Be fun. Be funny. Let them hit on you.* Be a cool friend, not a slimy pickup artist. If by the end of this minute-to-two-minute opening act, if a girl is interested she will respond; if not, move on. You are out to get good at this, so practice. This is the Photo Opener.

"Now to make it a mission: I want you to learn timing and tempo. Slow it down, act cool and collected—yes, it's an act, I know— inside, you are screaming, but outside you are like Fonzie, cool! Lean more toward using humor than being serious. You will need to do this opener a good fifty times before you understand the timing of this and how good it is. It seems natural ('Hey, I just got these pictures developed') and it's a wonderful beginning to play off of."

Adam asked, "Can I open with 'Hey guys, I've got to go in a sec, but get this . . .'"

"It's not enough," I replied. "You need a reason. I've played a lot with false time constraints. I'm the one who first came up with this and Style is the one who honed it.

"It's called a False Opinion Opener because I do not actually allow them time to respond. I immediately continue with 'Okay, get this. I can only stay for a second; I'm entertaining friends. Some woman in an elevator said . . .' and I go on into a story where a woman thought I was a devil worshipper because of my black nails and I gave her the middle finger. Then I launch into negs in 'throw and go' fashion, and stack into another story straightaway. As long as I'm doing the talking—I don't care for strangers' opinions—I'm conveying my personality, and hopefully demonstrating value up the wazoo. If they talk, I get little done, until I allow the target to attempt to win me over during qualification."

"Adam, I challenge you," I said. "Approach sets tonight. Initiate the chat, and try to keep the conversation going while not hitting on them. If it's not going well, leave, saying, 'Pleasure meeting you.' Then move on to the next girl. Remember also that most girls are in a group, so you must address the group and make everyone like you before you can select the target girl you like.

"It's just it can be so hard to get over that approach anxiety," said Adam.

"You're not the only one," I said. "It's the same for everyone. I must deal with many emotions before, during, and after I go out to meet girls. Before is loneliness. Sometimes I just want to stay in and mope. So I must force myself to solve the emotion and not just lie there. During the night, I am in that aware state where the girls make me feel so weird and I have to deal with that to act normal and in control. And then afterward, if I go home with nothing, I must have the strength to know that I am working with probabilities and know that by looking only at this day I am blinding myself to the big picture.

"Now is the time to stop just watching. Get into a fun mood— which I know is hard for the very first girl, but you can fake it—and walk up to many girls, attractive or not, and say hi. Remember to smile when you approach. Then, and here is the best part, say any *nonstereotypical opening line* you would like, and then after whatever banter you began with, say, 'Pleasure meeting you,' and walk off with a smile and a skip to your walk.

"Example: A girl is there. She's only a seven. Walk up and say, 'Hi. Did you know Elvis Presley dyed his hair? What was his original hair color? Guess? Nope, blond. Isn't that odd? Pleasure meeting you.'

"Then leave. Don't be a goof and overanimate yourself. Be natural and fun and in a good mood. Now do that to every girl you can. Attractive or not. You will meet many girls, and get over your fear of opening. Well actually, you won't ever get over it, but you will learn to pretend you don't have it.

"That is your mission. I would like you to do this and yes, this is going to be a different day than you've done before. The past does not have to equal the future. If you keep doing the things you've done then you'll keep getting the results you've gotten—and that means no girls. This is your mission. Talk to twenty women in one day. Go alone. Do not intimidate girls by having friends with you. Not one or two girls, either. Twenty. That is a realistic number. If you feel it isn't, then I'm telling you now you are completely wrong and your emotions are fighting you. You will control these emotions head-on.

"As for the 'go for it' attitude, this will only come *after* the first success in the day. You have to work despite not having this emotion for the first one. And if the first one doesn't come off as if you are a fun guy, then you still won't feel good. But if you finally get a fun response, then your success will give you the go-for-it attitude to now go to the next eighteen girls.

"This is the only trick to getting the attitude you wish. Too bad you can't get it for the very first, but if you could easily do it, then every other guy could, too, and that wouldn't be a good thing for you anymore. All the other guys would have gotten to the girls first. Remember, they always go up and act like typical guys. How many walk up and smile and be fun and then just leave without hitting on them? Again, this is your mission and I expect this to occur this week."

"Say you're in a club," said Adam, "and you look around, and catch a glimpse of a girl looking at you, but then looking away immediately. This may happen several times. What do you do? You can't wave, nod, or say hi when she's not looking. And tapping on the shoulder is generally considered intrusive, I've noticed."

"Smile," I said. "When she looks for the very first time, smile big and say 'Hi.' *That's* the Three-Second Rule. You will get used to saying hi and smiling to every beautiful girl everywhere you go. Now you already have come off as playful and pleasant. If you miss this first opportunity to do this, you risk staling-out the girl. That is what you keep getting yourself into. You stale the entry so you feel awkward to approach. Why? Because you know she knows you have sex on your brain. You have no other reason to approach her. That's stale. Now if you smiled and said hello in the first three seconds of seeing her, then you can immediately start chatting. It's natural this way.

"You may get the formality of the introduction over with only after you have broken the ice. Let's say they are laughing and asking you questions—a minute or two into it. That is when you can do the introduction. Unless they find you interesting, they don't need to know your name."

Adam asked, "Don't the women in the room notice that you're 'girl hopping' and get suspicious of you? Especially if you're handing out or taking phone numbers!"

"Nope. I do two places an evening. Six girls a place. Two hours to meet six girls. Very easy. And four of them (this is all averaged over time) will take up only two minutes or less. So there is *lots* of time to dance and meet friends and hang out. I don't attack and hit on women. I approach them. Chat in a very comfortable and playful way. Believe it or not, most girls appreciate me talking with them. I certainly don't bother them. Do I surround myself with women? Sure. Do I look like a ladies' man this way? Certainly. Do other women notice? Of course. Do I look slimy. No. I haven't hit on anyone. I've at most flirted a bit, but with my negs, I look rather valuable."

"What do I say to my friend who lives in a small town," asked Adam, "and he says there aren't enough girls to practice on?"

"Well, if excuses are what he's looking for," I replied, "then that is as good as any. He's right. He can't meet any of them—in case they start to think he likes girls or something."

"What if I don't have twelve hours per week to chase girls?" asked Adam. "I have a lot of other things going on in my life, but I can go out on weekends and practice this. Will I learn anything if I just speak with five or ten girls per week?"

I answered, "After learning about science and cosmology, I see a more grandiose viewpoint of where I stand in this universe. There is a great futility to the life of only one human. I have prioritized my life around women. It satisfies me. Other things are important, but getting a good job is to build a good nest so you can attract a mate to fill that nest with eggs. If you create another excuse that you don't have the time to allot to the most important thing in a human's life, you've got some prioritizing to contemplate. Go to college? Friday night. Saturday night. And then a Wednesday night. There's twelve hours of girl getting. Done.

"You will begin to self-sabotage your situation by waiting. Enter now! You have to do so many approaches you will literally become numb. You will merely ignore the feelings. You will put yourself in the aware state so much per week that it just doesn't matter anymore. It removes its own potency. I've crossed the barrier—honest! It works this way. I wouldn't shit you."

"Can I just practice this on women that I see every day?"

"I strongly recommend against doing that. The skill to improve is meeting the challenge of approaching strangers. Work on that. Don't expect her to give a shit about you until you have conveyed your personality to her. Talk for at least forty-five seconds and make her laugh, and have a smile, and look confident, before the name exchange. Don't ask her name. Tell yours and wait. But this is a test to see her interest, so you won't pass the test if you start with the test. I call a test like this a ping. You ping the user and wait for how long it takes to get a response. Tell her your name and you wait to see how she responds. It's called pinging.

"I have begun noticing I can close all the way to the number close and even the kiss close without trading names. I don't know the girl's name until I get her to write it down. Knowing her name is not essential to get the girl. Experiment with not asking it. If you ask her name, it means you are interested, and the jig is up. It's basically the same as using direct game instead of indirect."

"Can you tell me more about the guard that women seem to have up?" asked Adam.

"Yes," I said. "While it is true that the girls have a guard up in the club—I call it their shield, like in *Star Trek*—there are simple practical techniques to remove the shield. Once you remove it, you are in. Don't get mad about their shield. They all have it as a safety mechanism for all the stray men who approach. Don't be like those men and you will be fine."

"What are some ways to reduce the shield of a girl?" asked Adam.

"Well, let's see," I said. "A smile in your approach will lower the shield level by fifty percent. Seriously, I know. And by opening the chat with something that is not hitting on her, you open up the shield by making them curious. This reduces the shield by twenty-five percent.

"So you now have twenty-five percent more to go. This will get removed once you have made them laugh and made them conclude you are *not* hitting on them. You are just chatting for the fun of chatting—for the entertainment of talking. When they begin to enjoy the conversation, you then convey to them all the traits they would naturally want in a man (preselection, protector of loved ones, social alignments, etc.) and they will then pick you up. Serious."

"What I find really strange is," said Adam, "when women make eye contact and stare for a few seconds, then turn their attention elsewhere."

"At the moment of eye contact," I said, "give her a big grin. I mean really smile. This will make her smile instantly. Bam. You can now walk straight over there and she will get all nervous and you will open with something interesting, but not hit on her. That is the power of eye contact. Walk up to her and enter with the Elvis Script. She wants to talk with you, and once you make her feel at ease that you aren't a guy who is going to hit all over her, then you will be in. It's a money situation to get a stare like that from a woman, but you have to take advantage of it and play it right."

Adam nodded. "I get it," he said. "I think I get it."

"Another thing," I mentioned. "Always be in a conversation with someone. And if you aren't in set, open the first set you like within the first three seconds of seeing them. That's the Three-Second Rule. That way you'll always be in set, and therefore you'll always have maximum social proof. I believe strongly in getting into a club and getting into the action and approaching immediately. Waiting and scoping around is lame."

"Some people say they don't use the Three-Second Rule when guys are around, because no woman is worth getting into a fight over," said Adam.

"That is merely an excuse not to approach her," I said. "When you talk to her, since you aren't hitting on her, when he arrives, start talking with him. After all, you have to take the time to re-move him as an obstacle. He may be a brother or only a friend. And since you don't know, you have to find out and not assume he is the boyfriend. You would rather sit back and not approach a girl because maybe she has a boyfriend? Completely chickenshit.

"Consider increasing your statistical chances of success with women by increasing your chances at every phase. Get better at getting out more. Get better at approaching more and more quickly. Get better at the approach itself. Increase your chances with the attraction by dressing better more consistently. Increase your chances of succeeding past the next-day phone call by incor-porating your phone rules into your close. Increase this also by kiss closing instead of just number closing. And, increase your chance of success by approaching women when the variables are not all there.

"If a girl is alone, sure, she may have a boyfriend, but without finding out you are reducing your chance of getting laid. Don't let the opportunities pass you by this way. I used to do that but it feels so good to get a girl who was sitting with a guy. I once met a girl with a guy who were sitting really close together and any regular player would have assumed they were a couple. Or for fear of getting beat up they wouldn't approach. What did I do? Seeing as I couldn't tell for sure whether he was a boyfriend or not, I entered and approached him. I found out they met four days earlier!

"I ended up wooing her big-time and he could do nothing but let it happen as he had not yet established the relationship with her. And he liked me as a person, as I didn't alienate him. She and I were holding hands and everything in front of the poor guy. In fact, honestly, I ended up feeling bad 'cause he was a cool guy, so I let it go and told her she had a good guy. About fifteen minutes later, they were holding hands again. Sometimes you just have to throw back fish that are too small."

THE THIRTEEN STEPS OF THE APPROACH

1) Smile when you walk into the room. See the group with the target and enter, Three-Second Rule. Say 'Hi.' Smile.

2) Recite a memorized opener, if not two or three in a row.

3) The opener should open the group. When talking, ignore the target for the most part. This is *active disinterest*.

4) Neg the target with one of the slew of negs we've come up with.

5) Convey personality to the entire group (using stories, humor, anecdotes, games, vibing), paying particular attention to the obstacles. During this time, the target sees you are the center of attention. You may do various memorized routines, such as the photo routine, to an obstacle and say to the target, for example when she wants to look at the pictures, "Wait your turn. Wow, is she always like this?"

6) Neg the target again if appropriate.

7) Ask "So how does everyone know each other?" If the target is with one of the guys, find out how long they've been together. If a long time, eject with "Pleasure meeting you."

8) If she is not with one of the guys, say to the group, "I've sorta been alienating your friend [target]. Is it all right if I speak to her for a couple of minutes?" They always say, "Uh, sure, if it's okay with her."

9) Isolate her from the group by taking her one-on-one to sit with you. As you do, do a hand kino test. (Does she squeeze back when you hold her hand, directing her through the crowd?) Start looking for IOIs.

10) Sit with her and do a connection routine. That's your reason for isolating. Or an ESP test where you hold her hands (again looking for IOIs). Then do the digital camera routine.

11) Tell her beauty is common but great energy and outlook is rare. "What do you have inside that would make me want to know you more than a mere face in the crowd?" If she begins to give qualities, this is a positive IOI.

12) Stop talking. Does she reinitiate the chat with "So . . ."? If so, you've seen three IOIs and can . . .

13) Kiss close. Right out of the blue. "Would you like to kiss me?" If this is impossible to perform due to the situation, then time-constraint yourself and say, "I have to go but we should continue this." Number close, give phone rules, and leave.

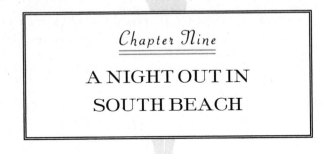

Chapter Nine

A NIGHT OUT IN
SOUTH BEACH

WE GOT IN THE CAR for the twenty-minute drive to South Beach. The location was our biggest mistake when choosing the house that we did. Our rationale was that for $2.1 million, you get a lot more house in Coconut Grove than you do in South Beach. But, although we pulled girls to the house quite often, the house was still just not "pullable," according to my standards. The twenty-minute drive turned every attempt to bring girls back to our house into a gigantic pain in the ass.

As we passed downtown, I was struck by just how many condominiums had their lights out.

"It's because nobody lives there," said Lovedrop. "All those dark condos have their lights off because they're owned by speculators. And look at all the cranes that have just been sitting idle for months. This bubble is gonna pop."

We drove onto the bridge to Miami Beach. More condos came into view, more beaches and strips of ocean water, palm trees dancing lazily in the warm, night breeze. I admired the twinkling glow of colors and city lights and the expensive cars everywhere. In spite of the flashy materialism, it *is* beautiful. It's a place with character.

"If you suddenly hear Kid Rock blasting at full volume," said Lovedrop, "that means Matador just roared past us in his Mercedes convertible."

The Rat said, "Oh guys, check this out. You're gonna love this. I invented a new kind of opener. It's called the 'On a Scale of One to Ten' opener. You guys know how opinion openers are all played out? You can't go up to girls anymore and ask them for a female opinion, because they've heard it so many times already. So instead, you do it 'on a scale of one to ten.' Watch. LD, gimme an opinion opener."

"Okay," said Lovedrop. "'Hey guys, I need a female opinion. Would you date someone who still talks to their ex? Get this, my friend—'"

The Rat interrupted: "Good, now check this out: 'Hey guys, on a scale of one to ten, would you date someone who still talks to their ex? Get this—' See? You can use the exact same opener again, without the cliché. It works for any opinion opener. You just say 'on a scale of one to ten' instead of asking for a female opinion."

"That's cool," I said.

"Cool?" said the Rat, "It's fucking awesome! Think about all the times that you can reuse that opener now. Over and over again. None of the chicks have heard that one before." He snickered. The sound reminded me of Jon Lovitz from *Saturday Night Live*.

"Personally," I said, "I like to open with 'Hi.' As long as you stay talkative, it works."

"Hey guys," said the Rat. "Have you heard of these new pheromones called phero-hypnol?"

"That's creepy," said Adam. "Is that like the date rape drug?"

"No, not that stuff," said the Rat. "This is pheromones. It's like cologne. But when women smell it, they get horny. They did studies. It's based on chemical signals in your brain."

"I bet it is," said Lovedrop.

I frowned. "That's like cheating. How will you ever get good at the game if you always let the pheromones do all the work? It's a handicap. They shouldn't let people buy it."

"I tried that phero-hypnol stuff in Chicago recently," said Lovedrop. "I definitely noticed an effect from it. This one girl, I had barely introduced myself to her, when my girlfriend walked up, Kacey, so I introduced them. And this girl squeezed Kacey's hand really hard. Kacey later made a comment about it. And then, get this, later on we were outside another club, somewhere else in the city, and I felt someone pulling at my hand, and I turned around, and it's the same girl! She said some excuse like, 'Uh do you know where we can get a cab?'"

"Are you kidding me?" asked Adam.

"Obviously girls never normally act like that," said Lovedrop. "I have to use game to get them going like that. That's what really made me notice with this girl because I hadn't gamed her at all. A few other weird things happened that night. I definitely noticed it. But you have to use that stuff in the right dosages. It's powerful, and it affects some women differently depending on the time of month, differences in your immune system . . ."

"Jeez," said Adam.

"Yeah," I said. "You'll notice things when experimenting with pheromones, if you get the right ones. And there are all different kinds, too. There are copulins, which you can use to create pre-selection because they occur naturally in women. There are testosterone-heavy blends, but those can cause aggression from other men. And there are a lot of fake products on the market as well."

"Oh, by the way," said Lovedrop, "did you guys hear? George Wu started a lingerie company. That guy who used to run Mystery's website."

"A lingerie company?" said the Rat. "Wow."

"He put up some money and found a designer in New York. Here's the deal. They do knockoffs. His designer just copies the designs of the top five or ten selling lingerie items at the hip stores.

Then he pays a factory in China to churn out the underwear. Right now he's having the boxes designed."

"Yeah? I like that," said the Rat. "That's how you do business. Check this one out. I had some friends who owned a moving company. They ran a scam where they would find a family that needed to move, and offer to move them. They'd come and pack everything up and get the unsuspecting family to sign a contract that contained all sorts of hidden fees in it. They would go and unload all of the family's possessions into a storage facility, and then send them some astronomical bill in the tens of thousands of dollars." He laughed. "If they didn't pay up, then they would keep all of their belongings as collateral. That's where I got that beautiful, big table I brought to the house when I moved in."

"That's fucked up," said Lovedrop.

"I feel dirty," I said. "You are the guy who would steal someone's wallet."

"Come on, Mystery," said the Rat. "I'm hurt. You know I love you like a brother, right? If you were hungry for Chinese food, I would fly to China just to get food for you, 'cause that's how I feel about you."

I bet you would.

"Hey, guys?" I said. "Where are we going tonight? Set?"

"Fuck that place," said the Rat. "They were assholes at the door last weekend."

"That's what they want you to say," said Lovedrop.

"Why do you say that?" asked Adam, his curiosity piqued.

"That place, they want to get the reputation as the hot new place that is impossible to get into." Lovedrop shrugged. "The door staff will deliberately fuck with you, so that later you will bitch and complain about it to all of your friends. It's how they create the word of mouth they need for the reputation they are trying to create."

"That's fucked up."

"What?" I asked. "That it works? Or that they take advantage of it? If you don't want to get screwed around with at the door, just don't go there. There are plenty of other places."

"Okay then," said Adam. "Why are bouncers such dicks?"

"It all depends on what the venue is trying to do. The bouncer is just doing his job. But if you act like he is a big asshole, it certainly won't open a lot of doors for you in this world."

"What do you mean, 'it depends on what the venue is trying to do'?"

"Well, for example, consider the Sagamore Hotel. That place has a great crowd. The doorman knows not to let in a lot of guys. If a guy wants to get in, he needs to bring some girls, or buy a bottle. So you can decide that the doorman is a jerk and get all bent out of shape, or you can do what I did."

"What's that?"

"I went out on the sidewalk, opened a two-set, got them laughing, and asked them to step in the hotel with me for a drink. The doorman let us in. He even said something like 'Now you've got it.'"

"How about Kress?" I said. "In Hollywood."

"That place," said Lovedrop, "it's in L.A. The door guy is a total dick when he's working, but he's not really a bad guy in real life. He does all kinds of things to fuck with the crowd. You should see it sometime; it's a hoot. For example, there's a huge, roped-off area at the entrance and he's walking around in it, holding his clipboard. So the people don't know where to line up. They all just form a crowd along the rope, and they're all trying to get his attention. That's on purpose. He's getting them to start freaking out and make a commotion at the entrance.

"Also, the entire smoking section is situated on one side of his roped-off area, just to make it seem like there is that much more of a huge crowd ringed around him, waiting to get into the club. But of course, the smokers are already in. It's just part of the illusion.

"Then he goes over to talk to someone, to let someone in, so everyone else crowds to that spot as well. They don't know where else to go. But then he walks off, and talks to someone else at a totally different part of the rope. So everyone freaks out and they rush over to the new spot. And so on. They don't know what to do; it's pandemonium.

"Another thing he'll do is let a group of girls in, but then he closes the rope while one of them is still trapped outside. Just to make them all freak out because they hate being separated from their friends. Everybody's freaking out. He does this to a couple of groups and then finally he lets the girls in at once, so the people waiting outside see a huge group of hot girls walk in at the same time."

"So what do you do to get in?"

"Understand, the whole situation is engineered to sell bottle service. When you see this huge group of hot girls going in, and everyone's freaking out, and meanwhile you're some guy with your guy friends, you just pony up and pay four hundred bucks and get a bottle. Or you leave, or you wait around outside like a chump, which I personally will not do, beyond reason. It helps them sell bottles to have me standing there, but I won't waste my night on that bullshit. In my mind, you shouldn't bother going to a place like that unless you already have a hookup to get in, or unless you plan to buy a bottle. They'll leave you standing out there if they want to, and they always think it's funny when you throw a fit."

"So how do you know we're getting in the club tonight?"

"Tonight we're going to Pearl, which is the VIP club above Nikki Beach. Matador is getting a bottle, so we'd get in no matter what. But we normally get in there anyway, because we know the doorman at Pearl. He had picked us out of the crowd, said we looked like 'artistic' types, and just started letting us in. The owners must tell the staff here to filter for 'cool' people and let them into the bar."

"That's us," I said.

"In fact," said Lovedrop, "if we don't have any girls with us, I'll grab a couple of girls from the crowd to bring in with us, because I don't want to make him look bad for letting three or four dudes go walking through the front door. Might as well walk in with girls. I've ended up pulling those girls before, at the end of the night."

"The universe provides," I interjected. "It's as simple as that."

"The universe provides?" asked Adam.

"I see the girl. I get the girl. I know I will see the girl. I know I will get the girl."

"But how do you know?" asked Adam.

"How? The universe provides. It has provided in the past. Sometimes abundantly.

"It all starts by getting out of the house, going to public gatherings, starting to get desensitized to social interactions. A lot of people didn't have the opportunity to be social, parents just never took them out, so they have to take it upon themselves to desensitize themselves, to acclimate themselves to social interaction, knowing they're surrounded by billions of people.

"For me, it's as easy in the bar as going to a brothel, I imagine. Go out to a place chock full of women, meet several of them, banter and merge, kino and roll off, build jealousy plot lines and social proof, pace yourself, and you will have a very fun night. Be fun. Accept the now as everyone else there does.

"As soon as I'm in the venue, I'm relieved. Even Mystery can get messed with at the door. I try to limit this: Roll with friends who are getting a bottle, roll with some beautiful ladies, and if your friends aren't bringing them, you better start texting, or hope the door guy loved your TV show. Don't ever get an attitude at the door. Just smile.

"I'm alone. What do I do? Open a set. I'm with a two-set I can't split. What do I do? Open another set. How can I trust the set will open? Because the universe is kind to those who have been kind to it.

"I will meaningfully engage in at least five or six sets throughout the course of the night. I know the women can save the step of knowing me very very well if I can demonstrate other women have already chosen me in the past, or in the present. That is why I make the first few sets 'dance' with me—for the benefit of later sets.

"I merge sets. It's more fun for everyone. I kiss the girls in several sets. They enjoy it. Preselection demonstrated. Opportunities to do so will present themselves. The universe will provide. Don't jockey for social position. Rather, let each moment present itself and dance with it. Ah the universe: She loves to dance with you.

"A simple rule: *Love* them. Love the next set. You don't know them yet; they're out on the town, bringing their friends, their social masks, their act and personality for when they leave the safety of their home. They are out together and bonded, huddling for warmth.

"They have been waiting for you to arrive and show them you, too, are in the know. You *know* they know. And they know that, too. Reach them.

"Holy shit! Here we all are! Crowds of people all over the world gather into rooms like this and play music and dance and meet each other. It's all happening in real time. Wow! We are a part of this thing, together. Strangers on the same ship. You and they have all the commonality of the world.

"Pace it for a few minutes. You are excited to meet them. You need nothing from them. Just enjoy getting out and seeing what exists. What came to be? Wow. You came to be! I have seen other things that moved me as I am moved by you. Let me show you. Perhaps you will show others. A seashell. This flower. My pupil. This song. This idea. This subtle feeling on your skin.

"Who wouldn't want a fascinated person as a tour guide of the world? Mind-map her future. In time you can add yourself into it. Be of use to her.

"You may open a single set. A girl by herself. These sets often transform into larger sets when her boyfriend returns from the washroom, the friends she's been waiting for arrive, or she reaches for her phone. And yes, if a girl is on the phone, that is a two-set. We must get good at speaking to people mano a mano.

"You may open a two-set. The target and her boyfriend. The target and her sister. The target and her ugly friend who is in love with the target. Keep the two-set together as if a single when locking in, throw your wing into the set a few minutes into opening it yourself to transform the two-set to a three-set so you can then isolate your target while not alienating her friend. And if the wing doesn't stick to the obstacle, your already having disarmed her before your wing came in will allow you to reengage without losing the set to a 'loose cannon' obstacle. Forward or backward merge to 'tie up' the loose cannon, then isolate your target.

"You may open a three-set. Two-thirds of all approach scenarios are three-sets. Here, let's run down some scenarios of different possible sets: If the set is all girls, consider opening with 'Hey guys.' As you speak, make eye contact with each in the set. Be prepared to roll off with your body as you speak. You will use these subtle back turns and weight shifts to convey your lack of interest in a balanced way. IOD compliance tests, on the open, work on tens.

"If it is two girls and one guy—respect the man. Is he a brother? Win him over and he will give his sister to you. Is he the boyfriend? Perhaps he cries out to have her taken off his hands. Perhaps the guy in the set has an ex-girlfriend you have to meet.

"More difficult, but definitely doable, is two guys and one girl. First you've got to neg her to disarm them. Ask what's so great about her; they will explain and thus supplicate to her.

"Remember, you are not merely attempting to bond with a single target, but to incorporate yourself into the group of people—a social circle that may include family members (specifically parents and siblings), the best friend, the gay friend, the gaggle of girlfriends surrounding your target.

"Your place in her social group will make life more familiar or not. You choose the target, then see what other bonds must be made to position oneself for target bonding. When you are speaking to a two-set, a triangle is made, or a line. Two-sets are more solidly held as a triangle than a line. A three-set, plus you, makes for different dynamics. A square, with diagonal lines. A four-set plus you connects like a pentagram.

"Six-sets readily decay into two three-sets. For instance: You enter into a five-set. You can either converse with one person, leaving four; two people, leaving three; three people, leaving two; but not four people, leaving one, since it alienates this person. Why not run the five-set, round down to two, then merge the obstacle into the remaining people to isolate the target?

"If you do tens of thousands of sets, you'll understand how they generally go. Go in with an opener. A short story. Rock out with your body as you speak. 'Oh by the way . . . ' Reengage. Pause your story to begin another. This is multiple threading. You can control the focus of many people in a set with multiple stories. Escalate physically, punctuated with roll-offs."

"We're there," said Lovedrop. "Let's see if Adam is learning anything."

CHECKLIST

Did you lock in by the third minute?

Approach despite your fears?

Engage the entire set?

Multiple-thread?

Use an opener? Stack openers? Go situational? Remember to neg?

Did you isolate your target?

Did you state interest toward her, then roll off and get IOIs?

Did you compliment her (IOI compliance test) and get a favorable response?

Did you qualify her? Did you make her work for it? Use Bait-Hook-Reel-Release.

Did you introduce your friends to her, and give her a brief rundown on their accomplishments?

Did you meet her friends?

Do they all want to hang out with you?

Is the sister jealous that she didn't get you?

Did you show her mind-mapping? Google Earth?

Did you smoke with her—sharing saliva?

Hug her from behind and she accepted it?

As we entered the venue, Mehow was already there getting warmed up.

"Hey man," I greeted him. "How's it going?"

"Not bad at all," said Mehow with a smile. "I've been playing around with that hug opener you taught me, and it works like gangbusters. Hopefully you guys can pull some girls tonight so you're not back at the house later trying to steal mine."

"I would never do that," I lied.

"Speaking of the hug opener," said the Rat, "you should see this crazy Russian guy I know. He just walks right up to the girls and grabs them. Sometimes they start freaking out but then he always hooks them. It's the craziest thing I ever saw."

"I don't think I could ever do that," said Adam.

"Actually," I said, "that sort of thing is easier than you think. You can definitely open with a hug, and that's no big deal. Try it."

"Try it?" asked Adam. "How do you even do it?"

"Here's how I do it," interjected Lovedrop. "I'll be standing near a girl, or even if one is walking by, or if I walk by her, and I just put my arm around her shoulder like she's an old buddy of mine, like it's no big deal. I look away with my face as I put my arm around her. That's the key. Then I start talking to her, just having fun, and meanwhile I also push her away with my arm, lightly, just to get the escalation started. The important points are that I look away when I do it, that I don't hold on for too long, that I act like it's normal, and that I immediately stack forward."

"I don't understand," said Adam. "You just walk right up and put your arm around her?"

"I'm telling you, as long as I come across disinterested and fun, that's the magic combination; then I get away with it just about every time. The Ghost and the Flame. I know it seems intimidating when you imagine it, but when you test it, it's really no big deal. The fact that you look away when you do it, the fact that you release before it gets weird, the fact that you have something else to talk about, these are the little details that help you get away with all these moves. Watch this."

I don't actually hit on a girl in the first ten minutes. I merely convey my personality (humor, wit, confidence, charm, etc.). When she realizes that I'm a great guy and therefore begins showing me indicators of interest, then I know she wants me, and I go for the kill.

The opener must really be natural though. The moment you find her, meet her beginning with a 'Hi.' Then use a memorized opener and go immediately into the next piece. It's one long, seamless set of events. Don't close unless the signs are there. If the signs are not there, then just leave pleasantly and there is no rejection.

Get good in clubs and the rest of the world will be yours.

Suddenly Lovedrop turned and put his arm around a woman standing nearby. He gave her a squeeze and pointed toward Mehow as he said, "I want to introduce you to my friend." He said it as if he already knew her.

"Hi," she said, smiling. "I'm Elizabeth."

"Lizardbreath, this is Mehow. Mehow, meet Lizardbreath." Lovedrop started laughing to himself and he pushed her away by the shoulder.

She laughed. "You crack yourself up, don't you?"

"Sorry," said Lovedrop. "I just can't help myself. I'm having fun tonight."

Next to Elizabeth stood a shorter girl. "I'm Kelley," she said.

"All right, give me a hug," said Lovedrop, rolling his eyes and turning his head away as he hugged Kelley.

"You guys seem fun," said Mehow.

"We *are* fun," they both said at the same time.

"You guys said that at the same time." Mehow smiled. "My fun radar just overloaded. I don't know if I can—"

SEVEN HABITS OF HIGHLY EFFECTIVE PICKUP ARTISTS

1. Be humorous!
2. Be enthusiastic!
3. Knock on more doors. Daily.
4. Focus on the pickup arts rather than getting the girl.
5. Do group sets. Let previous sets aid in the next ones.
6. Be playful in your approach.
7. Love women.

"—don't know if you can handle us?" interrupted Kelley.

Mehow raised an eyebrow. "You are sassy, aren't you? I bet I could put you in a Sass-O-Matic and make sassy juice out of you."

They giggled.

He continued: "When I'm president, and you and all your friends are my first wives, I'm going to keep you in the West Wing, and you in the East Wing, so we can keep the drama between you guys down to a minimum." He pointed at Kelley. "And I would put you in charge of the Department of Sass."

The girls burst out laughing.

"You're fun!" said Elizabeth.

"Yeah, well," Mehow replied, "that's because I am fun. I'm two hundred and fifty percent fun. How do you guys know each other?"

"We're best friends," said Kelley.

"Okay, for shits and giggles," said Mehow, "we're going to find out if you guys are psychic together. Are you ready? Here we go. All right, give me your hand, and give me your hand."

He reached out and grabbed a hand from each of them, so they were holding hands in a circle.

"All right," said Mehow. "Now we have formed the psychic position. I can totally read your mind. This one's thinking dirty thoughts; I fully encourage that. Now I want you to think of a number between one and four. The first number that pops in your mind. You got it? Don't say it. Between one and four. Now don't say it. What number was she thinking?"

"My number was three," said the shorter one.

Her friend gasped. "Mine too!"

"Yay!"

Mehow took over again. "Hold on. Are we ready to step it up?"

"Yeah!"

"All right, here we go. Gimme your hand. Think of a number between one . . . and one. But first—"

The girls burst out laughing.

"I am such an ass. Who'd you guys come here with?"

"Each other!"

"You guys can be fun," said Mehow, but then he acted suspicious. "But can you guys be chill? Like what if you have to chill with your friends. Can you do that?"

"I bet you I can," said Kelley.

"This girl's so chill, you're like so chill that I'm going to adopt you, as my bodyguard—"

"I'm good, I'm good."

"—and you will kill people with your chillness."

"Fuck yeah!"

Taking her hand, he said, "Now stand up, now spin around. I totally stole your seat!"

"You stole my spot!" she said, then, "We can share."

"Hold on," he replied. "We're gonna share. You may come here, you may sit on my lap. That's all you get for now. Just don't mess anything up, all right?"

"Okay."

"Okay, good."

"You know what we should do?" said Mehow suddenly. "Let's go commandeer that elevated couch right now. Let's go."

"We're wearing skirts, though," said Kelley. That was an IOD. He must have asked for too much compliance.

"Just cross your legs," said Mehow.

"Getting up there is dangerous," said Kelley. Another IOD. He's on the verge of blowing out his set.

"Yeah, that's bad. Look at all these fucking dudes here," said Elizabeth.

"Yeah," said Kelley. "Lots of dudes."

"Sharking the area," said Elizabeth.

Mehow said, "Okay, we're gonna have to go to the other bar, because the other bar has my bartender at it, and my bartender hooks me up." Another compliance test from Mehow. He framed it as if the girls created the double bind and he merely chose one of the options they presented him with.

The girls said, "Let's do it," and with that, they fell into his frame.

He continued leading. "C'mere, give me your hand; let's go. We're gonna do the train, all right?" He showed Kelley to grab Elizabeth's hand, and said, "So you have to get behind her."

And with that, they were gone.

"That was pretty cool," said Adam.

"What's that?" asked Lovedrop.

"You know, getting all those great reactions from the girls. Especially being, you know, as ugly as he is."

"It's flash game," I said. "Buying temperature."

"Flash game?" asked Adam.

"Listen," said Lovedrop. "All this flash game is cool and all, but in the long run you want solid game. You want to flip all the right switches. There are attraction switches, connection switches—"

I interjected, "Get ready for this line from girls: 'Are you a ickup artist or something?' or 'You must get all the girls.' It's a con- ience test. They'll use these sorts of congruence tests. I used to o deny being a player, but that's just digging a hole. You get further by going straight into the 'beauty is common' routine. That shuts up the whole issue in a flash."

"What is flash game?" asked Adam.

"Flash game," said Lovedrop, "is all about getting great reactions from girls. It's about getting them into a really emotional state. We call it buying temperature. But it's not solid; it's like a glitch in the matrix; it gets great reactions from girls. It's like crack for chicks. But it's not solid."

"What tactics, for example, constitute flash game?"

"Any push-pull tactics, where you alternate between qualifying her and disqualifying her. Cycling her between validation and de-validation in this way will ramp up her emotional state and get her giggling. Microcalibration takes advantage of this."

"Anything else?"

"Games, such as the physical escalation routines."

"Okay, what else?"

"Role-playing."

"Role-playing?"

"Yeah, like Mehow's 'sassy' lines, or Lovedrop's *Honey I Shrunk the Kids* machine routine, as well as Style's old 'you dress up like a nun and I'll dress up like a priest and we'll sell hot dogs on the beach' routine."

"Okay, I get it."

"That stuff is fun when you're first starting out," said Lovedrop, "because you can get easy reactions. Students love getting reactions. It makes it easy to hook the set at first, and it's impressive to students."

"But?"

"But to close, you need solid game. You've got to have all the pieces in place. You need to establish your value, you need to establish that she has value for you, and that there's a growing sense of connection between the two of you. You need to escalate properly, I mean physically escalate, and you've got to be able to have fun with her. You can't just make her giggle a few times; there's more to it than that. There are switches that need to be flipped. A lot of it is just about being normal and comfortable, and not being weird."

I said, "I don't use all that buying-temperature stuff at all; I just use the absurd."

STEP-BY-STEP GAME OVERVIEW

1) Engage entire group, paying attention to all, but least to target and most to guys.

2) Throw a neg at target within five to ten seconds to disarm the obstacles from thinking you are after her.

3) Demonstrate higher value to group while ignoring target (save for negs thrown at her). Lock her into her own set with a prop placed in her hand.

4) Three minutes in, begin to qualify her (in front of her group).

5) Move the entire group so you are leaning against a wall or bar or sitting on a stool.

6) Continue qualifying and find out how they all know each other (who's the brother, who's the boyfriend).

7) Begin kino tests. (See chapter 2, on physical escalation.)

"Let me ask you this," said Adam. "How would you sum up the entire game to me in a few short sentences?"

"Be entirely comfortable and at ease—remember the Ghost," said Lovedrop. "Smile and have fun—remember the Flame. Remember the absurd. Speak slowly, with pauses, and with enthusiasm. Sprinkle in DHVs and negs. Sprinkle in IOIs and IODs. And touch everyone. Always be escalating—use Bait-Hook-Reel-Release as your model."

"Remember to get locked in to your set in the first three minutes," I said. "Get situated so that you are physically as comfortable as everyone in the group, and preferably more so. Make yourself the central focus point of the positioning of the group. For example, if you are leaning against a wall and everyone is standing in a circle around you while you tell some cool story, perfect."

"Position is power," said Lovedrop. "The direction you face with your body determines where you are giving away your power. If you are facing someone with your body while he is facing away from you, then you are losing value relative to him. That's why we always open over our shoulder—to maintain the power position."

"Just don't lean in," I said. "That's the newbie mistake that will get you blown out."

"All right," said Adam, rubbing his hands together. "There's a

---

Let's talk about obstacles.

Think about what happens when a less attractive girl is with two other girls, and then you come and ignore her. She feels alienated and decides you are an asshole and becomes an obstacle to your getting her friends.

Therefore, you should give more attention at first to the *obstacles* than you do to the 10. That's how you get a 10. Here's the reasoning: The friends never get the attention because of the 10. So when you come and ignore them, they see you as just another guy. But instead, if you ignore the target (putting her in her place) and pay attention to the friends, they will like you for two reasons:

1) You are paying attention to them, which makes them feel good.
2) You aren't paying attention to the 10, which makes you look like you are in control and therefore a perfect match

for the 10. It's textbook. Remember, always remove the obstacles first.

Here is a good way to disarm an obstacle:
Grab the obstacle's hips and say, "Mmm. Yummy." Then ignore her for a few moments as you speak to the others. Then say, "You're voluptuous. I can't think straight around you." Then ignore her again for a moment. Now this all hinges on the delivery. Without perfect execution, it will fail.

That's about all it takes. Make sure the others in her group don't hear what you said or you'll blow yourself out of the set.

On the other hand, what if the obstacle is a guy? What if he has a crush on your target? Don't belittle him, *befriend* him. That's right, make him think you are awesome. The social proof she sees you have when it comes from him will make her switch out to you right under his nose.

two-set right over there. I'm going in. Wish me luck, guys!" He started walking toward the set.

"Walk slower!" Lovedrop called after him. "And don't fidget!"

When Adam returned from being in set, I gave him feedback on his body language and delivery. Then I pointed out that he should have befriended the guy in the group, instead of trying to "out-alpha" him.

"Befriend the guys," I said. "Neg the target. Then find out how everyone knows each other. Be the storyteller to entertain the guys and have them shaking your hand. She will witness the respect. You are the man of the group. Then another neg or two to make the boys laugh, and finally pay some attention to her, going physical with all the obstacles disarmed. This is advanced group tactics.

I succeed in these situations. Why? Because I go for the hardest situations just to see if there is a solution—and I consistently find the solution.

"I don't want to do the hardest situations when I have easier ones to work with. Yet it's the hard ones that are the most fun, and that you learn the quickest from. Suggest the next time you see an impossible scenario that you *mission-impossible* it, also known as *crash and burn*. You lose the set, but it's fun—and you learn so much for next time. In fact, most people don't do group sets at all 'cause they think they are impossible, but I excel in them now. The most beautiful women are always in group set with guys. It's the nature of the beast.

"Your gimmick must be your mouth. You have to talk so you can get a group of people around you and be the center of attention. Your target will then see that, and when you begin talking to her, she will have the desire to find out why all these people are around you."

"Here's a scenario I just saw here in this club," said Adam. "There is a girl with three guys sitting on the couch. The guys are paying attention to the girl a lot. Should I bring another girl into the set?"

"Yes," I said. "Pawns are very valuable when the obstacles are all guys, because you will screw up their system, because you have brought them new girls to keep them occupied. So if I have a group male set in front of me, I will pawn some women and bring them with me into the set. Then disarm the guys and go for the target."

"Okay," said Adam. "I screwed up that last set, but I think I'm getting the hang of it! I see a three-set over there, I'll be back . . ."

Chapter Ten

A STUDY OF ATTRACTION

ADAM HAD A PRETTY SUCCESSFUL FIRST NIGHT, but he still needed work. On the way back to Project Miami and well into the night, we kept at it. He definitely was one of the more eager students I'd had for a while, which I liked.

"Let's talk about creating attraction," I said as I grabbed a Red Bull from the fridge. "The most important concepts for attraction, in my opinion, are demonstrations of higher value (DHVs), being talkative, using the absurd, and negs."

Adam nodded. "Okay," he said. He kept scribbling away on his almost-filled notebook.

"The sales metaphor is wrong," I instructed. "We have used a metaphor in the past that seduction is like sales: You must sell yourself. But this is entirely the wrong frame. You want things set up so that she is trying to sell herself to you, and not the other way around.

"But beyond that, if you think of seduction as a sale, then you begin to find yourself handling her objections in a rational and logical manner. By doing this you play the entire game of seduction on a logical playing field rather than an emotional one. That is a mistake. The more you think about it, the more you'll realize just how important it is to stir emotions in a woman. Reach her emotionally. Make her *feel*. You have to internalize this a lot more.

"I have reaped far better rewards by appealing to her emotions. Don't counter her objections with logic. Rather, lead her emotions by having her imagine things. Tell her stories to stimulate her imagination, and describe sensations and emotions to her, and convey alpha-male characteristics."

"Okay," said Adam. "I think I understand."

CONVEY, NOT CONVINCE

Convincing her that you are what she wants is not the right way. *Convince* is not a great word. Better: *Convey* the personality traits she wants. And it's not just about the traits you have that she wants, it's about conveying the traits that all women want. These traits are consistent with all women.

I continued: "The old pickup theory had the pickup artist dealing with her objections about why she didn't want you, and then you had to counter with reasons why those objections were invalid. Truth is, those reasons she gives you count for shit. She is very likely to take her cues from her emotions, no matter what reasons you give her. A way to assist in this is to tell her, 'You know sometimes you just have to stop thinking so much and begin feeling—, too many people just analyze things to the point of paralysis; sometimes it's better to go with your feelings. After all, emotions were designed over millions of years of trial and error, and we are the result of the successes of correct behavior to those emotions.

Sometimes it's better to just shut the hell up and feel.' From there on you must only lead her imagination and — *bam* — you are kissing her in five minutes.

"Routines serve as vehicles to convey the pickup artist's important alpha-male personality characteristics — his demonstrations of higher value. We must convey those characteristics emotionally. You may sound intellectual but once you have shown her you aren't an idiot, it's time to reach her at a gut-wrenching emotional level. That is the playing field. *That* is the place to be.

"Discard the sales metaphor and adopt the emotional playing field one. It's not about tricking girls. It's about displaying and conveying your attractive qualities before closing and doing so in a way to make her feel you are a challenge. That's it, in a nutshell. *Be* a pickup artist. Get good at this. *Master* this. Don't cop out just when you are starting out. It's a lifelong pursuit. Learn how to manufacture her experience."

BE A CHARACTER

Train with the thought that your sexual attractiveness stems from your personality characteristics, and these must be conveyed. Getting girls is a performance. You have to become a character — an outgoing man of action for the entire time you are in the club. Find a character from a movie to role-model and then behave like him in the club. Thought: There is a difference between conveying and projecting your personality. Conveying is talking, projecting is visual. Have a look, have a personality.

"Okay," said Adam. "Let me ask you this. What step-by-step experience are you manufacturing for your target?"

I said, "Most chumps think, *I'll go in and chat her up*. And new-bies to the game learn to think more like *I'll go into her group, and chat them up while I disqualify myself with negs until I get indica-tors of interest*. But the pro has a lot more in store for her: pivots that walk by and whisper in her ear, 'I see he likes your type. Stay away from him.' A friend that says, 'He's dated playboy models.' Pea-cocking that screams tribal leader. Demonstrations of leading the men in the group. Jealousy plotlines as groups are merged into other groups. A step-by-step adventure. The list goes on and on. These are plotlines, and my game is full of them. If her adventure includes VIP access, meeting successful friends of yours, some of whom are recognizable, learning that you are the tribal leader, hav-ing a jealousy plot line infuriate her, bouncing back to your hotel with friends and partying, and her feeling social value by hugging you in front of the others, followed by a passionate make-out, just the two of you, then this is a good experience for her."

"Won't that stuff just make her angry?" asked Adam. "I don't want to screw it up with her."

"You have to be willing to screw it up," I said. "And yes, it will make her angry. But it works. In my experience, the emotional sys-tem of every woman is very similar. I'm concerned much less with her cultural influence than I am with her hardwired response. I'll trust she will behave in a consistent manner—all women respond similarly to their emotions—especially the major ones, such as jealousy.

"A woman will not know she is attracted to you until she feels a sense of loss. Jealousy is one such feeling of potential loss. Her brain attributes survival and replication value when specific char-acteristics have been demonstrated, even if she doesn't logically notice. You see, Mother Nature uses emotions to enforce certain biological imperatives, and those emotions are triggered by DHVs."

"Wait, hold on, I'm confused. What do you mean by a DHV?" asked Adam.

"A DHV," I replied, "is a demonstration of higher value that makes the woman notice that you are of higher value than the average next guy or the last guy. It activates an emotional switch inside her. You want her to notice that you are interesting. It doesn't have to be sexual, only curious. This is what allows you to later build comfort and trust with her."

"Personally, I have a few favorite DHVs," I said.

1. Preselection. Two women on your arms, or a story of a hot ex-girlfriend actress. Just examples.
2. Leader of men. She observes you holding court in her group. Other men comply with your requests.
3. Protector of loved ones. She detects that your emotional programming is healthy.
4. Disinterest. Using negs, roll-offs, and other IODs. Show willingness to walk.

"Either you demonstrate, or you tell a story to convey these four DHVs. I like to repeatedly trigger them with many stories and many demonstrations. Okay, demonstrating four is tough, technically, but it comes up when you merge sets, and spontaneous events allow this to unfold, as long as you are out playing.

"A woman's attraction switches are actually a survival-and-replication value-judging circuit in her brain. This understanding changed my game for the better. I now know that a woman responds to any potential impact to her survival-and-replication value. She will willingly give up her replication value for my survival value. This is an elegant model of reality, and from this overarching evolutionary perspective, the Venusian Arts is based."

"This actually makes a lot of sense," said Adam. "But it's still hard putting it into practice."

"This is a performance art," I replied. "Get out there. Flash a smile! Be playful, and coy. Use negs. Be surrounded by females. Maybe have a little lipstick on the cheek. Meet her, make her laugh. Be charming. That's it. Get those traits conveyed before you start hitting on her, and she will start hitting on you: smiling, well

DEMONSTRATIONS OF . . .

HIGHER VALUE (DHV)	LOWER VALUE (DLV)
Preselection	Isn't seen with girls
Social proof	Rolls alone or with guys
Popularity and status	Seeks approval
Holding court in a set	Wallflower, hoverer
Social alignments	No friends or connections
Disinterest (negs, etc.)	Needy, try-hard
Social intelligence	Doesn't "get it"
Storytelling (Flame)	Boring, doesn't add value
Creative expression	Talentless or a show-off
Unreactive (Ghost)	Fidgets, leans in, talks fast
Healthy emotions	Has weird emotional responses
Humorous and fun (Flame)	Kills the vibe
Dominance and strength	Weak, no ambition, lazy
Protector of loved ones	Not protective (miswired)
Competence and lifestyle	Incompetent, low-rent
Health and fitness	Soft, out of shape
Fashion and grooming	Dirty, unkempt, bad fashion
Wealth and resources	Broke, loser
Height and looks	Short, ugly
Embedded value	Brags instead of vibing

groomed, playful and humorous, willing to leave, confident, has social standing.

"It's rather easy, and you'd be surprised how often a guy will screw up on these basic things. A good seventy-five percent of guys in clubs don't smile when approaching. Then you've got the guys whose shoes are ugly. And they don't shave the back of their neck. Then they reveal their shyness by not going up to the girl with a smile right away. Then they are all serious, saying things like, 'Wow, you are so beautiful,' instead of 'I like Pearl Jam. I'm not ashamed.'"

"Do the girls ever feel like your DHVs are just bragging?" asked Adam.

"DHVs cannot be bragging," I said, "because they are demonstration-based and not language-based. When I am telling a story it is being told to the target's friends. It is the fact that her friends are interested in my story that is my demonstration of higher value. Then my target responds to the social proof I have created."

"Okay," said Adam. "I get it."

"And it's cumulative," I said. "In group theory, your previous approaches work on your behalf. You are seen with other girls by your future targets. This way you convey your personality before even saying hi. The use of negs throughout the conversation initiates both the challenge and the underlying flirting. There comes a time to match her speed. When she says something negative a bit, you punish her with a neg. When she says something like 'You have beautiful eyes,' you say, 'You're not so bad yourself.' Sometimes the only way to approach a girl and get her attention is be bold and bigger than life. You need other girls around you to get the real beauties. *That* is social proof.

"I recognize that women are drawn to a man who conveys social proof. Performing artists do this, and so can you, in a limited way. There was a girl yesterday at a club who was not so much into me until I joined her group of friends and in a matter of five minutes became the center of attention, and got the hand-shaking respect of her peers. From then on I could tell she saw me in a whole new light. Just having her recognize that I was the best choice in the small group worked to my benefit, and I got her number.

"One must convey social proof. To do this, you must pawn women. In other words, you must be willing to lose a woman in order to win the target. Imagine that an eight is into you, but you want the 9.5. You must reject the eight in front of the 9.5 in order to get the 9.5. That is pawning.

"The easiest way to get approached is also to use pawns. Get sevens or eights to hang around you and make them laugh, and the nines and tens will see you are socially viable. Then they will be attracted to the fun; they will stand nearby and be very easy to open. As long as the girls you surround yourself with are enjoying your company, with laughter and smiles—but not kissing you—it's all good."

"Everyone says that you are the master of jealousy," said Adam. "How do you utilize jealousy in your game?"

"That's a good topic for me," I said, smiling. "I learned years ago that it's okay to invite more than one girl to do something together. Invite the girls you met from last week's four outings over at the same time. Let them all meet. I recall inviting seven girls I'd had sex with over the past year to a barbecue I hosted on a Sunday afternoon. Music, burgers, drama. It was choice. If you don't let them all meet, you can't give your selection the gift of dropping all the others. I looked around and enjoyed watching some of the girls getting along smashingly while others got reactive and demonstrated jealousy, which only amped up the evidence of my survival and replication value to all the others."

"How did you learn about using jealousy?" asked Adam.

"I remember," I said, "I was sitting with a very cute Asian girl on a bar stool, with her sitting on my knee, cuddling and talking for about twenty-five minutes in a swanky club in Toronto. I was enjoying 'the Now,' and I wasn't concerned with losing her or anything. Then, a male friend of hers spotted her and she greeted him, telling me they knew each other from a long time ago. As they talked, I sat there politely waiting for the exchange to be over. I noticed that the two, after hugging, had not let go of each other's hands. The feeling of jealousy kicked in.

"After about thirty seconds, I simply said, 'I'm going to find my friends. I'll let you guys catch up.' As I rolled off to preserve value, I thought, 'Wow, I want her!' If it hadn't been for the jealousy, I would never have recognized it. I had invested nearly half an hour with her. If I had invested ten minutes or less, I quite likely would not have received such a jealousy pang from my emotional circuitry upon experiencing the appearance of a potential rival male.

"How can this be useful? Twenty-five minutes into your set, allow another girl to present you with IOIs, and your target will realize that she wants you. Merging two sets together allows for this easily. Good game plan. You want some examples?

"Invite last week's new girls all out to the same place. Let them meet. Or invite a girl over to your place to hang out with you and your friends. When she gets there, she finds out all your friends are girls. Merge sets. Each target will want you more if she notices the other getting reactive to her jealous emotions.

"You can say, 'Uh-oh. It appears you'll have to fight for me, but it's worth it.'"

"Virtually every set I've run in the last few years incorporated a jealousy plotline. Work a girl for ten minutes with accepted increments of physical escalation, roll off 'for a sec,' work another set, get to lock in with the new target, and while in a pleasant heated debate with her, allow the other girl to see this, and miss you.

"The girl you are talking to is having fun, and showing you IOIs, and occupying your time. Pang! Jealousy in target one. This jealousy may be evidenced through reactive behavior to the other girl, amping up your perceived value. If the reactive behavior is simply flirtatious, this may allow the second target to pang jealousy, if you are in the set for at least three minutes generally, though ten is better and twenty-five minutes in is great.

"Go after one girl, get nothing. Go after two, get them both. Why? They preselected you to each other. They invested in you. They both witnessed reactive, and therefore committed, behavior in the other. They both needed to work to win you. When did you become the prize? When you set up the jealousy plotline.

"I allow a woman to feel the gift of really wanting me whenever I feel she needs to feel that. Every three weeks or so into a relationship I feel it healthy to remind her that I continue to have options, and continue to choose her. When she thinks she has me, she grows complacent. Options exist. Pang of jealousy. Reminder just how much value her emotional system has weighed you in at. A little reactive behavior demonstrated. Win the prize. Happy again. Remember, though, that you are working with powerful emotions. Be responsible. How responsible? Know that you are the designer of her experience."

"Now I want to talk about making conversation with women. The secret to getting in with a woman is this: *Be talkative.* That's it. If you have so much to talk about and you bombard them with lots of fun and interesting material—where you show humor and opinion and passion—then you get to convey your personality. Thing is, a talkative person gets way more play than one who doesn't. So the secret is to put yourself into a talkative mood. Ever been in one? I was talkative today and I tell you it works. I thought about it and honestly, looking back to all the women I got, I got them because I was really talkative. I just yakked their ear off. Then after I saw the body language was all positive I would come out of the blue and say, 'Would you like to kiss me?' That was it. I would talk passionately about something. And talk and talk. I wouldn't talk about them. I wouldn't ask questions.

"Write this rule down, Adam. Enthusiasm is contagious. It feels good to be excited."

"What's an example of using enthusiasm?" asked Adam.

"Walk up to a girl and say, with an enthusiastic smile and tempo, 'Oh man, check this out. I've gotta show someone this.' What do you show? Well, photos of you and a star are good. 'I met Jackie Chan and we took this photo. I thought it wouldn't turn out, but I

EIGHTY PERCENT RULE

She won't want to invest her time unless you have engaged her emotionally to do so. That means you have to do the talking first. I believe 80 percent of the talking should be the guy. It's your job to convey enough personality so that she wants to be with you.

---

just developed these pictures today, and it did. Check these out.' Continue to talk about how you met the star."

"But what if I don't know Jackie Chan?" asked Adam.

"The thing is," I replied, "she never even has to know the person, the star. It could be just someone you feel enthusiastic about. Isn't that cool?"

"Ah," said Adam, "I get it. A Jackie Chan photo is just an example of something you can be enthusiastic about. It could be anything."

"Exactly," I said. "I might say, 'Have you ever heard of James Randi? No, well, he's this guy who . . .' It doesn't have to be someone she recognizes, in any way, for the routine to work. The idea is to practice your enthusiastic delivery to the point where you can make others feel that sense of enthusiasm just from your delivery. Maybe you're talking about the new Mars lander. Maybe you're talking about springtime in New York."

I paused, then said, "Also, get in the habit of role-playing."

"Role-playing?" asked Adam.

"Just begin," I said. "Like this:

"'You've been naughty.'

"Her: 'What?'

"'You heard me. You've been a naughty girl.'

"It's just something you do as a joke, but you keep doing it and she will jokingly play the game with you. Learn to suck people into your role-play. It will grow. In three minutes you will be saying, 'Now you need to get spanked.' She will laugh and so will you, but you keep on with the joke. Point is, the joke turns real.

"You can create *any* persona so long as it conveys a sense of adventure. For instance, and this depends on your target, of course, you can say you are a rock star, or singer, or performer, or actor, etc.

"Her: 'What do you do?'

"Me: 'I'm an adventurer!'

"Her: 'Really?!'

"Me: 'Yes. Have you ever played the game Dragon's Lair? Well, I'm Dirk the Daring.'

"Her: 'Oh really?'

"Me: 'And you are the fair princess Daphne. I'm here to save you from the evil dragon. Do you remember his name? Singe! I loved that game. I'm not a video gamer really but that game was one hundred percent cartoon, and way ahead of its time.'

"See?" I said. "No need to say 'performer.' No need to say 'pickup artist.' Pick what you want, just don't be boring and say, 'Uh . . . I'm a student . . .'"

Adam asked, "How will I know if my personality conveying is going well?"

"Stop talking," I said. "If she doesn't reinitiate the conversation, then you know there is something wrong with your personality-conveying routines. They aren't cool enough, not funny enough, not enough of the right energy."

"If she says she came with friends or family," said Adam, "then can I say, 'Oh so you don't have a boyfriend'?"

"Don't do it," I said. "Just assume the single status. I know, you just want to hear her say she is single. But the thing is, her telling you this is equal to her saying, 'I like you.' Don't put her in a position to have to decide right away. She will go for the safer 'I have a boyfriend' tactic because it's easier on her life, since she doesn't have to deal with the possibility that you are going to bother her. You may ask her, 'Who are you?' If she mentions she's single, good for you. If not, assume it."

Adam asked, "How about if I ask her, 'Do you attend classes here?' If the answer is yes, I'll ask her what her major is and then share my major and see if we have any classes or professors in common. Fluff talk."

"Everyone talks about school and majors and so on," I replied. "It's not original enough. There is no such thing as fluff talk. Everything you say has a purpose. What is the purpose of fluff? To build comfort? Then it's comfort-building material. But were you in comfort phase or were you actually in attract phase and running DHVs on her? Make sure you aren't using fluff talk just because you have nothing better to say."

"What are the best routines I can use?" asked Adam.

"Think topics," I replied, "and not word-for-word lines or routines. In fact there is no such thing as a line. Your routines should be loosely based outlines. No word-for-word memorizations. Remember the basic outline of the routine. Design routines that don't hit on the girl. She's expecting that from a guy. Just be fun and funny and confident and cool, and when she notices you aren't hitting on her, she doesn't know whether you are just chatting for the fun of it or what, so she will test you by challenging this. Don't take the bait and start hitting on her. Give a neg.

"Here's a good one after you have initiated conversation through a nonsexual topic and she has bitten into the game of chatting. 'Oh, check this out. Watch this. Here, pull my finger. This is good.' She will pull your finger and you go, 'Pft! Oh man! You actually pulled my finger! Ha! No, no just kidding, here, really, pull on my finger. No honest this is good. Pft! Oh man! That's twice! I can't believe you! My niece is six and doesn't fall for that anymore! Man, ha!'"

"Why does this work?" asked Adam.

"You were being playful and fun," I replied, "and you weren't hitting on her. She will now feel a little dumb, but you were just being playful so she won't hate you and call you an asshole. She will, however, know you aren't hitting on her, which pulls her bitch shield down, and so will try to restore her image in your eyes. She is trying to impress you.

"The pull-my-finger routine is a very good one for girls who are tens. You see, it seems silly and juvenile, but think about it: Nobody toys with them that way. They are so used to men behaving like boys and falling over them, that when you come and play that game, in a smiling, playful way, it is a wonderful neg. If she calls you an asshole, reply laughingly, 'I'm an asshole, but I'm fun,' and smile. You are displaying everything she wants in a man. You are different, yes? You are comfortable, yes? You treated her normally and not like a goddess, yes? You were having fun with her, yes? Playful? You showed her that even though she was hot, you were willing to walk away. Why would a guy be willing to do that? The only possibility is that he is crazy or that he is used to being with hot women. This is the Zen of Cool in action, the Ghost and the Flame.

"I am very good at what I do, and yes, I have used this even last Wednesday, and I got the number of a ten. My friend was there as a witness and it was really funny and coy and cool of me because here I am with a fucking ten, and I do this to her. It really brought her down to knowing who she was talking to in a very mild and pleasant manner.

"It's the fact that you performed this on a ten in the first place. You have the guts to possibly blow it with her. She gets people acting so proper and nervous every day. Tens cannot help being beautiful. She is used to being treated this way — it's just matter-of-fact for her. People don't treat her like a normal person because of it. And yet you do. You show her you are a man who doesn't buy into her beauty. In fact, I never compliment a woman's beauty. Every guy has said that before. Every guy and his father! So instead, compliment her on rarely complimented things, like her class or leadership within her peer group."

"What other things do you say when making conversation?" asked Adam.

"It's more about being a talkative person," I replied. "But here are some examples of things I might say. 'I bought my niece an ant farm. Well actually, I bought myself an ant farm. I never had one as a kid and . . .' (Keep talking along that thread.) Or talk about ESP and its impossibility. Talk about how you met a bear while hiking. Talk about how you were scared shitless rock climbing when your rope snapped, or the time you visited your friend's friend, and your buddy was almost beaten to death when the friend he visited had a boyfriend who came out, and there was a twenty-minute car chase through lights and you were looking for the cops but lost the crazed boyfriend before you found cops. Or the time you were in the hospital and it changed the way food tastes. The way birds sound clearer now. Or the time you hacked into a bank but chickened out and put the money into a charity.

"Or talk about the famous person you met.

"Does she believe in ghosts? Why?

"You like candles and incense. What does she like?

"Play the question game with her.

"Talk about the time you bladed down a steep hill and survived.

"Talk about the time you were onstage.

"Put a grin to everything you say and have the guts to try new material. Say things that are on your mind. Once a girl had lime-green shoes on and I said, 'Are you waiting for those to ripen?' Don't drink alcohol and your mind will be focused and aware for saying good stuff quickly.

"Follow up with 'Okay, get this. I'm . . .' and then tell a story about anything. Have you ever told a story to a friend about some-one who was a jerk to you that day? Well, tell it again, only this time make it seem like it just happened, and add humorous com-ments. 'I was with my niece in the roller-coaster line, and when I got to the grubby ticket guy, he said (whatever—make something up). Can you believe it? What would you have done? Well, I started to . . .' And so on."

"Another thing," I said. "Women do believe in Reiki and other nonsense, and for that reason one should learn to accept the irra-

MAKE A CHEAT SHEET

- 20 minutes: question game
- 5 minutes: music game
- 2 minutes: Elvis Script
- 15 minutes: ESP—Is it real?
- 5 minutes: *Titanic* connection pattern
- 5 minutes: the ant farm I bought for my niece and what I learned
- 10 minutes: My friend Tal likes this girl but is having problems . . .
- 10 minutes: My other friend's girl became a stripper—what do you think about that?

These are topics of discussion that together run over an hour.

Have you told any stories to a buddy on the phone? Give the story a title and write that on a list to put in your pocket or wallet. This outline of topics can be referred to while she is right there. You go into your wallet and check something, then continue talking. She won't know you have a cheat sheet.

tional nature of women rather than tell them they are wrong. If a girl believes in God or gods, then let her. Don't bother telling her otherwise. She can live life out in its entirety never understanding cosmology or the nature of the universe. Let her believe and use those beliefs to help in mirroring her. Months later, you can nudge her over to rational thinking by having her consider small ideas over time."

"Here's my digital camera routine," I said. "I have a digital camera. I take pictures of the girl and show her the images right away

---

JOKE

A guy and his girlfriend are in bed. They have just finished a red-hot round, and the girl screams out to the guy, "I want you so much, I want to have your baby! What should we name him?"

The guy gets out of bed, pulls off his condom, ties a knot at the top, and throws it out the window. He then turns to his girlfriend and says, "If he can get out of there, let's call him Houdini!"

---

on the back of the camera. Thing is, I purposely take really bad shots (mouth open, distorted 'I wasn't ready' faces) and when I show it, they get all embarrassed ('Oh erase that!') and I like to zoom into the worst part of the photo and show it around to her friends and they laugh and then I say, 'Oh man, every time I look at you, I'll think of this picture now.'"

Adam started laughing.

I continued: "That completely takes her off the pedestal she sits on in her head. Sure, ten guys hit on her before, but I then brought her to the emotional place I wanted her.

"I then take a shot of me and her, and when I show it, I say, 'That's better. You know what? We look good.' If she says 'yeah,' which is more likely now, you are in."

"What's your ESP routine that I keep hearing about?" asked Adam.

"Okay," I said, "this is one from my personal stash, so if you use it, don't tell them you learned it anywhere. It is supposed to look like you have ESP for real.

"Say, 'Do you believe in ESP?' Remember to smile when you walk up or you may startle her. Say, 'Just think of the first number that pops into your head from one to four. Don't say it. Just think it.

Now take that number and imagine that it is drawn on a black-board in your head. Have you done that?'

"She says 'Okay.'

" 'What's so neat about imagination is, we both have it.' (Pause.) 'On the blackboard, I see the number . . . three.'

"Whether you get it right or not, either way say, 'All right, let's try this one more time. This time think of a different number from one to ten. Got it? Picture it in white chalk on the blackboard. You are thinking of the number . . . seven.'

"If you got the first one wrong and the second right, you look like you finally got it, a one-in-ten chance. If you get both right, which is actually a ninety percent chance, seeing as it is a psycho-logical trick where most North Americans naturally choose three and seven as their first picks, that's a one-in-forty chance! '. . . and of course I don't stake my reputation on mere chance.'

"If you get the first right but the second wrong or both wrong, say, 'Proof! ESP does not exist!' then start to laugh, and say, 'And you believe in ESP!' A good neg to start. If she mentions that most people pick three and seven (most girls won't know this, though) just say, 'Really? Hmm. Didn't know that. Thank you Cliff Claven.' A perfect neg, the guy from *Cheers*.

"If you take the wording I have and do this exactly as stated, you will be surprised how well you will do. When they ask how, tell them, 'I don't know.' Tell her you can see the numbers on your imaginary blackboard. That it is not a trick. You hate magicians. If she wants you to do this again, tell her, 'Don't be greedy now.'

"Speaking of greedy: If a girl kisses you on the cheek and goes to kiss your other cheek, tell her, 'Only one. Don't be greedy.' This is a good neg. Mild but a neg nonetheless. If she says, 'Yes, but I'm French,' you reply, 'Are all French girls as greedy as you?'

"This is an excellent lead-in to the connection pattern. I use this and I swear I've slept with at least fifteen girls with this intro. No kidding. It's playful, fun, connects with their beliefs, and when you get it right, you are skilled with some weird intuition.

"Go rent *Comedian*, with Jerry Seinfeld. I mean it. Put this on your Netflix. It's a must. It will improve your game when you see this video. The parallels are astounding.

"Like a comedian, many bits come from reality but the comedian learns that part of the game is removing parts that aren't funny and changing things to make it more funny. Same with your routines. Maybe a story is a year old, but you can say, 'Earlier today . . .' just to make your routine concise. It doesn't matter that it was a year ago, so you remove that from the routine. Maybe your friend was driving the car but it's funnier and more concise if you say that you were. Change the stories any way you like. If you want to concoct entire stories, hell, do it!

"Remember, a carefully constructed first impression, conveying and demonstrating the characteristics of an alpha male, will get you the girl. You have to be more than just a guy. You can do that by not just saying 'My friend is from out of town' but rather by personalizing it. 'Mark here is visiting from Brazil.' See how this is more personality conveying? You can convey much more interest-

USING MAGIC TRICKS PROPERLY

Use a mind-reading routine to pull the target into isolation and dangle the carrot in front of her to get her to jump through some qualifying hoops first. Of course, you still want to demonstrate higher value before this. So you do magic, not to the target (which telegraphs you *trying* to DHV) but instead show something to one of her friends in her group. It is the social proof you want. That's the format.

1. Do a magic DHV to her peer group.
2. Dangle "Wanna see something unbelievably cool?" in front of target.

3. Isolate.
4. "Before I show you this . . ." Make her jump through qualifying (Bait-Hook-Reel-Release).
5. Show another magic DHV "just for her."
6. Now don't be the dancing monkey. Immediately drop magic and get a connection going. If you don't, you'll be seen as merely an entertainment, a curiosity.

ing things, such as '. . . and the soles of his feet are still burned by the lava rocks he walked on three days ago.' "

"What do you do," asked Adam, "when a woman asks you a question you don't want to answer?"

"Use frame control," I replied. "When asked a question that can be answered yes or no, most guys screw up by thinking they have only those two choices. There is a third, and I often take it to get out of the pickle. Is it to throw a question back at them? No, that's too evasive. The answer is to throw a statement at them. For example, if you're at a strip club and a dancer asks you, 'Would you like a table dance?' you can reply, 'Oh man, I'm not even here right now. You know what just happened to me? I was at . . .' Get it?"

Adam nodded.

I continued: "If I'm asked, 'Do you date a lot of women?' I'll reply, 'I bet you're a heartbreaker yourself.' Yesterday I got 'You wouldn't go out with my type, I bet.' I replied by ignoring it and just going into my next routine: 'You think spells work?' "

"Okay," said Adam, "I get it. It's like you're a sucker to think you have to take her thread when you can just start a thread of your own."

"Right." I smiled.

"I'm curious," said Adam: "Why do you have to neg the nines and tens? Just because she's attractive, I'm supposed to insult her?"

"No," I replied, "not at all. Negs are not insults. It has to do with how things normally go down during a pickup. Look, I've gone out with plenty of nines and tens. This is my particular standard. I have had relationships with dancers and models and bartenders and strippers, too. They have to deal with the daily barrage of men and are used to it. So when you neg them (remember, it isn't an insult) it gets them going.

"A ten is there surrounded by friends. She has put on this bitch act. Is she really a bitch? Unlikely. All my girlfriends were wonderful human beings—beautiful people have it easier because they are beautiful and oftentimes have better upbringings because of it. But she needs to have a standard to uphold when all of these nobody guys approach her. So her values are very honed and understood. When a man walks up and says, 'Can I buy you a beer?' she will be annoyed by this. While the guy thinks he's doing something nice for her, she gets this all the time. She is desensitized to this. You are the eighth guy today! So she is very good at brushing all these guys off. Shit, she has to be. She isn't going to sleep with all of them! So she may say no or act annoyed, and then the guy thinks she's a bitch and he walks off pissed and feeling like a failure. And that seems to work. Sometimes when the girl is particularly in a feeling of control, for example in a club, she will accept the beer and then flake the guy off. Hey, the guys are stupid enough to buy her one, she might as well take it. When she takes a beer from you, the girl is saying, 'I don't know you and I don't care about you. You are just another one of those typical guys and since I don't respect you, I'll take the beer from you before I snub you.'

"I was with my friend Diane, a ten, and her cute friend. A guy came up and asked, 'I don't mean to bother you but would you like to dance with me?' The friend, not being used to this, said, 'Um, ah . . .' and the guy gave a puppy-dog look. I was smiling at her, knowing how pathetic the guy was acting, so I saw the humor in the situation. The girl said, 'Um, why not. Sure.' The guy said, 'Really? Are you sure? Wow, I never get girls to dance with me.'

"She then started talking with Diane, and the guy just stood there and they never went for the dance. Weird, eh? He then said, to me, 'Can I buy her a beer?' I said, 'You can buy me a beer, but you'll have to ask her.' At this point I knew he was being a hassle to her, she wasn't interested in the slightest and felt uncomfortable. I thought it was great to see this occur in front of me—it was highly educational and, more so, entertaining. So I say, 'Hey, the guy wants to buy you a beer.' The girl goes, 'Um, no thank you.' Now Diane says, 'Yes, she'll take the beer.' So he buys her a beer. And then he never talks to her again! Weird eh? Well, that's how it went down. What on earth are these guys thinking?"

"Oh my God," said Adam. "I have actually done that before."

"I digress," I said. "A ten is so good at snubbing your approach. It's nothing personal, either. It is a strategy that is built over years of stupid guys approaching every day, and she will do the same to you. That is why snubbing them is important. You can't insult them, because they are used to all the hurt guys insulting them, so this rolls off their back.

"How do you snub them without insulting them? Well, let's say she has long nails that are most likely fake. Now why do tens dress so fine if they don't want the attention? Because they love the feeling of control sometimes. She's in a club with friends, and she wants to be the leader of the circle so she gets all the attention. The guys come and buy drinks for her and she gets off on knocking the guys down. It's all in a day's play.

"So she is wearing fake nails to look even better. Most guys will say, 'Wow, you are so beautiful.' Boring, typical, and in her mind by now (after years of the same shit) true. But imagine a guy comes along and says, 'Nice nails. Are they real?' She will have to concede, 'No. Acrylic.' And he says, like he didn't notice it was a putdown, 'Oh.' (Pause.) 'Well, I guess they still look good.' Then he turns his back to her. What does this do to her? Well, he didn't treat her like shit and insult her. He complimented her but the result was to target her insecurity. She thinks, *I'm hot. I'm beautiful* (especially in that emotional state of control as she feels in public) *but*

I didn't win this guy over. I'm so good at this. I'll just fix that little smear on my image that he has of me.

"Then you continue to show disinterest in her looks, as you give her a neutral topic like the Elvis Script. During this time her intention is to get you to become like all the other guys so she can feel in control and then snub you. Then you give her another neg, like this: 'Is that a hairpiece? Well, it's neat. What do you call this hairstyle? The waffle?' Smile and look at her to show her you are sincerely being funny and not insulting. You are pleasant but disinterested in her beauty. This will intrigue her because she knows guys. And this isn't normal. You must have really high taste or be used to girls or be married or something. These questions make her curious. So this keeps happening and is known as flirting. She gives you little negs and these tests are qualifiers. You pass them by negging her back. After all, you aren't like the others showing interest. But . . . why? To get control again, she asks, 'Will you buy me a drink?' Notice how she is trying to get you now! But she only wants to sucker you in enough so she can snub you. That is all she is about—this strategy is all she knows and it's not working, so she is trying to do damage control on the situation. But at the same time she doesn't quite understand why you don't think she is great. After all, her nails are fake. You say, 'Ah, that's so funny. Your nose moves when you speak.' (Pointing and being cute.) 'Look, there it goes again. It's so . . . quaint. Hee looky.' Smile. She'll say, 'Ah, stop!' Now she is self-conscious, and in this state is where you want her. You have with three negs successfully created interest and curiosity and removed her from her pedestal, thus removing her bitch shield. You were humorous, you had a smile, you dressed well, you were confident and everything she would want in a man. You didn't take her shit. And when she asked you for a beer, you said, 'No. I don't buy girls drinks. But you can buy me one.' You are qualifying her now. If she buys you a beer, this is symbolic of her respect for you. If not, you say, 'Pleasure meeting you,' and turn your back to her again. Don't walk away, just turn your back. You are negging her again, just when she thought she was negging you.

You are teasing each other. That is the first step to flirting. This is all textbook psychology.

"A neg is a disqualifier. The girl is simply failing to meet your high expectations. It's not an insult, just a judgment call on your part. The better-looking the girl, the more aggressive you must be with using negs. A ten can get three negs up front, while an eight, only one or two over a longer time. You can go overboard if they think you are better than them. You can drop the self-esteem right out from under them—just as most tens do to guys—and this isn't good. You have to get as close to the breaking point as you can without crossing the line. Once you have gotten her right there, you can start appreciating things about her, but never compliment her looks. There is a mutual respect now. Something most guys never get from the girl. This is how you remove a bitch shield. Three negs ought to do it within two or three minutes of neutral chat. Once it is down, you can, from a place of mutual respect, seduce her."

"Should I neg my girlfriend?" asked Adam.

I shook my head. "Not as a general rule. To use negs in a relationship is not what negs are about. Negs are for meeting a girl. They are used in the first ten minutes only. You only need three negs for a girl who is a ten, to show her you don't take her shit. Other than that, one or two will do. You don't keep negging her for years to come. You don't understand what a neg is. It's not a put-down. Put-downs and negs are completely different things. You only use negs to remove the bitch shield.

"The neg is about showing a girl that you do not appreciate being stepped on. That's it. It's not about calling a girl an asshole. It's about not allowing her to treat you like one.

"Negs should be sincere and fun and playful. I can see how complimenting her aloud shows confidence on your part. You aren't just being lame by complimenting her the same as everyone else. If you act it up, you come off with more control. You are saying it in a fun, playful way. It works. I've done it sometimes. However, to compliment a girl's anatomy is one thing, to compliment something else out loud is another. 'You are so classy! Wow! You've got . . . style! You know who else had style? Pierce Brosnan as 007. But I bet you'd make a better spy . . .'

"A ten wants a challenge. Why? Because it challenges her ego. Be an asshole to a ten, but do so only when you are the social center—when two or three people are listening intently to what you are saying. If they are girls, then it's even better.

"A ten must be negged. A neg is a statement that disqualifies oneself as a potential suitor. It's something that a guy trying to get the girl would never do. For example, 'Nice nails, are they real? No? Oh. Well, they're still nice.' See? It's not an asshole remark, just a hint of your not being impressed, like most guys are, by the ten. 'That's a nice hairstyle. Is that your real hair?' Say these things with sincerity, or else you look like an obvious asshole and then it won't work.

"Never hit on a ten at first. Be polite, but don't compliment her or anything stupid like that at first. I neg and otherwise am polite for the rest of the group. When she is testing me, I neg her, then I'm polite again. She quickly realizes that she gets more attention from me by being nice to me—and this gives her the opportunity to get her self-esteem back after the little negs. You get a ten through her ego issues.

"Rock stars neg big-time. The minute they get treated like shit from a girl, they put on their rock star attitude and the negs start— toying with the girl and being coy. So in a nutshell, to get a ten is to act like a rock star.

"When shaking hands with a beautiful woman, smile big, look into her eyes, and say, 'Nice to meet you.' However, before you finish, turn your head to someone else and immediately say, 'Hey did you know . . .' and go off into something else. This is a great neg because most guys try to impress her. She is accustomed to people paying more attention to her. But it seems you didn't even notice her beauty. As if maybe you don't like her. You were polite, but you didn't try to chat it up with her. As you speak enthusiastically about something to another person there, she will see that you are fun, are not in a sex mood, and so on. You are conveying your personality to her indirectly. I believe quite strongly in this indirect personality-conveying tactic.

"The girls are testing you when they neg. And you win by deflating the sails of each neg. A girl will say, 'What are you doing here—picking up lots of girls?' And you say, 'My friend Diane would *kill* me if I did that.' 'Who is Diane?' 'Oh, she's a really good friend and we used to go out but we are good friends and while we aren't an item, I know she still loves me very much and some interesting emotions take place in her brain when she sees other women taking interest in me. She knows she has no right to be jealous; it just comes through anyway. I had a girlfriend for a while after Diane and Diane had never met her because of this—but we are still very good friends.' I then point to Diane, who is a ten, surrounded by guys in the club. 'So why are you talking to me?' the girl may say. That's yet another neg. Respond with 'Didn't mean to bother you. Never mind!' and turn your back to her. This is a test to see if she will laugh and turn you around back to her.

"See how this goes? So yes, girls neg you. Most guys don't realize this, and they don't neg right back like they should. That is what flirting is all about. Testing and teasing.

"Blow your nose in front of her casually while telling a story to her friends. Ask them, 'Is she always like this?' Or ask her, 'Where's your off button?'

"Notice you aren't insulting her in any of these. You are just disqualifying yourself from appearing to be the next guy.

"Most important, when you neg, 'throw and go.' Throw the neg and then keep talking, without apparently watching for her reaction. Try it the same way that you practice multiple threading: Routine. Pause routine. Neg. Continue routine.

"Overnegging occurs when you neg and wait for her to respond. Instead, neg and then keep talking about something else like the neg was no biggie to you. Otherwise the jig is up.

"After doing a magic trick, I show both of my hands empty. I say, 'Nothing in my left hand,' and then I say, 'Nothing in my right

> I believe a burp is an excellent neg. A neg holds two pur-
> poses:
>
> 1. To lower the woman's self-esteem.
> 2. To convey lack of interest (which does 1).
>
> Burp and don't apologize for it. When she says, "You
> are a pig," you reply, "You think that? Well, my reputation
> precedes me!"

hand,' each time showing the hand empty. Then I say, 'What's that
behind your ear?' and I reach behind her ear. 'Is it? Just as I sus-
pected . . . dirt!'

"If you do it right, everyone laughs. Right at the moment she
thinks you are trying to impress her, you neg her.

"Any topic of discussion that can allow you to touch her is good.
Not just the complimentary 'You've got soft hands' talk, but the
'Do you believe in chi energy? Let's see if we can feel each other's
energy' talk. If they believe in spells they most likely believe in chi.

"Thing is, while humor is acceptable, it isn't really a neg if it
doesn't make her feel embarrassed a bit. My 'Nice to meet you—
Hey did you know' neg is brilliant. That one really gives you the
Zen of negging; just try it a few times. And the 'I like your nails, are
they real? No, well they are still nice I guess' is great. They aren't
funny but they work tremendously.

"When you embarrass within a joke, you acknowledge to her
that you know you are negging her. Thing is, it's more powerful if
she doesn't know you did it on purpose. That is why I say humor is
not an essential ingredient to a neg. Some negs *are* humorous,
though."

"I notice," said Adam, "that you often don't use routines when
you're talking to girls. You're just making fun conversation. And

USEFUL NEGS

- "Is that your natural hair color? No? Oh." (Pause.) "Well, it fits you."
- Bump her and say, "Hands off the merchandise."
- "You and I would never get along. We're too similar."
- "You don't have a chance."
- "That was weird."
- "Wow."
- "I've eaten girls like you for breakfast."
- "Don't make me come down there." (I'm tall.)
- "You have crooked teeth."
- "There's beauty in imperfection."
- Ask her, "What nationality are you?" If she says she's from a mix of more than two countries, say, "Wow, your parents really got around."
- Ask her, "If you were born a boy, what were your parents going to name you?" Now call her by that name all night.
- "Hey knucklehead."
- "Wait your turn." (Said even if she said nothing.)
- "You talk a lot." (Said even if she didn't talk a lot.)
- "Did you just roll your eyes at me? You little shit!" (Smirk and put your dukes up.)
- "You need to wash that dress already."

you are so funny when you talk to the girls! How can I learn to be funny spontaneously, without having to use memorized routines, like you do?"

"It's all about practice," I replied. "But my secret is, I use the Absurd. Adam, I want to tell you something powerful: As long as it comes from the right place inside of you, the inner game of humor, you can make up anything you want and it will work. I am not saying that you should lie to people and they will believe it. Rather, I am saying that you can improvise conversationally, even to the point of the obvious nontruth, even if no one even takes it seriously; it will still work. All it takes is that you are actually laughing inside when you say it. Literal truth and factual accuracy are not necessary for vibing and conveying value. When they are vibing, people only care that it feels good. Here's an example from Lovedrop that will help to illustrate the concept.

"Somebody says, 'One day I'm going to buy my own house.'

"Lovedrop says, playfully, 'One of these days, I'm gonna have my own *town*. Just like the bad guy in the movies.' Lovedrop takes the thread to the absurd, and people laugh. 'And I'm gonna name it Loveland. I'll staff the city government with all my loyal friends. Of course I will also build a massive castle to live in. I'll even have my own henchmen, and I'll own the cops, and everything. Just like the bad guy in the movies. My own town!'"

I smiled. "Notice a few things about what Lovedrop has said: First, it's not literally true. This is immediately obvious to everyone listening. Yet it still works. People still laughed along and enjoyed it, even though they didn't literally believe it."

Adam nodded. "Okay, that makes sense."

"Also," I continued, "notice that Lovedrop is flipping attraction switches, including status and resources, social alignments, and healthy emotional programming—such as ambition. Notice the way that he naturally assumes these value indicators in his words, to embed those attraction triggers.

"Of course, his actual value, his actual accomplishments, and his actual alignments and resources are unknown and cannot be known. This is why bragging is a worthless and vain effort. Anyone can lie. Even if you are rich and powerful, trying to convince people of this will only convey lower value since trying is a demonstration of lower value, or DLV. People don't hear your literal words anyway—they hear the DHVs and DLVs embedded in your speech. What are they?

"This is the same reason why you can invent bullshit off the top of your head, embed value indicators in it, and even though everyone knows it's bullshit, they will still feel attracted to you—because the value indicators are processed at an *emotional* level. How cool is that?"

"That is pretty amazing," said Adam.

"The key is to realize that you can say anything you want, even if it is not literally true. It will still induce whatever feelings are described, and paint whatever picture. As long as it feels good, be creative and people will vibe to it. Realizing this simple truth will set your conversations free."

"What do I do if my mind goes blank?" asked Adam.

"Well," I said, "the first thing that usually happens when your mind goes blank is the Interview pops into your head. It's the mindless stream of questions, such as 'So what do you do?' 'Where are you from?' 'What music do you like?' But every time you do this, you are indicating interest in the target.

"Use the Interview as a tool instead of letting it tool you. When the question 'Where are you from?' pops into your head, turn it into a statement. Use it as an opportunity to practice the absurd.

"Instead of asking, 'Where are you from?' perhaps you say something like 'You know, you guys look like East Coast girls to me.' (calibrating.) 'Maybe it's those shit-kicker boots, or that look in your eye, like you mean business . . .'

"Instead of asking, 'What's your name?' perhaps you say, 'You look like a Georgette to me.' See how this adds more value than simply asking?"

"Yeah," said Adam. "That makes sense."

"Notice the pausing as well," I said. "The exact line is not important. In fact, it doesn't even have to be that great. What's important is that you are using the Interview as an opportunity to add value in a more spontaneous way using the absurd."

"I get it," said Adam. "It's a creativity exercise."

"Yes," I replied, "and here is something very powerful: Make it a practice to agree with every statement, and then to build upon it creatively. Disagreement stifles creativity, as anyone knows who has studied improvisational comedy."

"Agree with everything?"

"Well, maybe not everything, but certainly as an exercise. Here is a game that can be learned in any improvisational comedy class. The rules are simple:

1. Say something fun and creative. Something absurd.
2. Next, your wing must agree with you, saying "Yes, and . . . " following up with a creative statement that builds on what you said before.
3. After this, you must agree with whatever he has just said, saying "Yes, and . . . " followed again by your own opportunity to improvise.
4. And then he must agree with you, and has his turn again, and so on, back and forth.

"Notice how I don't argue with what is said," I pointed out. "Instead, I *agree* with it and then push it even farther."

Adam nodded.

"When someone throws a thread at you, simply agree with his thread, and then direct his conversational momentum to your own aims, by taking it somewhere creatively absurd. This is my secret of humor.

"This is also the way that I use absurdity in order to control the frame. For example, if someone says to me, 'You're an asshole,' then I reply, 'I'm an asshole, and I'm fun.' Everyone laughs. I accept what is said and then take it in my own direction. This is so important!"

I glanced at the clock and it was well into Sunday morning.

"All right, I think that concludes our session. You have an early flight tomorrow, yes? Do you have any questions for me before we go to sleep?"

"Not right now," said Adam. "To be honest, it was a bit of an overload. My mind is racing right now, trying to connect everything together, but I already feel like a new man. I wish I could learn some more. I feel like the new me is just beginning. Maybe we'll catch up another time."

And with that, Adam crashed face first on the couch pillow. He left before I awoke the next day.

Chapter Eleven

THE PLEASURE BUBBLE

WITH ADAM GONE, I was reminded of the nice little life I had made for myself. The business was doing well, the show was set to premiere soon—nothing seemed to go wrong. I'd finally realized my dreams. We eventually decided to leave Project Miami behind and so moved on to California.

We all sat in what we'd named the "Pleasure Bubble"—an apartment we decorated while staying in San Diego to produce a new video set. Me, Matador, Lovedrop, Lovedrop's girlfriend Kacey, and our friend and Internet marketer extraordinaire, Jim Pike.

Matador was his usual animated self, telling a story. ". . . So we were at Project Miami, and Mystery's back in his bedroom with this girl," he said, "the girl he met at the Bondage Ball. This is the girl, remember, who was writhing around on a pool table while some guy dripped wax all over her naked body . . ."

It was easy to get lost in the vibe of the Pleasure Bubble, a dreamy timeless place full of good feelings, comfort, safety, happiness, and fun. We had built it out of sensations: cleanliness, lighting, scent, music, luxury, and abundance.

"Anyway," said Matador, "they were in the back with the door closed, and suddenly she comes flying out of Mystery's room like a bat out of hell. I was downstairs in bed, but we heard it across the whole house. She slammed his door, and then I heard the sound of my vase smashing."

"Those vases were expensive, too," said Lovedrop. "Our decorator picked them out."

"What'd you do to piss her off?" asked Kacey.

"She was pissed because he wouldn't have sex with her," said Matador.

"You wouldn't have sex with her?" Kacey turned to me, a confused expression on her face.

"She kept biting me," I said. "It hurt. It was irritating. I told her I didn't like it, and to stop, but she kept doing it. So then I wasn't in the mood anymore."

"She was *pissed*," said Lovedrop. "She went tearing outside like a banshee."

"I was lying in bed when it happened," said Matador, "and then I heard her car start up, and she revved it a couple of times, and then there was this loud crunch. Of course by then I was running outside, my shirt off, and I could see she had just rammed my car. My Mercedes SL 500 convertible. Oh, my God!"

Kacey giggled. "You guys are ridiculous."

Matador continued: "Then Mystery comes walking outside, and meanwhile I see her backing up, 'cause she's going to ram it again. Motherfucker, she's going to ram it again! I ran over there, waving my hands, shouting 'No, no!' but she rammed right into it again."

Chuckling, I chimed in: "That's when I told her, 'It's not even my car!'" I held up my hands and shrugged. I mean really, the irony of it all is quite striking. She's didn't even ram the right car.

"You crazy magician!" exclaimed Matador, exasperated. "You couldn't tell her that *before* she rammed my car?"

I finished the story: "As soon as she left, she called back and made some of the nastiest, scariest, weirdest, creepiest threats you ever heard. She said she was a witch, she said she would come back to the house and trash it, I mean on and on. I actually put it on speakerphone and recorded it just to be safe."

"Jeez," said Kacey. "That's psycho."

"There's a lot of weirdos out there," said Lovedrop. "You never know. For example, the San Diego Weirdo has roamed these parts for many years, but he's never been caught."

"The San Diego Weirdo?" asked Kacey.

Jim Pike took a long, bubbling toke from a giant bong and then said, "Oh, by the way, listen: It's really important to my partner Matt that his place is thought of as cooler than mine. So I know you guys turned my place into the Pleasure Bubble, and it's like a giant magnet for girls, but Matt is really rigid sometimes in his thinking, and he just needs to believe that certain things are true."

"Even if they aren't?" asked Lovedrop.

Jim shrugged. "Matt needs to think that his place is more pimp than mine. His mental state is important so he can do all of his brilliant marketing stuff and pull off this launch. Plus, I don't want to piss him off right now . . ."

"Sounds like you're walking on eggshells around this guy," said Lovedrop.

"Um," said Jim.

Just then, the Rat walked in carrying a couple of shopping bags. "Hey guys," he said in his whiny voice. "What's shakin' at the Pleasure Bubble?"

"I've got something to shake at ya right here, pal," I replied.

"Anyone know where I can get some Roxies?" The Rat walked over and took a seat beside me on the suede couch. "My back hurts like a bitch and my prescription is about to run out."

"Maybe you shouldn't take eight of them at one time," said Lovedrop.

"Hey Jim," said the Rat, "check out these badass shoes I got for you at Marshalls. They look just as cool as the ones LD wears, but they were like five times cheaper." He handed Jim a shoebox.

"Wow," said Jim. "Thanks." He opened it and held up the cheap shoes, looking at them momentarily as if wondering, *Why did this guy buy me a pair of shoes?*

"Hey LD," said the Rat, "check out these jeans I made for you." He held them up. Lovedrop winced; they were god-awful. The cut was all out of style, and the Rat had tie-dyed them and rubbed them with sandpaper to put holes all over them.

"They're okay, I guess," said Lovedrop. They were the ugliest jeans he had ever seen.

"Just 'okay'? They're fucking badass!" said the Rat. "Come on, put them on. Let's see how they look. Come on!"

I expected Lovedrop to try to weasel out of it, but instead he smirked and put them on, right there on the spot. Lovedrop gets a kick out of hanging people with their own rope.

"I don't know about those jeans, man," said Matador.

"Those jeans look like shit," I said.

"Thanks for noticing," said Lovedrop with a smile, strutting around in his shitty new jeans. "You just wish you had these jeans when you were filming the show."

That's right! My show would be on the air soon.

"Wow," I said. "I'm going to be famous."

"Yeah, you're going to be famous," said the Rat. "Hey Mystery, do you think you could get me on the next season of your show? You know I love you like a brother."

"Dude," I said, ignoring him, "isn't that amazing? I'm going to be on TV! Isn't that weird?"

"It's going to be great for our upcoming product launch," said Jim.

Matador grinned at the Rat. "You sure wanna be on TV, don't you?" Matador liked poking him. "You know, someday, they'll ask you what Matador was like. What are you gonna say?"

"Come on, seriously guys," whined the Rat. "I want to be partners with you; come on." He was very pushy.

"Well, that's a sad cowboy song," said Matador. "But seriously, tell me something. When I walk in the room, do you feel a shiver of electricity run down your back?"

The Rat was getting irritated. "Oh, you're a big star now?" he asked.

"I'm hungry," said Kacey. "Is anyone else hungry?"

"I'm starving," said Lovedrop. "I could eat a horse."

"Hey guys, listen," said Matador. "I wasn't going to say anything, but this morning I got up to pee . . ." His voice took on a conspiratorial tone. "I wasn't gonna say anything, but I saw Kacey sneaking some Twinkies into her purse."

"Oh my God I did not," exclaimed Kacey. "That is *such* bullshit. You are so full of shit!"

Lovedrop reached over to open a nearby pizza box.

My thoughts drifted to my last girlfriend in Miami. "I miss Cassondra," I said, reminiscing. "I fell in love with her. I knew it would piss off Amanda. Oops. But Cassondra was a beautiful young girl, and talented and smart, sassy and social, funny, all that great stuff."

"Kacey," said Lovedrop suddenly, as he held open the empty box, "please tell me you did not just eat that entire pizza."

"Of course not! Matador and Jim had like three pieces each!"

"Damn, Kacey," said Matador. "You sure can eat. Did you guys know she clogged up the toilet again last night?"

"He is lying right now," said Kacey. "You guys know he is totally lying."

"I wasn't going to say anything," said Matador, "but last night, I had to make a phone call. I wasn't gonna say anything, I walked by the kitchen, and I saw Kacey hiding a doughnut in her bra . . ."

Kacey rolled her eyes. "No one believes you, Matador."

"Your ballooning weight problem is really the issue here," joked Matador. "When we found you, you were eating chicken salad and celery sticks. Now you can't make it halfway through the day without cooking up a huge batch of chocolate-chip pancakes."

Kacey laughed. "You are such an asshole, James. I am the cutest girl you know; I'm sorry if you guys are used to your whores who like to go to bars and fuck guys like you every night but—"

"Hold on a sec," interrupted Matador, raising a finger toward her as he turned away.

Kacey paused, a dumbfounded look on her face.

Matador turned back to face her. "I'm sorry, go ahead?"

But as she started to talk, he turned away again with a wave of his hand. "That's it. I've heard enough!"

Everybody burst out laughing.

Just then, in walked Jim's partner, Internet marketer Matt Wilde, who was, in his own mind, the most brilliant Internet marketer in the universe. Smacking loudly on a piece of tofu, unshaven and dumpy, he wore a T-shirt with "Affliction" written across the top in large Gothic letters.

The first thing out of his mouth as he entered the room was "How do you like my baseball cap when I wear it sideways like this? Isn't it *baller*? I—" He broke off as he looked around the room. "Holy shit!" he exclaimed. "What happened to this place?" Wilde seemed to go into a state of disbelief as he turned around several times to let the new decor sink in.

We had spent the day setting everything up. Yesterday, Jim's apartment had been a disgusting bachelor pad, but now it was like the Garden of Eden. How could that have happened so quickly?

Wilde started pacing back and forth, and hit himself repeatedly in the head with his right fist. He said, over and over again, "This is fucking with me. This is fucking with me . . ."

"He's not used to this sort of reevaluation of his assumptions," said Jim.

" . . . This is fucking with me. This is fucking with me . . ."

Wilde was crazy as a loon. He had previously gained notoriety for cheating in Dungeons and Dragons tournaments, and unbeknownst to us, he would become an enormous joke in the world of online marketing in less than six months. Nevertheless, our plan was to produce a new video set for these guys to sell.

"I've got to say," said Jim, "the boys really did an amazing job putting this whole place together. We filmed everything; we figured maybe we could use the video somehow as part of our launch."

"Right," said Wilde suddenly, pulling himself together. "I need to get into a marketing head space, okay." He started rubbing his temples.

"Good idea," I said, smiling. "I want to talk about how I will look on this video. I want it to look pro. I'm on VH1, man! I'm famous!"

"And what should we call this new product?" asked Lovedrop.

"Okay," Wilde replied. "Let's brainstorm. First things first. The two most important customer questions are 'Will it work for me?' and 'How do I get started?'"

"Students want to learn this technology," I said, "because it's been proven. Or they want to see for themselves that it really will work for them, because they have limiting beliefs."

"I've got it!" exclaimed Wilde triumphantly. "We'll call it, 'Seeing Through Mystery's Eyes'! It's perfect! That's really what the customer wants. He wants to *see* the things that Mystery sees, to *understand* the way Mystery understands."

"How did you come up with that?" asked Lovedrop.

"It's a function of my genius," said Wilde. "I have certain foundational assumptions, and based on the certainty of those, I am able to extrapolate far enough out that I can see an entire empire stretched out before me. In fact, I believe that I should be the ruler of the earth." He nodded with ultimate certainty.

"Wow," said Lovedrop. "The whole earth?"

"That's a big responsibility," I said. (I mean, it really is.)

"It is," said Wilde. "Decisions have to be made where billions of people live or die. Big decisions." He paused for effect and then said dramatically, "And if any man thinks he can stop me, let him try, Mystery. Let. Him. Try."

("I will merely assume," I later said to Lovedrop, "that he has Tourette's syndrome and can't help being such an interesting character. He reminds me of the crazy guy who teaches Patrick Swayze how to move stuff in the movie *Ghost*.")

Wilde started looking around the room. "By the way," he said, "I still can't get over the vibe of this place. It's really fucking with my head."

"Yeah," said Kacey. "How do you guys make it feel so good in here?"

"Well," said Lovedrop, "let me tell you. The first tip is, keep it clutter free, and I mean completely. Next, it should be hygienically clean. Overclean. That's what creates the golf course feeling, which is *so* relaxing and peaceful."

"What else?" asked Matt.

"Sweep up the pubic hair in your bathroom," I said.

"Gross," said Kacey.

"I know this seems obvious," I continued, "but for some, it is the elusive obvious. Anyone can make a mess like this, but it takes a man to clean it up. Or fifty bucks, and call a maid. When your target comes over, do not subject her to the experience of seeing anything nasty around the toilet."

"Remember," said Lovedrop, "you want it to be super clean."

"Stock the fridge," I said.

"Yeah, keep the Pleasure Bubble stocked to the gills," said Lovedrop, "with alcohol and beverages of all types, food, bathroom supplies, towels, every type of medicine, moisturizing cream, tampons, toothbrushes, contact solution, etc. It is this overstocked 'extra mile' that creates the luxury and abundance feeling. This feeling makes a woman feel safe, protected, and taken care of. It makes her feel like her every need is met, like magic, inside the space of the Pleasure Bubble. The Pleasure Bubble, where there are no clocks and where time does not pass, and where she never wants to leave."

"I have to admit," said Kacey, "that when I first came here, I never left. I literally did not sleep at my own place for a month. I always ended up crashing on the couch or on one of the LoveSacs. I just like being here."

"When I'm shopping," I said, "I think to myself, *Who do I expect to come over in the next week?* I got Corona for my good friend Neil, Diet Coke for Matador, I personally prefer Rockstar, and some fruity wine coolers for Kacey."

"I enjoy a nice protein water," said Lovedrop.

"Fair," I said. "Okay, also, prepare your home for guests. Do you have a guest room? If you were to have guests over, ones you were not going to sleep with, where exactly would they stay? How comfortable do you think they would be? Is the bed comfortable? Is the bedding clean? Did you buy a few extra toothbrushes? Is there soap? What about a cozy blanket to curl up in on that comfortable couch of yours?

"Girlify your guest bathroom," I continued. "I once had a girlfriend who took over the guest bathroom as hers for a time. She made everything pink. The towels were pink. The mats were pink. Even the items on the shelves were purchased solely because they were pink. Of course, when my girlfriend and I broke up, and she moved out, I was left with a pink guest bathroom. Whenever I would have female friends visit, they would no doubt see the pink bathroom. Providing evidence in your home that you happen to have had women in your life before this particular girl will corroborate the prior preselection demonstrations she witnessed in the club."

"Tickle the senses," said Lovedrop. "The Pleasure Bubble smells good because I took out the trash, emptied the sink and ran the dishwasher, wiped down the counters, lit scented candles, and I use a fan to keep the air circulating in the room."

"Yes, make your apartment smell pleasing," I said. "The next time you've been away from your apartment for a while, when you come back, take note of the scents your apartment bathes you in. Is it pleasing? If not, let's fix it. Aside from sanitizing your kitchen and bathroom, get the trash taken care of. Get three scented candles. You really only need one, but three scented candles slam the point home. This house is cleansed."

"The Pleasure Bubble looks good because I use ambient light," said Lovedrop. "Candles, lights pointed at works of art, colored lights behind plants, and so on. And it sounds nice in here as well, because I have a playlist going on the iPod."

"Build a good musical playlist," I said. "Have you created a comfort-building playlist yet? The type of music that can be played in the background while she sits on your comfortable couch and tells you about her dreams? Have you created a must-share playlist? You know, the songs that have moved you. The songs that your best friend just has to hear. Show her what bands you like."

Lovedrop said, "Notice also the furniture is comfortable and soft, with lots of pillows and blankets. There is a shag rug in front of the couch. There are plants. The Pleasure Bubble tickles the senses."

"I've had good couches," I said, "and I've had shitty couches. At some point you're going to have a woman in your apartment. Like the new cat being introduced to a new apartment, so too will the woman be similarly uncomfortable. The cat must see all four corners of the place, see all the rooms, and take account of all other sentient beings in the vicinity, before settling on your lap. If the couch doesn't make her want to settle in for a while, you need to look at getting a new one. The difference between a good couch and a bad couch is maybe the difference between seeing that girl again and not."

"We got Jim's furniture at Mor Furniture for Less," said Lovedrop. "You should have seen the shit he had before." He shook his head sadly.

"Get a plant," I said. "Now remember, if you can't take care of a plant, how in the world will you be able to take care of a girl? What does it say that you can't take care of your own plant? If you have plants in your apartment right now that are dead, first off, shame on you. And I will fully forgive you if you recover those pots, get rid of the evidence, and go run out and buy yourself a plant; one you will take care of this time. One she will take care of for you. This plant will become a subplot to your next romance.

"Display meaningful art," I said. "Again, you don't have to spend a lot of money. Or any in fact. It just needs to be meaningful, to you. May I suggest you take your favorite digital photo, printed out large, and frame it. A curious and interesting picture from Google images, when blown up to indicate its importance to you, grows in perceived value. Generally, the bigger the image, the more apparent investment is in its display. Or if you want to convey your brilliance, why not show her the Bedini motor you built from plans off the Internet. Proof that energy can be free."

Matt nodded as he continued to listen.

"Prepare a sensations kit," I said. "This consists of items that assist you in giving her a specific experience. The subtle sensation of butterfly kisses, that is, fluttering your eyelashes on her fair skin, or of a feather lightly brushed on the arms and shoulders and stomach for five minutes. How heavenly. Since you and her are alone with no one to judge how you entertain each other, why not do so with a light touching session?

"Set up your Google Earth. At some point I'm sure you'll want to show your potential new girlfriend all the different places you've been. Were you to set up a series of Google Earth bookmarks of locations you grew up in and had specific experiences at, such as your first kiss, the creek you jumped over in grade seven, and the specific spot where you built your first underground fort, you'd be able to transport her into your life, by way of your upbringing. How powerful is that? Of course it is even more powerful to take the time to visit her personal locations on Google Earth, and the stories that go with them.

"Create an inspirational YouTube playlist. Perhaps she hasn't seen the video of dolphins blowing ring bubbles. Perhaps she hasn't yet seen the one about the giant water lilies.

"Have massage oil by your bed. Sure, it may be there in anticipation of things to come, and reveal your intent, but if the bottle is half empty, it conveys preselection. Consider adding a male pheromone to the massage oil. Phero-hypnol is the best one. Using a male pheromone in your home to merely amp up your new girlfriend's already aroused state seems ethical. I believe pheromones are very useful in the seduction stage. What better way than to infuse it into your massage oil?

"Remember," I concluded, "you are the one in charge of setting the activities you will share with her when you are alone together in your apartment. Make her comfortable. You should be prepared with at least a dozen specific comfort- and rapport-building gambits. Whether it's rummaging through your toy box, showing her Google Earth, or scratching her head as you watch *Family Guy*, know that you are the designer of her experience. In doing so, she helps to design yours. And the best part is, they know what they are doing, too."

Later on, I was standing in the hall by my room when the Rat came up to me, crying and whining about Matador. "It's Matador, man, he's always interfering. He's always in my way. I don't like him. I want to move freely in Venusian Arts."

"Talk to Lovedrop," I said.

But the Rat, a guy who only helped us on a single boot camp, would soon set out to start his own pickup company: Rat Method.

Why is it that the seduction community seems to attract these people?

Chapter Twelve

A PARTY IN THE HILLS

"I THINK YOU MADE A WRONG TURN," Sondra said to Lovedrop.

We were on our way to a party in Beverly Hills, and I sat in the backseat with my friend Sondra. She always had fun events lined up, like this party. Since we moved back to Hollywood after the show aired and we found more success, we often went out with Sondra to various red-carpet events.

"Baby," said Kacey, "are you sure you weren't supposed to turn left back there?"

"That wasn't the road," Lovedrop replied. "Trust me. I have a map."

"I should have driven," said Sondra.

A real sweetheart, eh? But she's not my type. Objectively, though, she's a lovely girl. In fact, she was recently on a Super Bowl commercial.

I looked out the window. We continued winding our way up the hills. Beautiful houses of all shapes and sizes passed by on both sides. A Tool song played on the radio, and I sang along with the words:

fret for your lawsuit . . . and fret for your pilot

After a while, I asked Sondra, "So who is this guy that's throwing the party?"

"He's really rich," she said. "He's like the second-biggest pornographer in L.A."

Kacey snorted. "What a distinction," she said derisively. "I mean, really?"

"Seriously." But Sondra was talking about the money. "His place is like a copy of the Playboy Mansion. He's got monkey cages, tennis courts, a game room, a bowling alley; he even installed his own grotto."

"Eww," said Kacey. "A grotto? It's one of *those* hills houses?"

"I hope there's a gym up there," said Lovedrop. "I wanna do my triceps."

"This party's great for meeting people," said Sondra. "He throws it every other week. Erik, you're going to like it. He always has hot girls up there. He put me on the list."

I felt a pang. Suddenly I could see how things worked at this house.

"Oh dude!" I said. "This is all wrong."

"What's the matter?" asked Kacey.

"You should have given me some advance notice," I complained. "I haven't brought any girls."

"What are you talking about?"

I sighed. "He's built a system," I explained, "It's not my system. It's the way Hollywood types do things. He's got his mansion, he throws his parties, and he gets girls to go up there. I get it. And I'm the guy who's showing up at his house to mack on his girls."

"I think that's a little extreme," said Lovedrop. "We are bringing girls. There are two girls in the car."

"Yes, but the general rule is, it should be two-to-one. If you're a cool guy going to the party, you need to make sure you have two girls with you: one for yourself, and one for the party. Or at least just one for the party. And Sondra isn't the value that I'm contributing to his event, because she was there last week. *She's* bring-ing *me*. So I would expect him to be pissed because I'm not en-riching his party. I'm not bringing any girls."

"Erik, it's no big deal," said Sondra. "Trust me. I go to these things all the time."

"This guy is a rich pornographer," said Lovedrop. "Right? His place looks like the Playboy Mansion, right? He probably hooks up with a different chick every night. What does he care if we only brought two girls to the party? There's no way he'd even notice."

I sighed again and tossed my hands, then smiled ruefully. "Oh well," I said. "The universe put me here, so . . . I'm just going to enjoy the Now."

When we arrived, I had to stop and admire the house, and the view.

"Wow," I said. "You can see all of L.A. from up here."

"This place looks like it cost thirty million dollars," said Love-drop.

"Yeah," said Sondra, "it's really cool. And you can make good connections at this party."

Tanned bodies frolicked everywhere. There were tennis courts and an infinity pool, girls in bikinis laid out in the sun. Sets of two or three people stood at the open bar, while men in shorts and T-shirts exchanged business cards. Young hardbodies of both sexes played volleyball on a patch of sand and a pretty girl posed nearby for a photo shoot.

"Are there professional photographers here?" I asked Sondra. Photo shoots are often just a ruse to get women. In fact, I recom-mend to get into photography and make it one of your hobbies.

"Half and half," said Sondra. "He actually gets some pretty good photographers up here sometimes. It's worth it to come up here."

I looked over again at the girl in the photo shoot. She posed this way and that, and flashed a pretty smile to the camera. Then I no-ticed that she wasn't just pretty, she was quite possibly one of the most beautiful women I had ever seen. Her face was absolutely gorgeous. Have you ever met one of those women who is so beautiful that you can't even look her in the face? When she's a 10, it's like staring at the sun.

I found myself getting sucked into her beauty. She had a perfect body. Fit but voluptuous, with long, dark brown hair. And her face! This girl was a 10.

"Hey!" said Sondra, knocking me out of my trance. "Come over here. I want you to meet the owner of the house."

"There's a gym in that building," said Lovedrop, "next to the bathrooms." He pointed toward the game room. A few pinball machines were situated around the entrance. "I'm going to go do my triceps," he said. "I'll be back in a few minutes."

Sondra grabbed my hand and started pulling me toward a patio set nearby. "Oh, and I should warn you now," she said: "He's kind of a dick." I followed along but I still couldn't stop thinking about the girl.

The owner of the house sat with a small group of fat, middle-aged men. He looked like he was in his fifties or sixties, with scraggy hair and a thin, weathered face, like a surfer.

He didn't like me. When Sondra introduced us, he immediately started making comments in my direction. "So you're Mystery, huh?" He adjusted his dirty baseball cap and squinted at me. "The Pickup Artist?"

"That's me," I said. "Pleased to make your acquaintance."

"I don't know if I believe in all that pickup shit," he replied. "Where's your girls now?" He delivered it with a bit of a joking manner—but within every joke is an element of truth. He obviously felt irritated by my presence. Which, I might add, if you have ever spent any time with me, you would know is very unusual. I'm fun!

I looked over at Sondra as if to say, *I told you so.*

"I'm just enjoying the Now," I said. "Sondra invited me."

A group of blondes walked by in bikinis made out of the Swedish flag, making their way toward the grotto.

"Sondra, huh?" He picked his nose.

"This is a beautiful place," I continued, "and were I to indulge in bringing some women up here, I'm sure a good time would be had by all."

"I'm gonna have to take Sondra off the list," he said. "As far as I can see, you're like a tractor. You just come up here to pull the girls out, but I don't see you bringing any girls back in."

The way he delivered that line, I could tell he had delivered it many times in the past. It was his warning to stray dogs that they weren't welcome unless they brought girls. It was also rude, but then again, I had decided that I was definitely going to pick up that girl from the photo shoot and take her home with me. Then he would have a reason to be pissed off.

"Pleasure meeting you," I said, and then I made my way to the next set.

Later on, I was talking with Kacey and Sondra, and Lovedrop walked up to us, laughing and shaking his head.

"What's so funny?" asked Kacey.

"It's nothing," he said.

"Tell me!" she reacted.

"Yeah, come on," I said. "What's so funny? Let's hear it."

"Really it's nothing," said Lovedrop. "Just when I was walking back from the bar, I passed a circle of people, and the owner of the house was talking. And as I walked past, I heard him saying, 'We're going to bring her up here, we're going to fuck her ass . . .'" Lovedrop started laughing again.

"Eww, and then what?" asked Kacey. "What was he talking about?"

"I don't know," he said. "That's all I heard when I walked by. 'We're going to bring her up here, we're going to fuck her ass . . .' I didn't even hear him finish the sentence." He chuckled. "It was a snapshot of time, but strangely appropriate for that guy."

"Hey," said Kacey after a moment, "do you guys notice something about those guys over there?"

Sondra glanced over. "The really good-looking ones?"

I looked over and there they were, near the owner of the house, like two pet dogs. They looked like the California ideal. Blond hair, sunglasses, tanned and in shape, and overly good-looking. It just looked like too much.

"Yeah," said Kacey. "Do you notice anything weird about them?"

"I do, actually," said Lovedrop, "but I just can't put my finger on what it is . . ."

"They keep looking at us," said Sondra. "Maybe that's what's creepy about them."

"It's their arms!" said Lovedrop suddenly. "They're way too big."

"Oh, my God, you're right!" Kacey exclaimed.

He was right. Their arms were muscled and huge, but the rest of their bodies looked completely normal. They just had these huge arms, like crabs. Kacey and Sondra both started giggling.

"Now that you mention it," said Kacey, "it's really obvious. Eww."

"Only in L.A. do you get these types," said Lovedrop.

"It's funny," I said, "because you know every locale has its freaks. Especially small towns. But only in Hollywood do you see these."

"I swear," said Lovedrop, "this town warps people. I bet you they hang out up here all the time, too."

"Oh, I wanted to tell you guys," said Kacey: "As soon as you went to the bathroom, a really old guy came up to me, and he started asking me if I ever did any modeling. And I looked at his face, and . . . I mean you could really tell he had a lot of plastic surgery—a *lot*. He just looked like he'd been . . ."

I said, "Carved up?"

"Yes! Exactly. His face looked like carved-up meat. And then he offered me coke."

"Gross," said Lovedrop.

"There's a lot of people up here with weird plastic surgery," said Kacey. "And also, those girls over there, I mean, I'm not trying to be a bitch, but if you don't got it, don't flaunt it. Put some clothes over that cellulite."

"Kacey!" I said.

"Well," she said, "it's true. And this place is weird. Everyone just wants to get something."

"What's wrong with that?" asked Sondra. "I'm here to get something, too. Like connections for my modeling career. Everyone has something to offer. It's value for value. The party's a resource; you just have to see what you have to trade and what you can get out of it."

"Well, I'm ready to get out of it anytime," said Kacey. "I want to see my doggy; I miss his little face. Plus, I'm getting hungry. I haven't eaten anything today and there's no food here."

"Okay, but let's go to the bathroom first," said Sondra, "and then I want to smoke this joint before we go."

The girls walked off toward the bathrooms.

Soon after, Lovedrop's iPhone rang.

Matador came on the line. "Hey, is Mystery around?"

"Yeah, he's right here."

"Go somewhere the two of you can have some privacy, and put me on speakerphone."

"Okay, it's just the three of us," said Lovedrop, after we'd secluded ourselves.

Matador's disembodied voice came through loud and clear. "Two things, gentlemen. Number one, our former friend, the Rat."

"Oh boy," I said. "My favorite person."

"Since he quit the company," Matador continued, "he's been going around talking a bunch of shit, and saying he was our lead instructor for years."

"Lead instructor?" exclaimed Lovedrop. "Are you kidding me? He's only been to one boot camp with us!"

Blah blah blah. I was losing interest in this conversation. Matador is always at war. I glanced over at the tennis courts. I thought, *I wish I could play tennis. Then I could try out the tennis court.* I scanned my gaze toward the pool and saw the girls again with the Swedish bikinis.

I could hear Matador and Lovedrop talking in the background.

I was already bored of this conversation. I wanted to get back to the task at hand: getting women! *Remember women? Think about the smell of peach perfume. The soft skin, the perky nipple in your mouth. The tender but firm ass. The taste of her.*

Through the speakerphone, we heard Matador take a long drag from his cigarette. Then he said, "Motherfuckers better hope I never get cancer."

No one spoke for a moment. I could hear the faint sound of an airplane in the distance, somewhere far overhead. My thoughts continued to wander . . .

> The universe is not really what we experience it to be. It exists as mathematics, wave patterns, and probabilities. It only seems graphical to you because your dream circuits are creating that experience for you.
>
> From quantum mechanics, I learned that a particle isn't really in a specific location until it is observed. Until then, it exists as a fuzzy probability cloud. It's only when a sentient being *observes it* that it actually collapses into a specific particle at a specific location. Experiments show that it is the act of observation *itself* that makes the probability collapse and become "real." We are the sentient beings who interact with those probabilities and make them real.
>
> What's amazing is that it's all being computed in real time! When you drop a drop of milk into your tea, notice the absolute utter complexity and beauty of the impact, of the upside-down unfolding mushroom cloud. All those molecules, all that motion—all that *math*!

"So what's the good news?" Lovedrop asked.

> What is your experience, really? When you have a
> dream, it feels so real. But it's not real; you're asleep. It's
> all in your head. There must be circuits in your brain
> that are responsible for that experience. Those are what
> I call your "dream circuits."
> But if you think about it, the same circuits are also in
> use when you are awake. The waking experience is also
> going on inside your head, though constructed from
> sensory data instead of imagination.

". . . Oh yeah. You guys are gonna love this. I was on the phone
with the lawyers, and they told me they slapped down that lawsuit—the guy from Scranton." Chuckling.
"Just like that?"

> Your body, that was given to you, is part of the universe.
> The behavioral system, that was given to you, is part of
> the universe, too. When you were born, the universe
> flooded you with experience, with mathematical, graph-
> ical experience. And from birth until now, you've been
> getting a steady stream of input.
> A woman you meet is the same way, just like you.
> She has a DNA machine as complex as yours. When
> you realize she too has a spirit, for lack of a better word,
> the two of you can turn off the girl/boy dynamics and
> you can reach her spirit. That is the most amazing
> thing. It's communion. When you reach the spirit, it's as
> if you're in sync with your best friend.

". . . yup, just like that. We are all set, fellas. So what do you
think is gonna happen next?" asked Matador's voice on the speakerphone.

Reality is literally a waking dream. You can control the dream. You can create moments. Moments filled with pain, loneliness, war. Moments of absolute bliss. Watching your firstborn open her eyes for the first time. If you're kind to the universe, the universe will be kind to you. It's your choice. It's filled with potential. And I know by helping you to see it, my grand work here will be far-reaching when I'm gone.

Lovedrop nodded. "Of course it worked out. You're *Mystery*. Think about it. The Universe provides."

What were we talking about, again?

As I looked around, at the girls playing volleyball, at the impossibly good-looking guys with the huge arms, at the Swedish bikini team splashing around in the pool, at the sneering owner of the house, standing in a circle of his friends, old men with faces marred by plastic surgery, all around I could hear the sound of laughter. Beautiful, tanned people frolicked all around me. A butterfly fluttered past, a flash of color in my peripheral vision.

I couldn't help but notice all the *math*! The universe calculating in real time! I became conscious of the smell of the breeze, of the deep blue in the sky, and the sunlight that shone down on the hills like beams of gold, warming my skin, with the entire city spread out before me in the valley below.

This is what really matters. Here I was *now*, with good friends, feeling nothing but love, and I was within seconds of meeting a beautiful woman in a bikini who would become my next girlfriend.

As the universe danced for me, I heard Lovedrop's words again, "You're *Mystery*. Think about it."

And I thought: *He's right! I am Mystery. The universe provides.*

I turned and saw the girl again, the one I wanted. The 10. With her perfect body, and her face like the sun—she looked like an angel. As she stepped out of the pool, she ran her fingers down the elastic of her bikini and smiled in my direction.

I thought, *Who cares about all the rest of it?* I started walking toward her.

And just before I mesmerized her, the words flashed through my mind: *The universe provides.*

Chapter Thirteen

CODA IN NEW YORK

ADAM WAS RIGHT. A year later, after all the dust had settled, we took a trip to New York, and I decided to call him up to check in.

As we approached the city from a distance, the skyscrapers of Manhattan first appeared like a mountain range across the horizon. The city seemed to stretch as far as I could see in both directions.

"Jeez," said Lovedrop. "Look at that thing. It's unbelievable."

"It's a modern-day Babylon," I said. "Just like a giant ant hive."

Each moment the great city loomed a little closer; it gave me a nagging, ominous feeling.

I thought to myself, *I appreciate interaction with other humans because I am a part of society. If I were an ant, I would prefer to live in an ant farm with other ants than all alone. That is just how ants were designed through, literally, billions of years of evolution. They weren't designed to be alone but, rather, within a collective. I am part of this glorious collective and whenever I am separated from people for too long, like a lonely ant, I am not most happy.*

"Every time I see New York," said Lovedrop, "I can't believe that such a place actually exists on the face of the earth." He shook his head incredulously. "But there it is."

"What other city is like it?" asked Matador.

"No other city can even be compared to it," said our friend and host for the weekend, Dr. Malik, flashing us his winning smile. He knocked on the partition to alert the driver. "Washington!" he barked. "Stop by the condo."

When we got to the condo, I went straight to Dr. Malik's massage chair and set it to the highest deep Swedish setting. "Ah-ga-yea-yeah."

Malik grinned. "You like that chair?" he asked. A portrait of Malik hung on the wall behind him. It looked exactly like him.

"This is my favorite chair," I said, and I meant it.

"That's the best one you can get," said Malik. "Most expensive anyway." He poured himself a glass of Johnnie Walker Blue.

Outside the window, the Empire State Building towered before me, the centerpiece of Malik's view. I felt like I was sitting in a garden of skyscrapers. The massage chair continued to work its magic all around my neck, my back.

"It's amazing," I said. "When you look out your window in California, you can see the ground six feet away. But when you look out your window in New York, it's fifty stories down."

Lovedrop poured himself a glass of whisky and clinked glasses with Malik. "Cheers, brother," he said.

When Adam arrived, it was amazing to see how far he'd come. He was dressed much better than he had been in Miami, designer jeans, shined shoes, a nice sport coat, and he carried himself with a lot more confidence.

"I've been practicing my game a couple of times per week," said Adam, after I greeted him. "I just feel so much more comfortable in my own skin."

"That's good," said Lovedrop. "That's how it's supposed to be."

"I've seen some amazing transformations," I said. "It's always neat to see students come into their own, and to know I had a part to play in that."

"Well I'll tell you what," said Adam. "It's a hell of a lot of practice. Until I got good, I had to look at it like going to the gym. Just set in a routine, getting out there. But now I have a couple of girls that I'm seeing. I'm still practicing, but I'm a lot happier than I was before. I have a life."

"That's wonderful," I said. "As for myself, recently anyway, I have succumbed to feeling a tad underwhelmed, so I haven't gone out."

"Oh yeah?" said Adam.

I nodded. "I stayed in for a while, just screwing around on the Net and watching movies. I felt down, so I went out last week to see if it would break the spell. And it did! God do girls make me feel good. The girl I met last week was exciting—it was an adventure to take her from the club to a coffee shop, and get to know her, and to play with words. It was something I needed. I got her number and that makes me feel good. Why? Because of all the girls in the place, she was the one I wanted. I would have felt good just trying for her. I was almost about to leave because the place was shit, except for that girl, but I couldn't find a good way in to her group, so I just went in anyway and it all went good around me. It was awesome. I'm in love."

Adam chuckled.

"He's always in love," said Lovedrop.

"I suggest we all find time in our schedules to get out more," I concluded. "Going alone is even okay. Honest. I went out alone on a fucking Tuesday, and I got a number."

"We're going out tonight," said Adam. "Right?"

"You're fucking right we are," said Malik.

"Malik," said Lovedrop, "I didn't know you were a boxer." Several championship boxing belts sat on display above the TV.

"It's true," said Matador. "If we get into any trouble at the club, Malik can kick their ass."

Malik said, "I'm not gonna have problems at the club over some idiot, though. If someone makes problems at the club, I'm gonna say 'I'm sorry, my fault.'"

"What if he insults you?" asked Matador.

"What if he has a knife?" Malik replied. "I'm not gonna have problems like that, over some idiot. No. I'll say, 'Please excuse me, I'm sorry,' and then I'm gonna go talk to security, and have them throw his ass out of there. Or maybe they take him downstairs, if he's a problem case." He grinned. "They straighten him out, though."

"So Mystery," asked Adam, "are you going to hang out with that girl tonight, the one you're in love with? Is she in New York? Coming out with us?"

"Well, no," I replied. "She is in town, and I'll probably have her come over at some point, but tonight we want to try to meet some new girls, and pull them back here. You see, what I meant before was, I find myself feeling so much better about myself when I know that a girl likes me enough to sleep with me. I'm not saying it's healthy, I'm just saying that my motivation for being with women is for ego boosting. Oh, and the sex. I love the adventure of a new girl. It's awesome."

"That it definitely is," said Adam.

"I feel wanting when I haven't been with a girl," I said. "It's around girls where I feel most me. It's like a girl in my life allows me to act and be the way I want to be. When I'm alone in a room, looking in a mirror, I see just a schmuck. But when I'm in the presence of women who treat me like 'performer Mystery,' then I can get lost in the role, and I feel great when they think I'm great.

"Again, it's unhealthy, but my strategy to feel normal and good is to be with a woman or women. I can't seem to find a better solution. I think that is why I perform. You are looking into the screwed-up mind of not only a pickup artist, but a performer. I perform for the acceptance of women. Sure, I reap many rewards, some cash, some adventure, handshakes from guys. But it's the attention from girls that really gets me all cranked. And when I'm alone in bed with a girl I feel most myself.

"Enough ranting. Most performing artists have the same issues. My dad was an alcoholic asshole who smacked me around once too many times or something. I don't blame anyone for my current state; I live with it. Thing is, as long as I am appreciated by a girl, I feel elated. The ups are worth it enough to have some downs. Depression, elation, depression, elation. Ups and downs. Longer ups and shorter downs are the goal. Three girlfriends ensures little downtime. Once I'm having sex regularly, I then have the mental energy to focus on other things like my performances and my goals. I actually have big plans. I'm in L.A. for a reason, not just the warmth and the babes, although that's reason enough. I read that all comedians are depressives. The owner of a large chain of comedy clubs said that in a magazine interview. Of course, I'm not a comedian, but I know many of them, and I have to agree."

"Girls really make you that much happier?" asked Adam.

"God, it's magic," I said. "Isn't it a blast to see a girl and go through the process of obtaining her? I love that. Thing is, every time I go to a public gathering, it's like starting over from scratch. There I am at the beginning of the night with no numbers. No options. Just like any other guy who goes there. I know I can just as easily waste the night not getting a single option. Not talking to a single person even. I've done that in the past, more than once. But, if only I would work the room, I know what a blast it would be. I know I could get some options if I only tried. And so I put forth effort into consistently sharpening my skills, so I don't have to go home empty-handed like so many guys out there. And do you know what the reward is, for focusing? Well, besides your ego getting boosted, you end up getting laid. The adventure of a new girl. The scent of a woman.

"The girl I was with last week has an awesome body but she was shy about her ass," I said. "But if you saw it, you would love it. Weird, eh?"

"I find myself passing up opportunities, sometimes," said Adam, "when I'm just not interested in that woman. But it feels good to have more options."

"Oh wow, look at how far he has come," interrupted Lovedrop. "The student is now a master! Do you know what that means?"

Adam stared back in confusion.

"We need to give you a name! Mystery, any suggestions?"

"Dean," I said proudly. "Like James Dean."

"Dean! I love it," Adam said. He grinned.

"Now remember," said Lovedrop: "You can use that nickname among us and on our Web forum, but don't use it in real life because that's weird."

"I don't know," I said. "Some people have really bad names. Adam isn't bad, but I've definitely had some students where I had to recommend they actually go by a different name in real life. If a girl has to ask you to repeat your name, or pronounce it, that's bad."

"I've got to say," said Adam, "this stuff really does change you, gives you more self-confidence to be yourself. Being a pickup artist is really about just vibing with women as yourself and being comfortable with who you are. And I love the chase!"

"I enjoy having the women chase *me*," I said. "But, you know, sometimes even I go home with nothing. Yes, if you can believe it, even Mystery sometimes has dry spells. I go to the wrong places, it's been a long weekend and the city is dead. It was raining. I was tired. Or my emotions get control of me where I just feel down or bad. If I get rejected by twelve girls in a night, yes, I can feel like a schmuck. But I know that this too will pass."

"What do you do about the pain?" asked Adam. "I mean, let's say you just got out of a relationship."

"When the pain gets bad enough," I answered, "you will move on. And then you will feel more pain from the next girl you can't get. And then the next and the next. Finally you will begin to feel a little numb, and not allow your emotions to get you until after she is your girlfriend. And then you will notice that because you don't let women step on you emotionally, that you will seem a bit like an ass and this attracts more women."

"Actually that rings very true," said Adam. "Especially the period of time after my boot camp. I had just gotten out of a relationship at that period of my life, and after I went out with you guys that weekend, everything finally started to gel in my head. I still felt a little clumsy in the field. But after I kept practicing, it all started coming together."

"That's how it works," I said. "Like dancing. You're clumsy at first. I failed a lot, I mean a lot. There was a time I didn't understand how to have sex in a way that would make her want it with me again. There were times I didn't understand last-minute resistance and would get stuck there. I mean a *lot* of times. That is the worst, getting a girl into your bed but not closing. Or not knowing how to arouse her. Or how to get her comfortably into your bedroom. Or how to take the time to build comfort, to convey vulnerability, to construct jealousy plotlines. Or how to properly execute a physical escalation ladder. Or how to bounce to another location. Or how to isolate the girl from her group. Or how to merge groups for social proof. I think you get the idea. I failed at many points along the game plan. And I had many relationships that, when they failed, burned me bad. I cried. I cried a *lot*. Really. And twice it was so bad I considered suicide. How fucked up is that?"

"Wow," said Adam. "I had no idea you were ever at such a low point in your life, over women. You're Mystery."

"Yeah," I said. "I'm Mystery, and I *did* go through low points, but it was worth it all. Which is strange because there were times I thought it was all pointless. But Adam, I'm telling you, keep going, keep practicing. It *will* reach a critical mass, like it has for me. I am, in my personal life, very fulfilled. I have love, happiness, options, validation, and a lot of drama." I laughed. "Quality problems. Mind you, I may have more tough times ahead, but no matter what, it will be worth wading through, in order to get to the other side, where more adventure awaits."

And then we were off into the night.

Congratulations

Dear Reader,

There's something you should know . . .

You're one step closer to your goals and to mastery of the Venusian Arts.

But I've got some **Bad News . . .**

The moment you put down this book, that's when the excuses will start and the distractions will come. You'll have all of the BS reasons to forget your goals and aspirations and any commitments you made while reading this book. The path to mastery in this world isn't reading. If you really want to master this, you need to engage yourself in its application.

Reading is one thing and understanding is another. But application is where the real game is played. If you want to impress your friends, then stopping at "understanding" is okay. But if you want something bigger, something better for yourself, something crazy (like a rock-star sex life with multiple women, or *the one perfect girl who will do anything for you*), then ACTION is key.

Don't worry! The book you hold in your hands, *The Pickup*

Artist, is merely the companion to a multimedia experience and life-changing program—all of which you can access for free. These tools will help you not only to master the information inside, but also to apply it to your everyday life.

How can that be? Check it out. Don't even put the book down. **Walk over to the nearest computer and enter this URL into your web browser:**

www.ThePickupArtistBook.com

It will take just a few seconds to set up your free account with us, and you'll have instant free access to the full PickUp Artist Multimedia Companion videos and other related programs. This is important! Now that you own the book, we've made all this available to you absolutely free of charge, so do this now.

ENJOY THE FREE MULTIMEDIA EXPERIENCE AT
www.ThePickupArtistBook.com!

— MYSTERY

Glossary

ACCOMPLISHMENT INTRO: Mentioning one of your wing's notable accomplishments as you introduce him to the group.

AMOG: The "alpha male" of the group.

ANTI-SLUT DEFENSE (ASD): A logical trigger in a woman's mind that activates to interrupt whatever is happening whenever she feels that her social value could be compromised.

APPROACH ANXIETY: The anxiety that many men feel when they are about to approach a group of strangers to start a conversation.

AVERAGE FRUSTRATED CHUMP (AFC): The typical "loser guy" who is unsuccessful with women. Coined by Ross Jeffries.

BAIT-HOOK-REEL-RELEASE: A metaphor describing the basic concepts of microcalibration. See chapter 2.

BITCH SHIELD: The rude attitude that some women use in public to blow off the men who approach them.

BODY ROCKING: Using your body language to cause the group to feel like you are leaving even when you aren't, in order to preserve comfort levels in the group, allowing you more time to hook them.

BOUNCE: To leave the current venue, usually with your target, and go to the next venue. Normally the entire group will bounce together.

BUYER'S REMORSE: The sense of regret that a woman will feel if you push for too much physical escalation before qualifying her properly. The pickup artist who causes buyer's remorse will complain that, although he was kissing his target the night before, now she won't even return his phone calls.

BUYING TEMPERATURE: A temporary emotional state, associated with higher levels of compliance, that can be installed into women through gaming focused on stimulating the emotions. Characterized by giggling.

CANNED MATERIAL: Routines that have been practiced in the past and are "in the can" and ready to be used when necessary in the field.

CHEAT SHEET: See "Stack."

COMPLIANCE MOMENTUM: The process of baiting your target to jump into progressively larger and larger hoops, and thus giving you a higher and higher level of compliance.

COMPLIANCE TESTING: The actual tests, verbal and physical, that a pickup artist uses to bait the target to give more and more compliance. Compliance testing is part of the microcalibration process.

CONSPIRACY: A sense between two people that they are "in on something" together that other people are outside of and wouldn't understand. Conspiracy is a connection switch, which means that using it installs and deepens a sense of connection between two people.

CRASH AND BURN: Approaching a group and being rejected. Often a new pickup artist will do "crash and burns" ten or twenty times in a row just for the learning experience and to desensitize himself to rejection.

CUTTING THE THREAD: Changing the subject of conversation by ignoring someone's thread and instead introducing a new thread of your own. Usually, people just go along with it.

DEMONSTRATION OF HIGHER VALUE (DHV): An indicator of higher evolutionary value, triggering attraction. See chart in chapter 10.

DEMONSTRATION OF LOWER VALUE (DLV): An indicator of lower evolutionary value. See chart in chapter 10.

DISARM: To neutralize an obstacle in the group, usually by winning over the group.

DISQUALIFIER: A statement or action disqualifying oneself as a potential suitor to the target. See "Neg."

EMOTIONAL STIMULATION: The use of sensory and emotional descriptions, rather than logical recitations of fact, to stimulate the imagination of the listener and install various emotional states.

FALSE TIME CONSTRAINT: Mentioning that you need to leave soon, for some logical reason. This is done for the same reason as body rocking: to preserve comfort levels in the set, allowing more time for the pickup artist to hook the set.

FIELD: The social gathering, usually a public venue such as a bar, where a pickup artist goes to practice approaching women.

FIELD REPORT: A report of a night in the field, usually written. Video and audio field reports are not unheard-of.

FIELD-TEST: To test a new tactic or idea in the field in order to ascertain its usefulness in pickup.

THE FLAME: The Flame is an inward vibe where you are happy, smiling, playful, having fun, adding value, positive, talkative, you make things happen, warm, friendly, enthusiastic, appreciative, and a little crazy.

FLASH GAME: Game that, while flashy and impressive to the observer, is superficial and only based on a temporary emotional state of fun. See "Solid Game."

FLUFF TALK: Mundane conversation used for "passing the time" when you have nothing better to say.

FMAC: Find, Meet, Attract, Close.

FRAME: The context through which something is interpreted.

GAMBIT: A memorized routine used to accomplish a certain piece of your game. Usually a funny story used to captivate the group and demonstrate value to the target.

THE GHOST: The Ghost is an inward vibe where you feel comfortable and relaxed, unreactive, unaffected, content, satisfied, not needy, not trying to impress anyone, and without agenda.

GROUP THEORY: The process of becoming the center of attention in a group, and demonstrating value to the group, usually through storytelling, while negging the target, in an attempt to disarm the obstacles and create attraction in the target.

HIRED GUNS: Women who are hired for their beauty. This category can include exotic dancers, bartenders, shot girls, hostesses, and so on.

HOOK: You can say that you have "hooked" your target when she is starting to give you IOIs instead of IODs.

HOOP THEORY: Hoop theory is the concept that people are constantly putting up hoops, metaphorically, and trying to get other people to "jump into the hoop." Part of having power in the conversation is about understanding when this happens and being able to control it.

INCONGRUENCE: A funny feeling that people get when the words you say, and the way you say them, don't line up. This goes away with practice.

INDICATOR OF DISINTEREST (IOD): An IOD is a cue that your target will give when she is not attracted to you or interested in what you have to say. She will turn away, look away, disagree, and so on. See the chart in chapter 2.

INDICATOR OF INTEREST (IOI): An IOI is a signal that your target will display when she is attracted to you and/or interested in what you have to say. She will smile, ask questions, touch you, continue the conversation when you let it drop, and so on. See the chart in chapter 2.

INNER GAME: This is your inner confidence and intuitive grasp of the game.

INTERRUPT: An interrupt often occurs when you are talking to your target, and suddenly one of her friends appears out of nowhere and they start talking to each other. A skilled pickup artist will have a gambit ready to use for such situations.

INVESTMENT: The amount of time and energy that a woman has put into her interaction with you, including how emotionally involved she has allowed herself to be. The more invested she is, the more compliance you will get.

KINO: A euphemism for the sense of physical touch.

KINO ESCALATION: Physical escalation. See chapter 2.

KISSING: A romantic embrace related to erotic love. See chapter 2 for instructions on getting the kiss.

LEADER OF MEN: A demonstration of higher value, triggering attraction. Pickup artists demonstrate leader of men by taking over the group with storytelling, or by winning over the men in the group and vibing with them, or by teaching them some trick in order to demonstrate authority.

LOCKING IN: A pickup artist is "locked in" when he has physically positioned himself as the central feature of the group, and when he is physically more comfortable than the other people in the group.

LOCK-IN PROP: An item that you hand to your target in order to "lock her in" so that she has to sit and watch while you ignore her and demonstrate value by telling a cool story to someone else.

MERGING BACKWARD: Introducing the people in your new group to people that you have previously gamed.

MERGING FORWARD: Merging forward is accomplished by opening a new group while in set and then introducing both sets to each other. Often this is done by putting your target on your arm and then taking her as your pawn into your next set; you have merged her forward into the next set.

MICROCALIBRATION: A process of interpreting signals from the target and responding with the appropriate indicator, whether a DHV or an IOI, or an IOD, or a compliance test, that will be most effective in that moment, so that over time the pickup artist will gain more and more compliance from his target.

MOVE: A good pickup artist will move his target to different parts of the venue in order to build the sense of comfort and trust between them. He will take her to the bar, to the dance floor, to meet his friends, back to her friends, and so on.

MULTIPLE CONVERSATIONAL THREADS: A good pickup artist will introduce multiple conversational threads and shift between them comfortably, as friends do when speaking. This is as opposed to speaking only about one conversational thread at a time, which will make people feel like they are talking to a stranger, a common mistake made by inexperienced pickup artists.

MYSTERY METHOD: See Venusian Arts.

NEG: A statement or action disqualifying oneself as a potential suitor to the target. See "Disqualifier."

NICE GUY: The guy who builds comfort with his target but fails to build attraction. He often ends up as her "friend."

NUMBER CLOSE: The act of obtaining a woman's phone number. A pickup artist will view this as perfunctory, and not as important as building attraction, qualifying the target, escalating physically, building comfort and trust, and so on. A newbie will place too much emphasis on the phone number itself and not enough emphasis on the emotional process that the target must undergo in order for her phone number to have any real value to the pickup artist.

OBSTACLE: A jealous friend of the target or otherwise member of her group who acts to block approaching men from picking up the target. Often an unattractive friend or a male friend.

OPENER: A gambit that a pickup artist uses to start a conversation.

OUTER GAME: The various tactics and techniques of game.

PAWN: A woman who is paraded about, without her knowledge, by a pickup artist so that he can demonstrate preselection to his real target. The pickup artist will be willing to lose the pawn in order to demonstrate to his real target that he is willing to walk away from a woman. A skilled pickup artist will also use pawns to create jealousy plots with the target.

PEACOCKING: Wearing at least one attention-getting item in order to cause murmuring about oneself in the field, and to give women an excuse to say something. Peacocking also attracts social pressure, which enables the pickup artist to demonstrate that he is accustomed to, and unreactive to, such attention.

PIVOT: A woman friend you use to convey preselection and to make groups more receptive to your approach.

PRESELECTION: A powerful DHV. The target will feel more attracted to the pickup artist when she sees that other women are giving him IOIs.

PROXIMITY: One IOI that women use when they want you to approach is that they will give you proximity by standing nearby. You may also notice them talking louder as you walk by.

PUSH-PULL: Alternating between IOIs and IODs as a way of pumping buying temperature in the target.

QUALIFYING: Showing approval or interest as a reward, usually timed to come just after the target has demonstrated value to you, or complied with escalation, or otherwise jumped into one of your hoops.

ROLL-OFF: To turn as if to walk away. Often a pickup artist will turn back into the group again after a roll-off, using the move as a quick IOD as part of his microcalibration.

ROUTINE: See "Gambit."

SET: A group of people that a pickup artist approaches, usually at a social gathering.

SOCIAL ALIGNMENTS: A powerful DHV. Your friends, hookups, connections, employees, sources, and other forms of social value. You can directly demonstrate social alignments, and you can also embed it as a DHV in your stories.

SOLID GAME: As opposed to flash game, which is superficial and only stimulates temporary emotions, solid game involves demonstrating evolutionary value in order to trigger attraction switches in the target. After this, a skilled pickup artist will bait the target to jump into his hoops, building more and more compliance and physical escalation between the two of them.

STACK: A series of routines, often listed on a Cheat Sheet, that a pickup artist uses to practice his delivery. See "Cheat Sheet."

STATEMENT OF INTEREST (SOI): An overt statement of desire for the target. A great move if done at the right time, which is usually not the approach, but rather after the target has been working for your affection.

STICKING POINTS: The parts of your game that are giving you trouble and still need practice.

TARGET: The woman you want to win with your current approach. She is the one you are negging. Her friends are the ones you are winning over in order to disarm as obstacles. She is the one you are using Bait-Hook-Reel-Release on and escalating physically.

THREE-SECOND RULE: Within three seconds of entering the venue, approach a set and get warmed up. If you are later not in set, and you spot a set worth approaching, then you have three seconds to approach. This will put you into a talkative state and will avoid problems where girls sense you "hovering" before your approach. Try it.

TIME BRIDGE: The act of making date plans with your target and visualizing those plans together, instead of merely getting her phone number.

VENUSIAN ARTS: Mystery's system of pickup and his flagship school, located at **www.VenusianArts.com**.

WING: Short for "wingman," from *Top Gun*. Your wing is your pickup artist buddy who goes out with you so that you can help each other to pick up chicks. Usually girls who want to meet someone are out in pairs as well, so it works out.

THE ZEN OF COOL: See "The Ghost" and "The Flame."

Acknowledgments

First and foremost, thanks to everyone at the VenusianArts.com forum for participating and keeping the community alive, and also to the guys at ThePickupArtistBook.com, as well as the staff at AttractionBlogs.com and AttractionWiki.org for your hard work and professionalism. It does not go unnoticed.

Special thanks to our brother James Matador, who has our back, as well as our superb editor, Ryan Doherty, who did a brilliant job on this book, and everyone else over at Villard Books and Random House: Katie O'Callaghan, Chris Sergio, Evan Camfield, and Mark Maguire, as well as our cover model, Alhia Chacoff. Thank you for your hard work and professionalism. Thanks also to Dustin Sinkey for his excellent work in support of this book. Special mention as well, of course, to Kacey and Pickle, who keep things so fun at home. (Congratulations, Kacey, on your first movie role!)

Our eternal gratitude to our literary agent, Marc Gerald, who made this book happen. (Congratulations, Marc, for all of your latest successes. You truly have a knack for books.) Thanks also to

Sarah Stephens, Caroline Greeven, and everyone else over at The Agency Group.

Erik sends his love to Christa, Rolf, Martina, Shalyn, KK, Amanda, and Dakota. Thanks also to our TV agent, Alec Shankman; our PR, Eileen Koch, and her beautiful daughter; and to Adam Greener and everyone else at 3-Ball Entertainment, VH1, and MTV Networks.

We are so grateful to Neil Strauss for his advice and guidance. Neil has now written two—count them—forewords for us, and has remained a good friend. Thanks also to Matt, Bravo, Gypsy, Evolve, The Sneak, and everyone else at Stylelife. Honorable mention goes to Robert Greene, David Faustino, Ron Jeremy, Tom Green, Ghita Jones, and all the other characters Neil has somehow brought into our lives.

This section would not be complete without mentioning our very good friends and legal counsel Jack Nash ("Uncle Jack"), Don Rosen in Chicago, Julian Chan, Mark Goldsmith, "Cousin David" Byassee (the best attorney in Orange County), "Uncle Steve" Odom, "Aunt Carolee" Martin, the brilliant Jay Adkisson, who wrote us personally, and, last but not least, Hartford Brown, all of whose counsel and support we have found most helpful and to whom we are most appreciative. Thanks also to Amelia Zalcman in the Random House legal department, Mari and David at the Klinedinst P.C. law firm, and Ingrid Hernandez and Ana Gonzalez at Fragomen, Del Rey, Bernsen & Loewy in Miami.

Special thanks to our very own Shaun Adams, aka "Discovery," who is a rising star; Caddy, a scholar and a gentleman; and everyone else on our U.K. team, as well as Kosmo, winner of season 1 of *The Pickup Artist*; our coaches Mohammad and Wemerson, who both kill it in-field; Derby Perez, our made man; Lizzie (ElizabethEgan.com); and our friend Mehow ("Poppadopalous"/"Poppashallskee"/"Poppa-rama-ding-dong") (and for the record, Mehow, "Denial is not just a river in Egypt" is Lovedrop's line).

Shout-out to Ross Jeffries, Hypnotica, David DeAngelo ("What can I do for you, what can you do for me?"), Craig Clemens (who always hooks us up), Johnny in Miami, Arcane in Australia and L.A., Mike Sartain in Texas and Atlanta, our good friend Dr. Malik in New York City, who does not fuck around, the "Rich Jerk" Kelly Felix, and of course "Magic" Ryan. Also our marketing director, Jason Adams; Dave Bass; Jim Kwik; Jason Mewes in Hollywood; J. J. Pantztar in Miami and West Palm Beach, who is a fashion genius, an amazing guy, and a great friend; Dan Axelrod, a man of integrity; Benedict Chen in the Bay Area; Drew Kossof; Adam Gilad; Thundercat; Dave Miz in Miami, who was the secret force behind the origin of Venusian Arts as a company; Daniel Rose; Mike Hill; Mark Goodman; Aaron Penasbodi; Richard "Gambler" LaRuina over at PUA Training; Sin; and DJ Fuji.

Special mention also of our friend Owen "Tyler Durden" Cook, an excellent PUA and an all-around great guy. (Owen, I have now released my third book—count them—so when do we finally get to read *The Blueprint?*) Also a quick shout-out to everyone else at RSD, especially Papa, Ox, Christophe, Tim, and Jlaix, who just released a masterpiece, the book *Nine Ball*. May the world discover it.

We'd also like to give honorable mention to MrSex4uNYC, Steve P., Neo-Rio, Swinggcat, Maniac High, Toecutter, Zan, Juggler, IN10SE, Wilder, Sensei, Herbal (Tynan.net), Cameron Teone, and Dreamweaver. (Seth, we miss you and wish we had visited more when we had the chance. The last time you came to our place, you told us of the unimportance of things that people waste their time fighting over, and we enjoyed your company tremendously. May you rest in peace.) Also to Roadking, Nightlight9, Maddash, Formhandle, TokyoPUA, PlayboyLA, Sickboy, Gunwitch, Barry Kirkey (aka Extramask, TwentySix), and everyone else from the old days of the pickup and seduction community. This book is for you.

ABOUT THE AUTHORS

MYSTERY is the author of *The Mystery Method*, the star of VH1's *The Pickup Artist*, and the founder of Venusian Arts.com, the top pickup training organization in the world. He has appeared on *Late Night with Conan O'Brien, The Daily Show with Jon Stewart, Jimmy Kimmel Live!*, and a wide variety of media including CNN, *The New York Times*, and *Playboy*. Mystery lives in Los Angeles and enjoys his travels.

CHRIS ODOM, aka Lovedrop, has traveled with Mystery for years, coaching students in the field and speaking at pickup seminars and conferences all over the world. He is the author of *Revelation*, the co-writer of *The Mystery Method*, and a founder of VenusianArts.com. He lives in Los Angeles with his girlfriend.

A NOTE ON THE TYPE

This book was set in Electra, a typeface designed for Linotype by W. A. Dwiggins, the renowned type designer (1880–1956). Electra is a fluid typeface, avoiding the contrasts of thick and thin strokes that are prevalent in most modern typefaces.